IMAGES
of America

MONROE

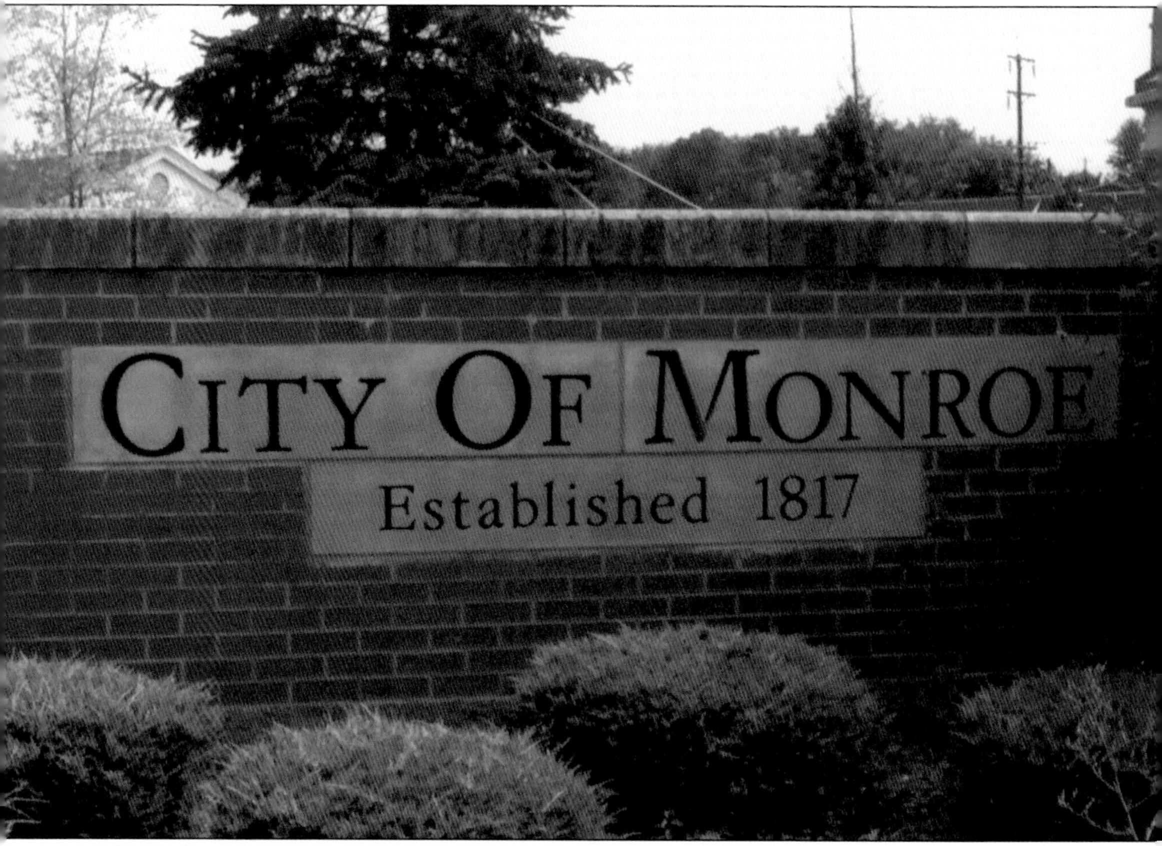

This is the enhanced entrance to the city of Monroe.

On the cover: R. E. Keever Bakery was located on West Elm Street next to the Dr. Charles Macready house. Keever delivered baked goods locally using the horse and buggy pictured here. Robert E. Keever Jr. is seen on the left; in front of him is his son, Robert. Sitting on the wagon is Robert E. Keever Sr. The bakery was a family business. (Courtesy of Boyd and Virginia Smith.)

IMAGES
of America

MONROE

Marcia McCartt

ARCADIA
PUBLISHING

ISBN 978-0-7385-6138-7

Published by Arcadia Publishing
Charleston SC, Chicago IL, Portsmouth NH, San Francisco CA

Printed in the United States of America

Library of Congress Catalog Card Number: 2008931399

For all general information contact Arcadia Publishing at:
Telephone 843-853-2070
Fax 843-853-0044
E-mail sales@arcadiapublishing.com
For customer service and orders:
Toll-Free 1-888-313-2665

Visit us on the Internet at www.arcadiapublishing.com

To my parents who nurtured my love for history.

Contents

ACKNOWLEDGMENTS

I would like to thank the Monroe Historical Society Board for generously allowing me to use their images for this book. I thank Norm Hayes, Anna Hale, and Gene Williams for their encouragement and support of this project. I thank Boyd and Virginia Smith and Ed and Marge MacDonald for graciously allowing access to their personal collections. Thanks to Gloria Hendrickson, Judge Robert Hendrickson, Angela Wasson and Kristina Mayes at the Monroe City Building, Chief Mark Neu II and Assistant Chief John Centers of the Monroe Fire Department, and Sue Goodpaster of the Monroe Swim Club for their assistance in this project. My husband, Larry McCartt, well deserves recognition for his undying support and historical input. Special thanks to all who contributed photographs: Carmon Hacker, Joe and Joyce Patrick, Liz Hutton-Taylor, Mary Jo Russell, Herb Davis, Gloria Miltenberger, Sylvia and Phoebe Lindsay, Nancy McNabb, and Michael and Melissa Giffen. Thanks to Joe Beatty for allowing me to research the Lion's Club's scrapbooks, to Lisa Warren, editor of the *Middletown Journal*, for granting permission to reprint several photographs, and to Lloyd Little for his team photographs. Thanks to Eckerd alumni and friends Sterling Watson, Dennis Lehane, and Ann Rittenberg for all their advice and support over the years.

Introduction

Monroe was platted by John Piatt and Nathaniel Sackett Jr. in 1817. Piatt was a merchant in Cincinnati, and probably never lived in Monroe. Sackett was born about 1769 in Fishkill, New York, to Nathaniel Sackett and Mary Rogers. His grandfather Samuel Sackett was a Presbyterian minister in New York. His father, Nathaniel Sackett Sr., was a member of the committee of safety and head of the Secret Service at Fishkill during the Revolutionary War. Nathaniel Jr. married Elizabeth Terboss in Fishkill, New York, around 1792. In 1816, with his wife and two children, two horses, provisions, and other needed goods, he set out for the 700 mile journey on a route through wild and sparsely inhabited country, ending up in Cincinnati. He had originally intended to make Cincinnati his home, but upon arrival decided to settle on a farm within marketing distance to the nearby city, since land was cheap and easily cultivated. At this point, he joined John Piatt in purchasing a tract of land in what was called Baker's Hill in Butler County. In 1820, four years after settling in the area, Nathaniel wrote a letter to his brother. The transcription of this letter appears in Charles H. Weygant's book, *The Sacketts of America*:

> We are in a favored land. But I have nevertheless had many a heartache since I saw you last, thinking of relatives and friends and native country seven hundred miles away, and I, with my little family among strangers in a strange land. We live in a thickly settled neighborhood of friendly people many of whom came in this country when land was cheap and now have large and well cultivated farms that are worth many times what they cost. If some of you would only come and spend a little time with us how it would sweeten our solitude and cheer us up. I have laid out a town on my farm and sold a number of lots. There are already 20 houses up and two stores and two taverns, and there is a Presbyterian Meeting-house in sight. I have called it Monroe.

Nathaniel's observations still ring true today. Large, well-cultivated farms are still prevalent in our area, the Presbyterian meetinghouse is still in sight, and there are still neighborhoods of friendly people. On April 6, 1964, the *Cincinnati Enquirer* noted that Monroe "is one of the fastest growing towns in all of southern Ohio. It has built that growth on friendliness." Sackett Jr. named his town Monroe, after the newly elected U.S. president, James Monroe. He continued to live here and is buried in the Mound Cemetery, which is located at the south end of town.

Stagecoach was the means of travel until the railroads were built in the 1850s. The Great Miami Turnpike between Cincinnati and Dayton was built about 1825–1830 and Monroe was midpoint on the route. It soon became a major overnight stop. The Red Onion Hotel was a popular stop on the route. Red onions hung at the doorway identified the stop for some illiterate stagecoach drivers. Across from the hotel was a huge livery barn. An old milepost can still be seen at the south end of town.

A tornado came through town May 10, 1969. It was the Saturday before Mother's Day, and happened right before dinner. The town pulled together in the aftermath of this crisis. Churches helped displaced families and neighbors helped their neighbors. The steeple of the Methodist church was ripped off, and the old Red Onion Hotel suffered extensive damage.

Monroe was a town where everyone met (and still meets) at the stadium for football games; a town that gathered at the Christmas tree burnings (this was always a fun gathering for children). It is a town where you could walk to church, the bank, the grocery, and usually ran into several of the community leaders; a town where you practically knew everyone; a town where you never locked your doors.

Monroe, once a part of the Middletown City School District, has a new school district that was established in 2000. This is attracting many young families to our community. The first-known schoolhouse was a one-room brick school that was located at the corner of East Elm Street and East Avenue. The academy at the Presbyterian church was probably the high school, as Judge Todhunter went from there to college. Dr. James Macready started Monroe High School in 1881. The building was razed in 1912 and a new one was built, and in 1948, the south wing was added. This building was continuously being added to, and in 1967, the 1912 building was demolished. Monroe eventually merged with Middletown City Schools and remained that way about 48 years, until the Monroe Local Schools was founded in 2000.

The large statue of Jesus located at Solid Rock Church is becoming quite the tourist attraction. We are growing, but also have managed to retain the close-knit, safe community atmosphere that was prevalent during the 1960s. This is due to the many men and women who love this city and donate their time to the various service organizations that make this town vital. Special thanks to the many people who have given so much of their time to insure that our community continues to be a good place to live, with the hope that it will remain that way for many generations to come.

The police department and fire department keep the community vital and the local churches contribute to the spiritual well-being of the community. Author Merle Constiner and country musician Matt Basford also deserve mention, for their creative contributions have benefited not only our society but the nation as well.

If you want to talk with the mayor, just hop down to the Red Onion Café for a burger. That is the beauty of our town. The leaders are very accessible to the citizens. You do not need an appointment to see them, you run into them everywhere: the Red Onion, the grocery stores, the Fourth of July celebration, or Christmas on the plaza. They will always take the time to smile and say, "Hi."

Monroe has experienced massive growth in the past 50 years, making it difficult to include everything within these pages. Any omissions are unintentional. More books need to be written in order to cover all the fascinating people and events that make this city vibrant and to preserve that history for future residents. I thoroughly encourage all interested parties to become more active in the community, the Monroe Historical Society, and to further expand upon this work.

One

Early History

During its first century, the village of Monroe was a small farming community. In addition to farms, Monroe consisted of a post office, volunteer fire department, the Red Onion Hotel, four churches (Methodist, Catholic, and two Presbyterian), a physician's office, blacksmith shops, grocers, a school, and a lodge of the Independent Order of Odd Fellows. After the dawn of the 20th century, the growing village acquired a bank, a cannery, and had erected a small village hall. More service organizations were formed and thrived throughout the new century. The introduction of the automobile forever changed the lives of Monroe citizens, and local blacksmiths acquired new skills in order to remain competitive in the new market. Blacksmith shops became auto mechanic garages. Barns, which were once stables for the horses, became housing for the automobile. Monroe was in the midst of change.

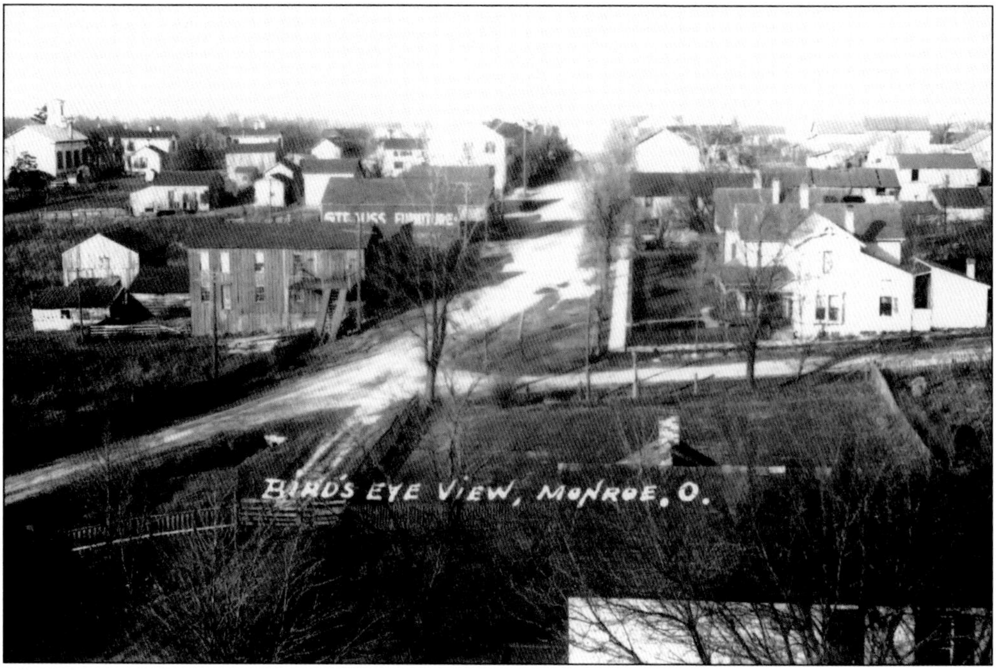

This photograph was taken around 1912 and is titled "Bird's Eye View, Monroe, O." The section originally platted by John Piatt and Nathaniel Sackett Jr. in 1817 lies to the east of Main Street. The western section was platted by 1819. The Mount Pleasant Presbyterian Church can be seen on the upper left side of the photograph. (Courtesy of the Monroe Historical Society.)

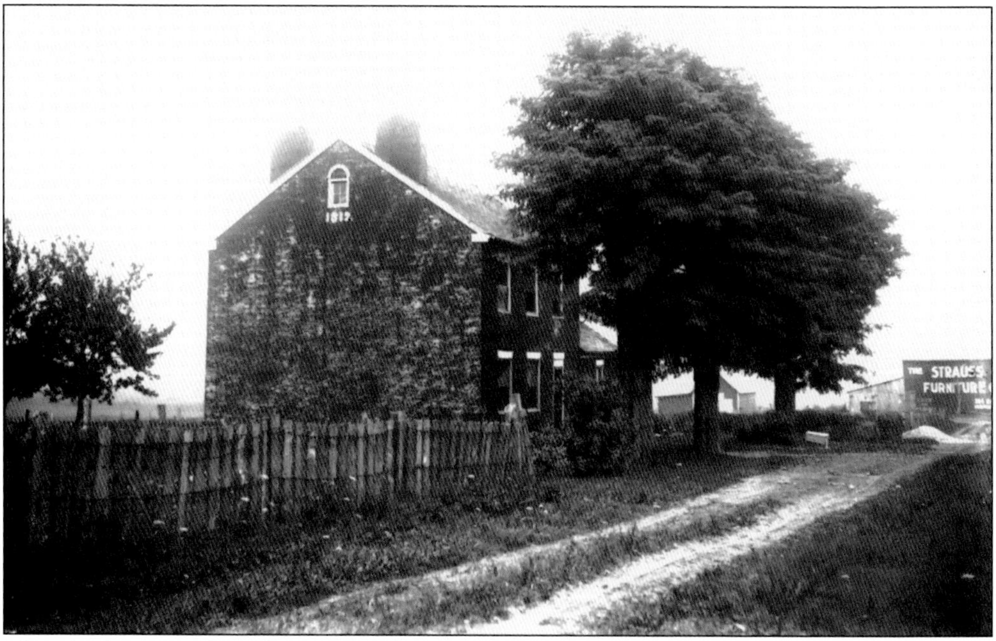

This 1812 house on the Bake Farm was located on Cincinnati Dayton Road, on the old stagecoach route. The Strauss Furniture Company can be seen in the background of this photograph. This house was built before Piatt and Sackett founded Monroe and is a typical example of architecture of the period. (Courtesy of the Monroe Historical Society.)

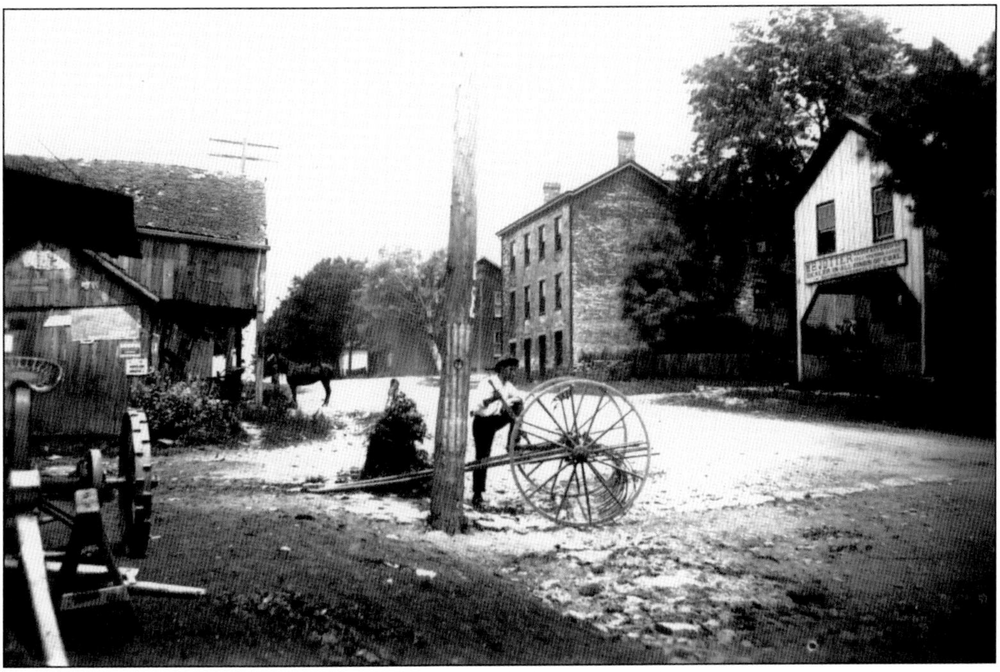

Clarence Warner is making repairs in front of the Warner Blacksmith shop. The JB Jotter Hardware store stands next to the old Red Onion Hotel building. The Red Onion was a popular stagecoach stop between Cincinnati and Dayton. It is now the home of the Brandywine Inn, which was created by owners George and Doris Bernas with friend Steve Morgan, and the Red Onion Café, which is owned by Mark Bursley. The Bernases and Steve Morgan renovated this historical building. (Courtesy of the Monroe Historical Society and Boyd and Virginia Smith.)

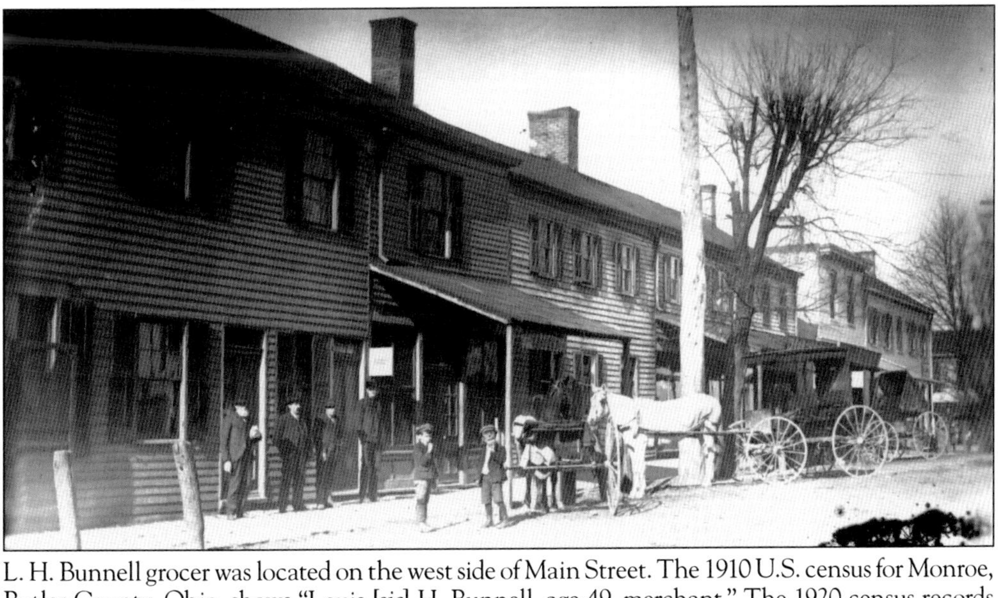

L. H. Bunnell grocer was located on the west side of Main Street. The 1910 U.S. census for Monroe, Butler County, Ohio, shows "Louis [*sic*] H. Bunnell, age 49, merchant." The 1920 census records show that a Louis H. Bunnell lived on Lebanon Avenue and was postmaster. On November 29, 1930, Lewis Bunnell died of a bullet wound, which was deemed by the coroner to be homicidal. He was still postmaster at the time of his death. (Courtesy of Boyd and Virginia Smith.)

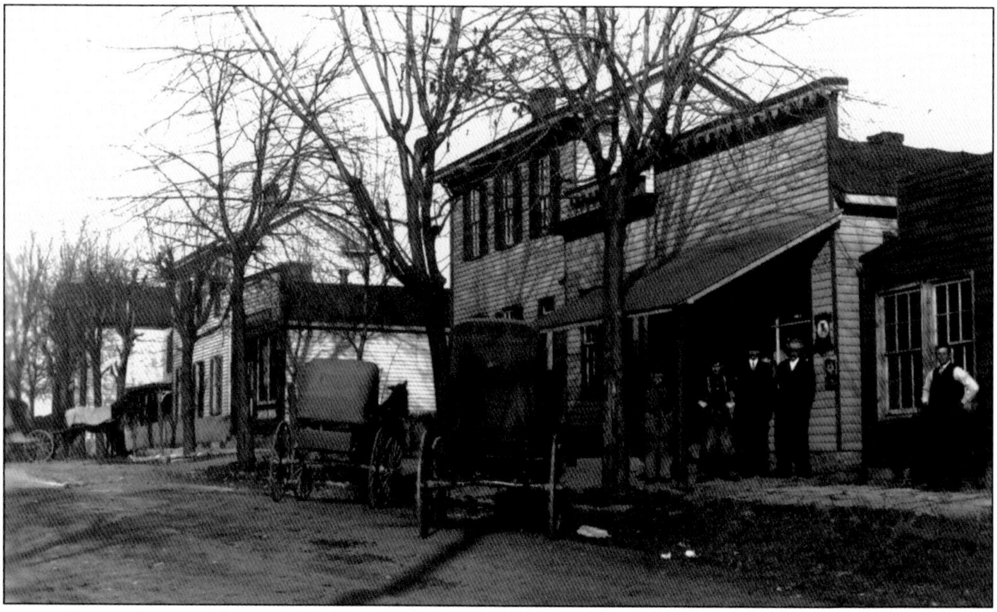

Main Street had not been paved in the early years of the 20th century. It is interesting to note that the horse and buggies are parked at an angle. Across from the grocer, on the east side of Main Street, is the Monroe National Bank, which was the first bank to operate in Monroe. The bank is the small building to the left, center, from where the men are standing. (Courtesy of Boyd and Virginia Smith.)

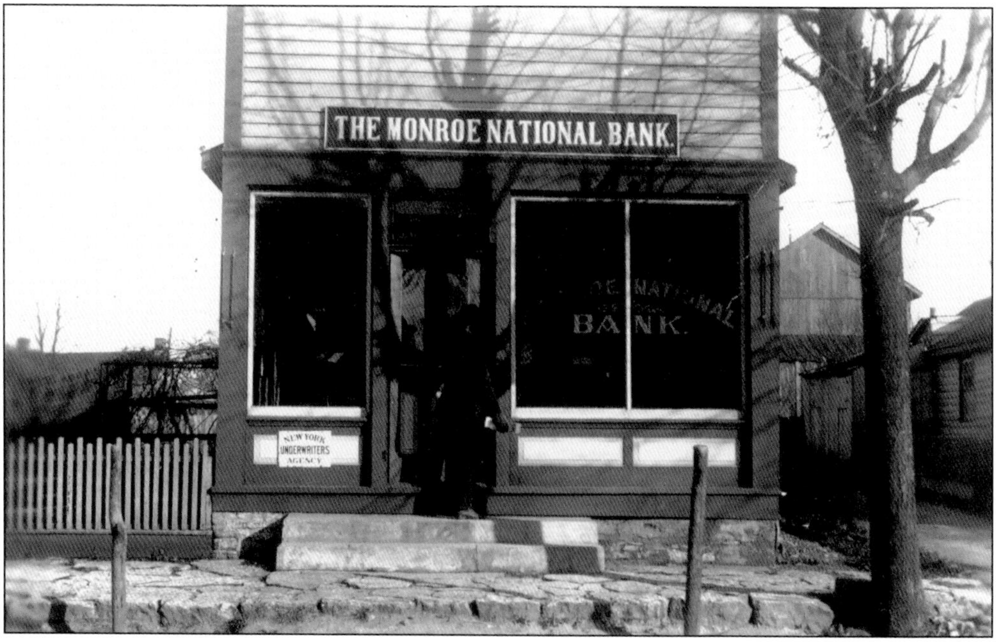

The Monroe National Bank was founded in 1905. On August 15, 1905, Austin T. Smith called a meeting to organize a bank and elect the board of directors. The bank opened its doors for business on Saturday, November 4, 1905. The first officers were James E. Compton, president; William Stewart, first vice president; J. W. Kitchen, second vice president; and Austin T. Smith, cashier. Smith served as cashier until his death in 1943. (Courtesy of Boyd and Virginia Smith.)

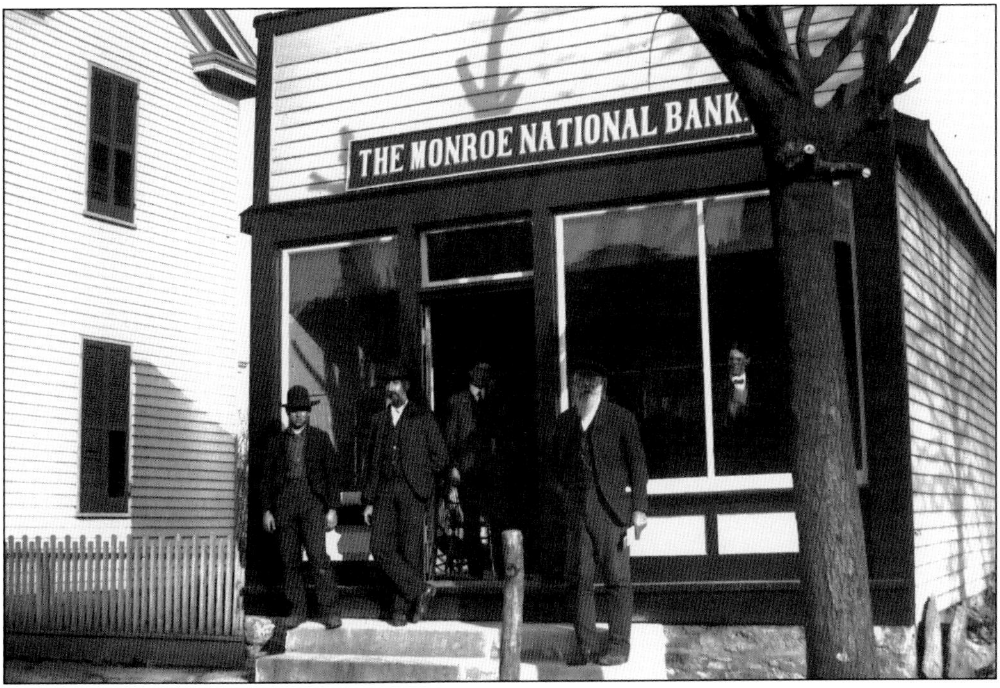

Unidentified customers stand in front of the bank. The first directors for Monroe National Bank were James E. Compton, William H. Compton, Horrace Q. Gallagher, F. M. Hughes, Samuel K. Hughes, J. W. Kitchen, C. S. Longstreet, Austin T. Smith, and William M. Stewart. Bank presidents were James E. Compton, 1905–1906; William H. Compton, 1906–1938; William M. Stewart, 1938–1951; and Charles E. Yost, 1951–1953, when Monroe National Bank merged with First National Bank of Middletown. Yost became director emeritus of First National Bank. (Courtesy of the Monroe Historical Society and Boyd and Virginia Smith.)

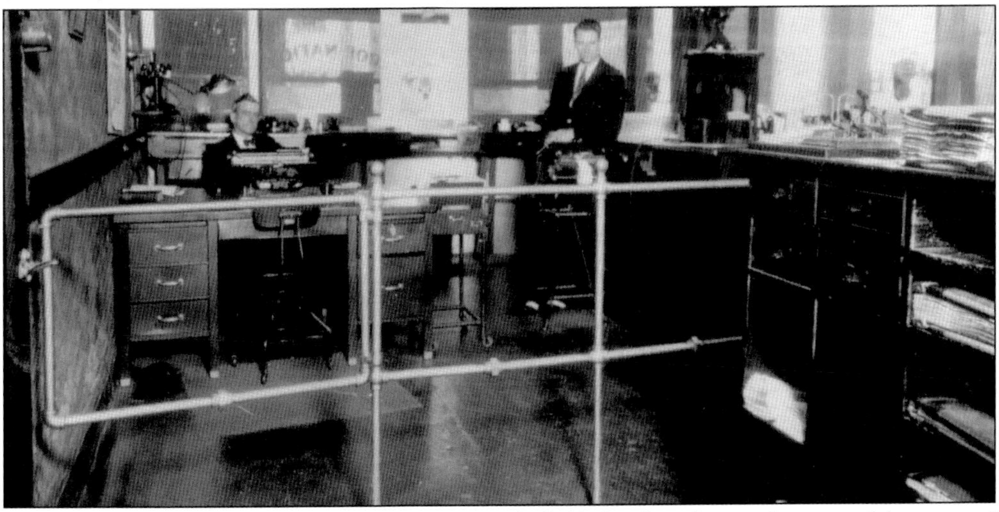

In addition to his banking duties, Austin T. Smith (left) developed several areas in Monroe and helped with financing for the homes. Austin Smith Drive is located in an area he helped to develop and still bears the family name. He became involved with other companies, such as the Butler County Canning Company and the Oakland Grain and Lumber Company, according to local historian Roger Miller. (Courtesy of Boyd and Virginia Smith.)

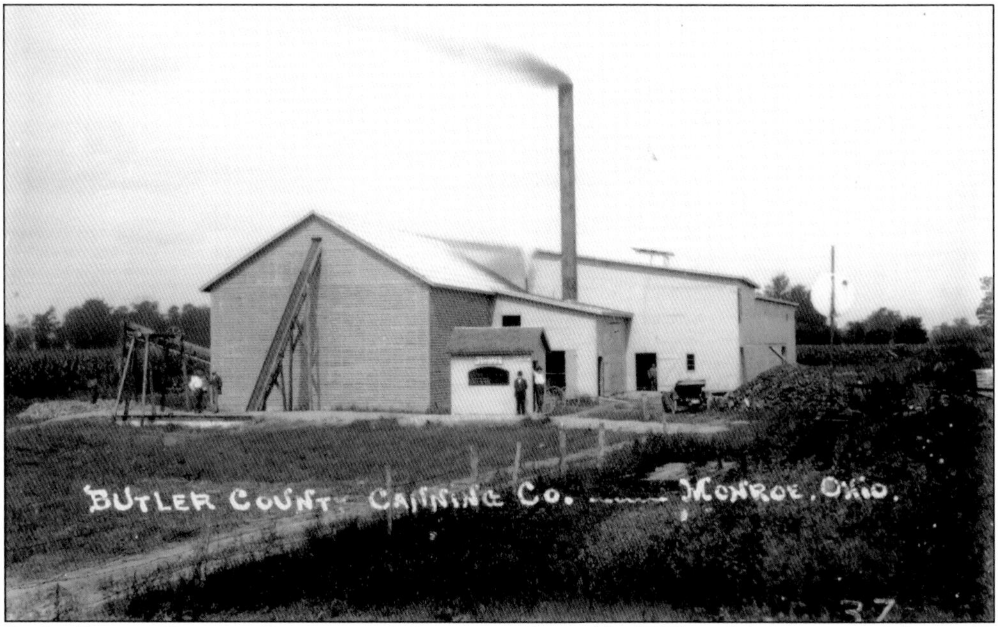

Butler County Canning Company in Monroe was formed by William M. Stewart and Austin T. Smith, both officers of the Monroe National Bank. By 1933, the canning company employed 90 workers and nearly all were women. The canning company provided much-needed income for the farmers during the depression. The canning company packed pumpkins, tomatoes, green beans, and corn. (Courtesy of the Monroe Historical Society.)

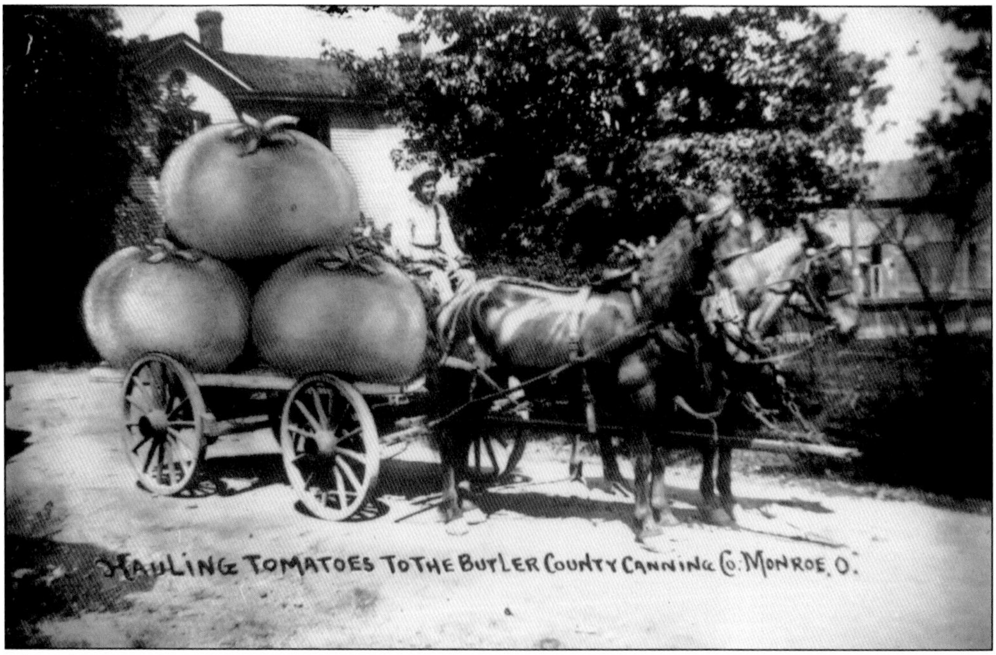

The photograph titled "Hauling Tomatoes to the Butler County Canning Co." was made into a comic postcard after 1912. The huge tomatoes are the focal point as Charles Shafor and his horse-and-wagon team head toward the cannery to make delivery. It is interesting to see the changes that were made from the original photograph. (Courtesy of the Monroe Historical Society.)

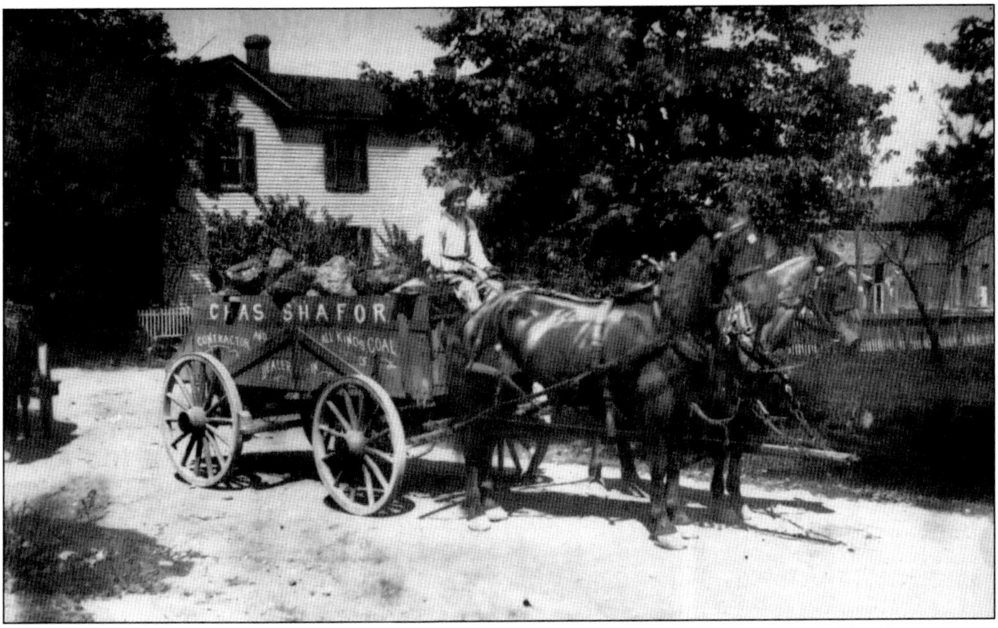

Charles Shafor is photographed with his horse and wagon around 1912 on West Elm Street near the Macready house. According to the 1910 U.S. census, he lived in Monroe and was a farmer and contractor. He died April 28, 1941, and is buried in the Mound Cemetery in Monroe. This is the photograph from which the comic postcard was created. (Courtesy of the Monroe Historical Society and Larry McCartt.)

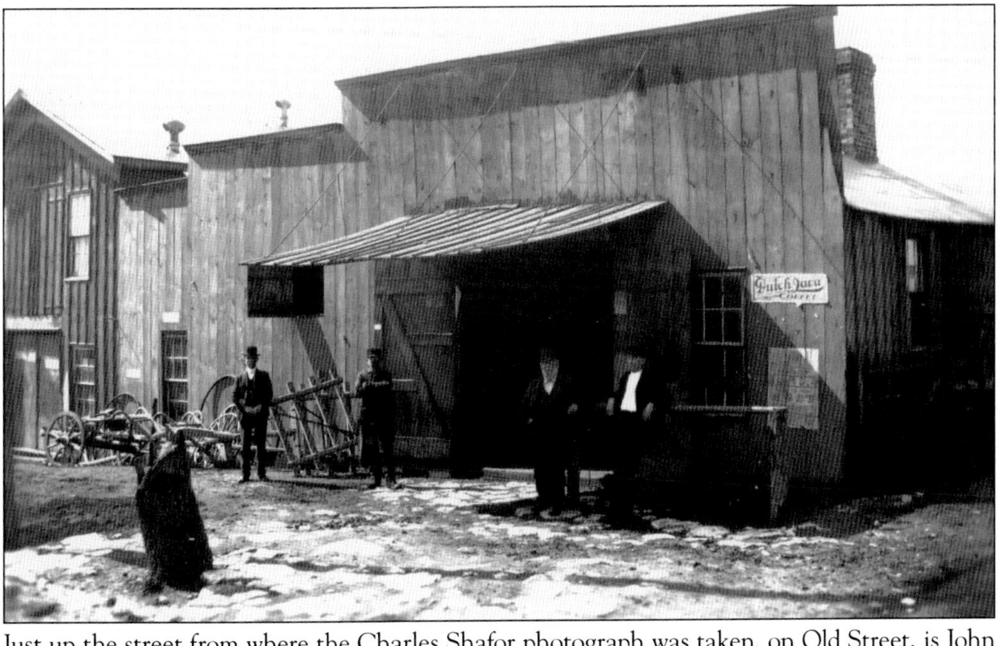

Just up the street from where the Charles Shafor photograph was taken, on Old Street, is John Boyd's Blacksmith Shop, which was in operation around 1910–1920. Notice the rail the men are leaning on. It was used to tie up the horses. John Boyd died December 20, 1926. He is buried in the Mound Cemetery. Boyd's daughter, Beulah, married Austin T. Smith. Boyd Smith is the son of Austin T. Smith and grandson of John Boyd. (Courtesy of Boyd and Virginia Smith.)

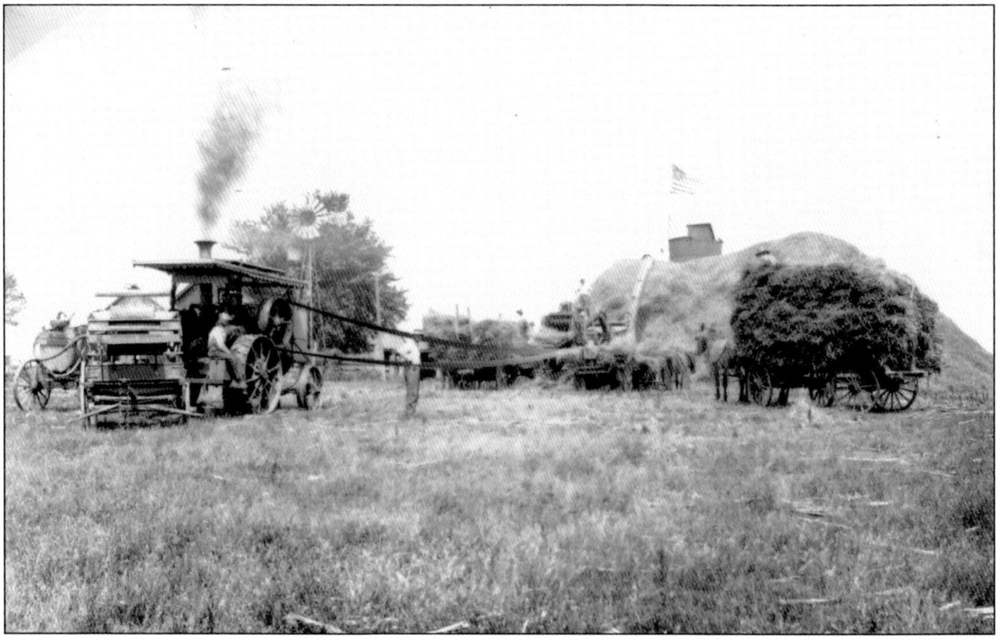

The threshing of wheat, oats, and barley also provided jobs in the community. According to Ruth Cast, there were 68 threshing jobs in 1851. In 1854, there were only 37. Threshing time was in the middle of summer, when the weather was hot and dry. Women worked long hours in the kitchen to feed the men in the fields. (Courtesy of the Monroe Historical Society.)

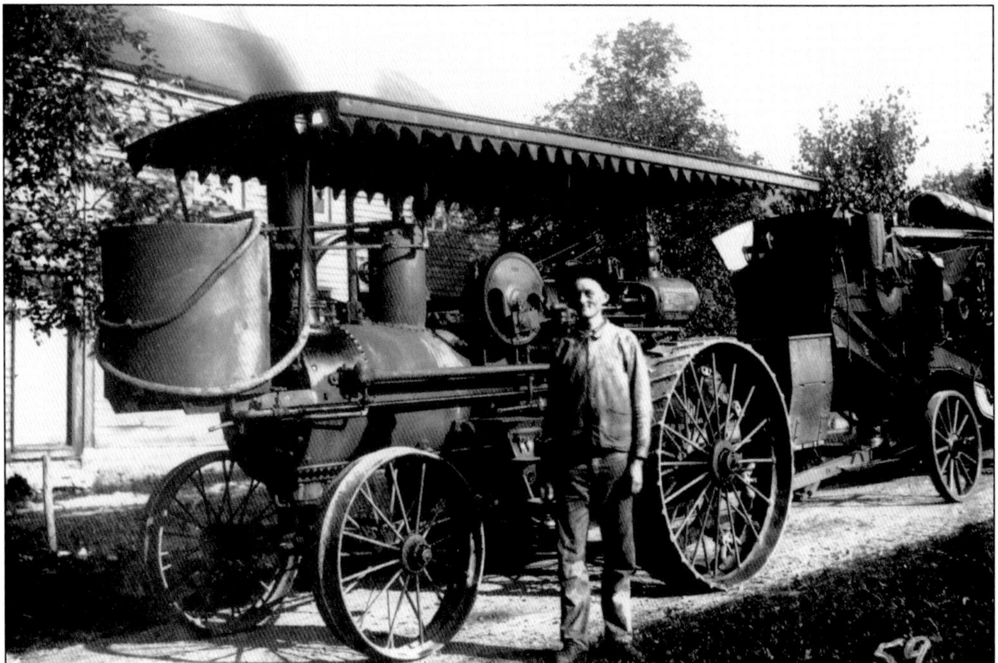

Seen here is a close-up shot of the threshing machine. Note the water tank in the front. The threshing machine was steam powered and was not horse drawn. This machine was used in Monroe during the early 1900s. (Courtesy of the Monroe Historical Society.)

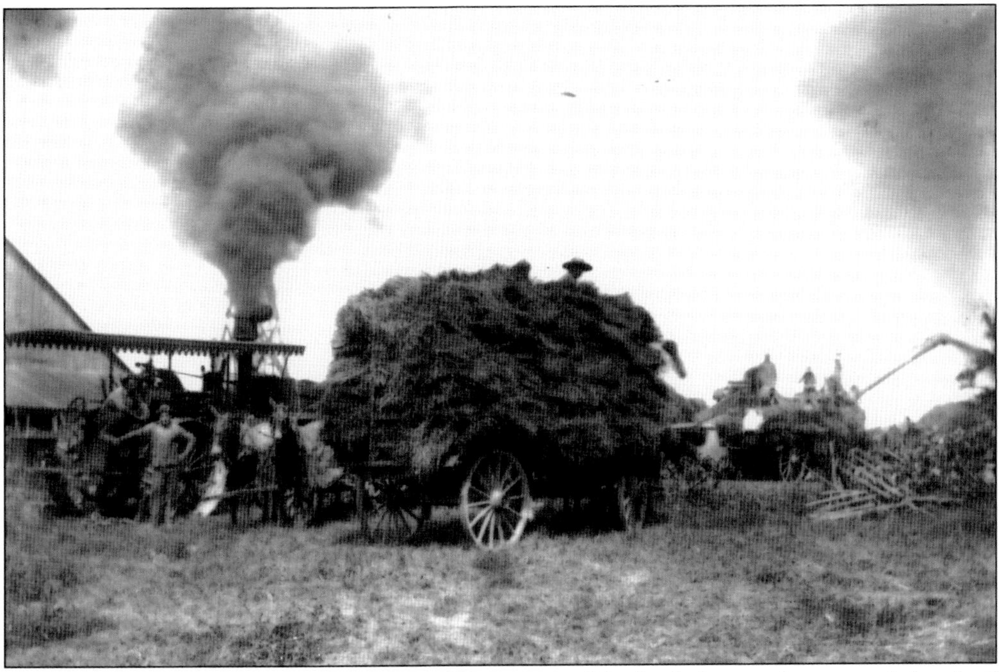

Local farmers take a break from threshing. The grain will be hauled to an elevator and the chaff bailed. (Courtesy of the Monroe Historical Society.)

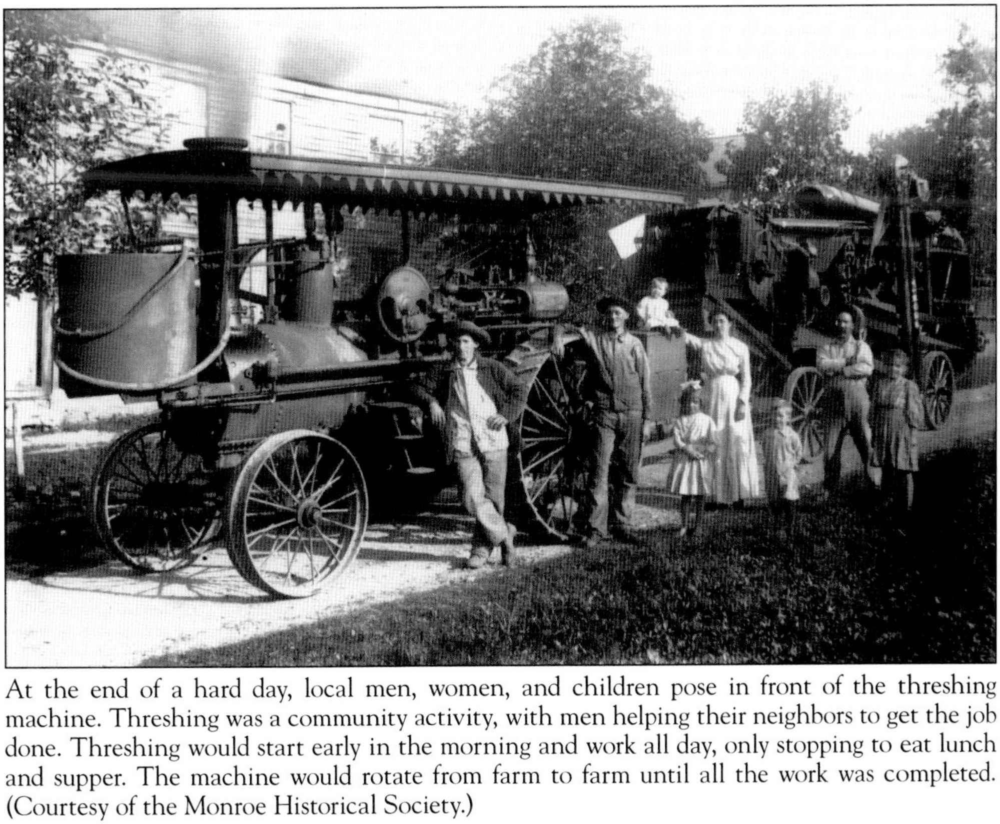

At the end of a hard day, local men, women, and children pose in front of the threshing machine. Threshing was a community activity, with men helping their neighbors to get the job done. Threshing would start early in the morning and work all day, only stopping to eat lunch and supper. The machine would rotate from farm to farm until all the work was completed. (Courtesy of the Monroe Historical Society.)

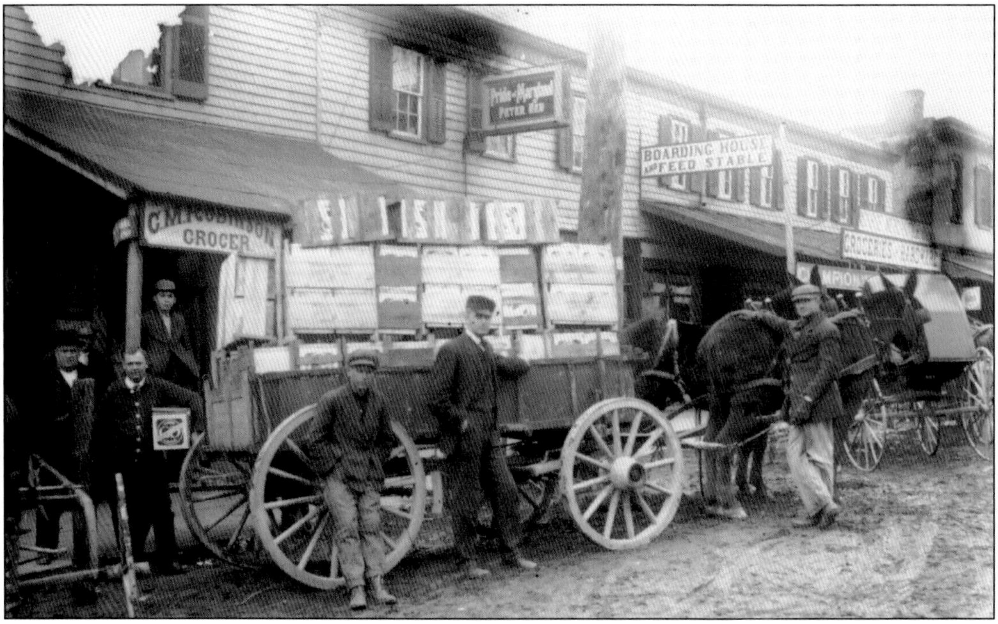

In 1913, the west side of Main Street was reminiscent of 21st century strip malls. From left to right are the C. M. Robinson Grocer and Hardware; Peter Neu's Pride of Maryland; a boardinghouse and feed stable; and Monroe Mercantile Company, Groceries and Hardware. According to the 1920 U.S. census for Butler County, Monroe, Ohio, Peter Neu owned a cigar shop. Neu was born in Monroe on December 17, 1873, and died January 27, 1953. He is buried in the North Monroe Cemetery. (Courtesy of the Monroe Historical Society.)

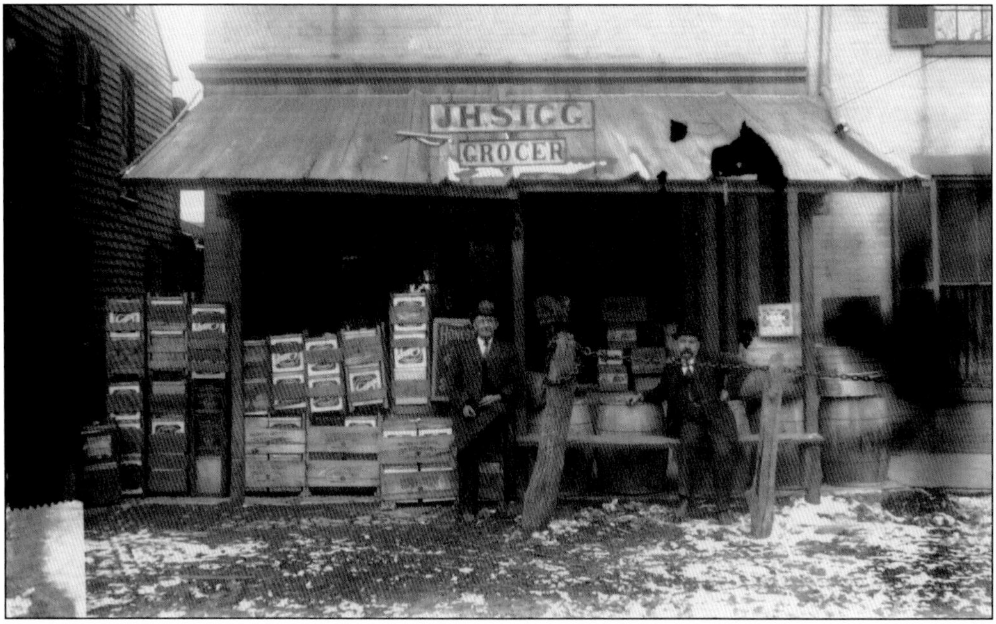

J. H. Sigg became postmaster after the death of Lewis H. Bunnell. During the early years, the post office of Monroe was located within a grocery or drugstore, as shown in this photograph. The post office later moved into the Monroe National Bank and remained in the bank until the current building was erected in 1967. (Courtesy of the Monroe Historical Society.)

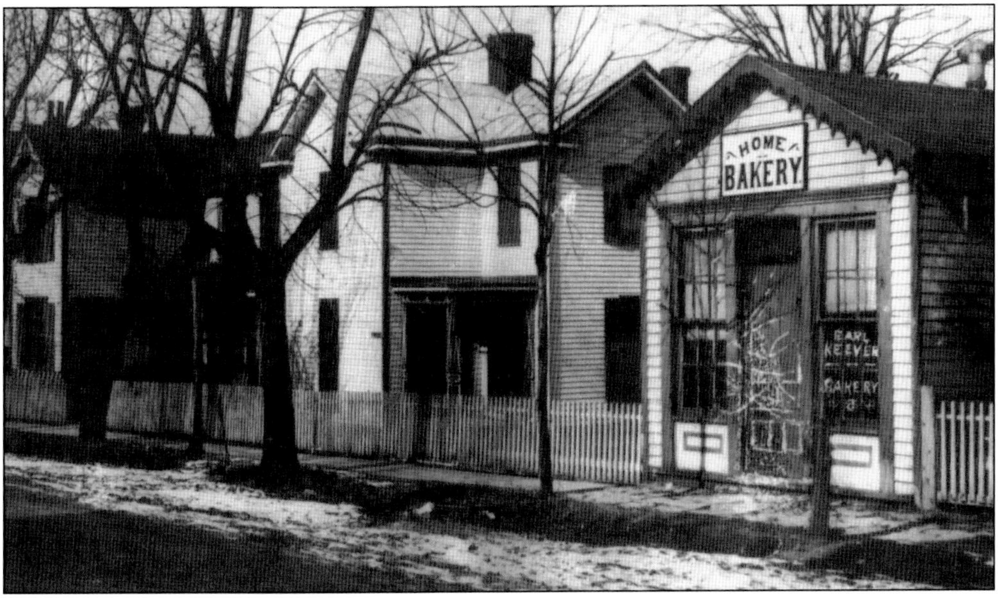

The Keever Bakery sat beside the home and office of Dr. Charles Macready on Maple Avenue, which later became West Elm Street. According to the 1920 U.S. census, Robert Keever Jr. was owner and baker, his wife Lou was clerk, and Robert Sr. and wife Katherine were also bakery clerks. Dr. Macready's father, James Macready, was an assistant surgeon during the Civil War. He built the two-story house in the mid-1870s and used it for his medical practice in Monroe. (Courtesy of the Monroe Historical Society and Boyd and Virginia Smith.)

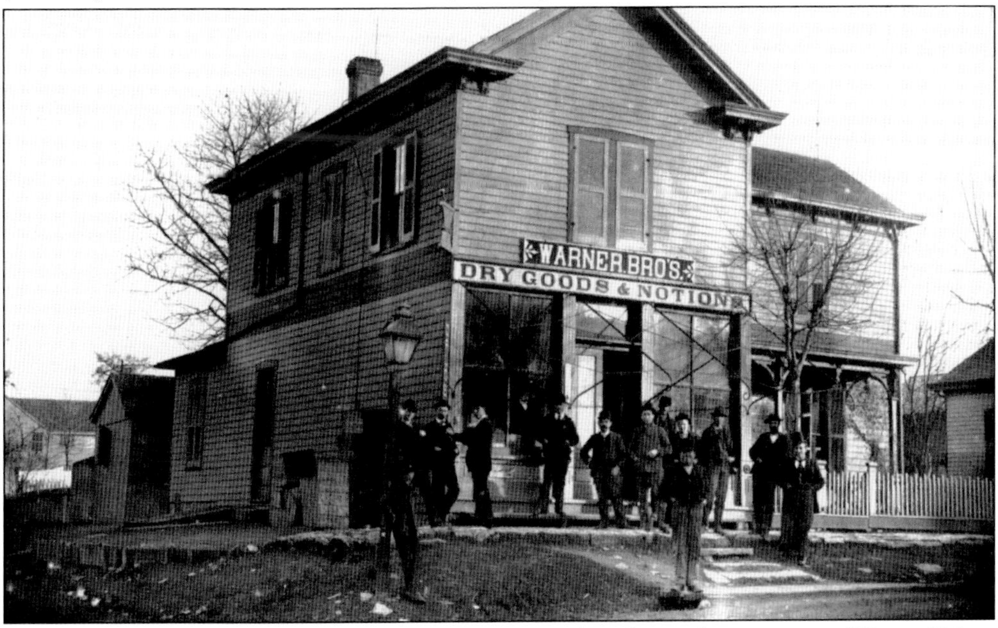

The Warner Brothers Dry Goods and Notions store stood on the southeast corner of Elm and Main Streets, where the First Financial Bank is now located. This *c.* 1895 photograph indicates that the Warner store was also a drugstore. The 1900 U.S. census for Butler County shows that "M. G. Warner" was a druggist. Marion G. Warner was born October 31, 1861, and died November 2, 1922. He is buried in the Mound Cemetery. (Courtesy of Boyd and Virginia Smith.)

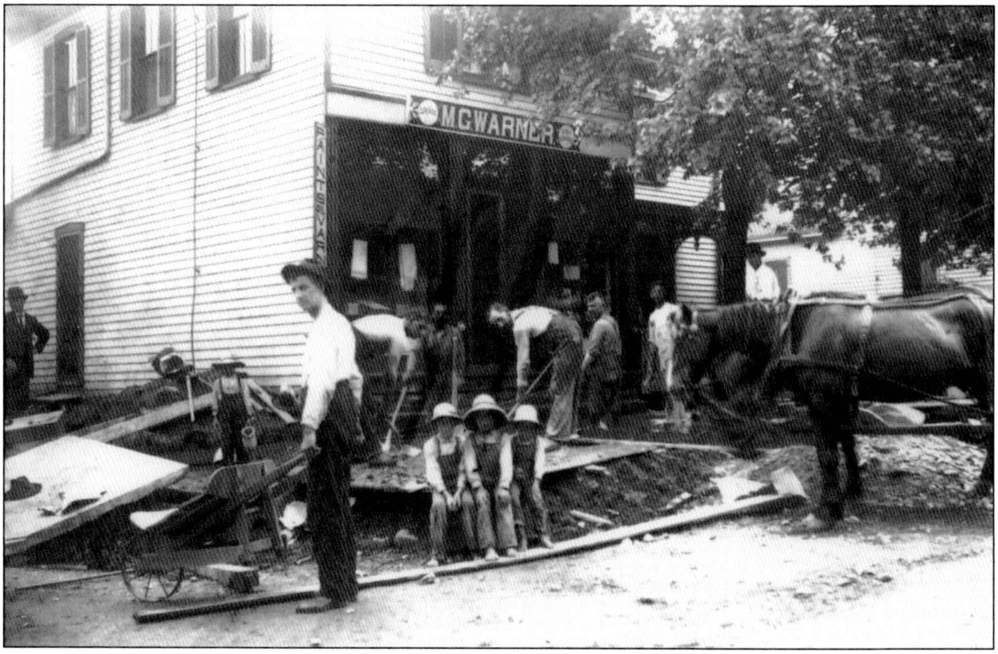

The sidewalk construction in Monroe was evidence of a growing community. Gas lines were also laid at the same time. This photograph was taken in front of the M. G. Warner store. Sidewalks were laid on both sides of Main Street. (Courtesy of the Monroe Historical Society.)

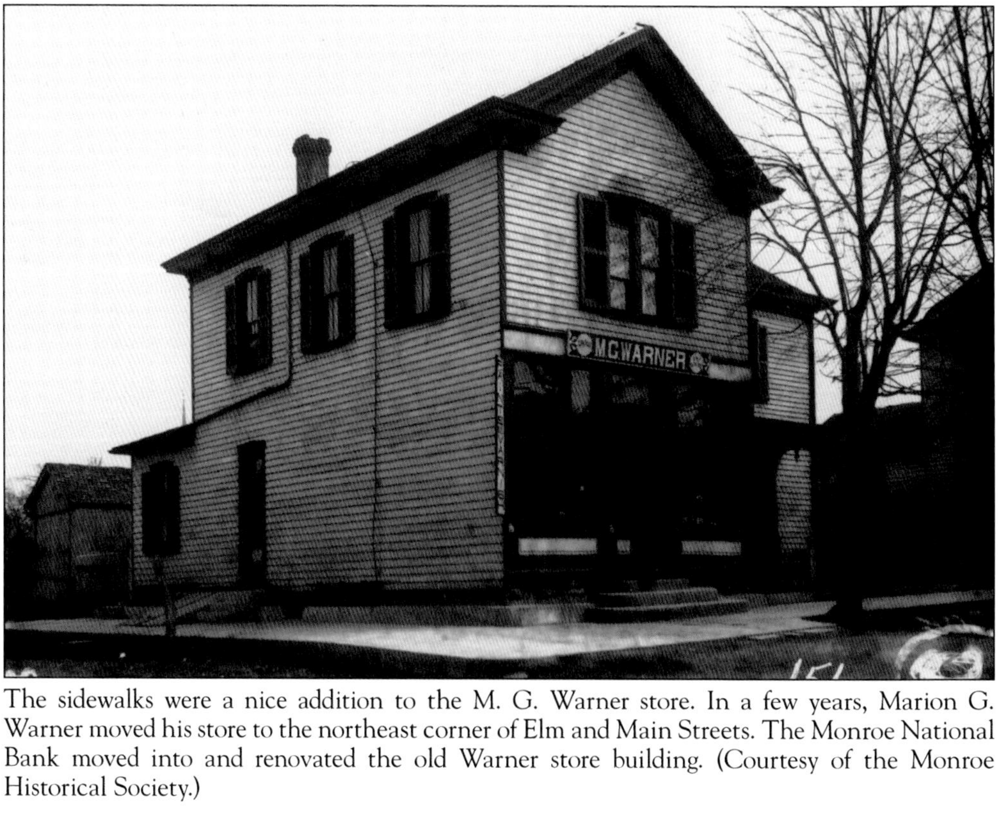

The sidewalks were a nice addition to the M. G. Warner store. In a few years, Marion G. Warner moved his store to the northeast corner of Elm and Main Streets. The Monroe National Bank moved into and renovated the old Warner store building. (Courtesy of the Monroe Historical Society.)

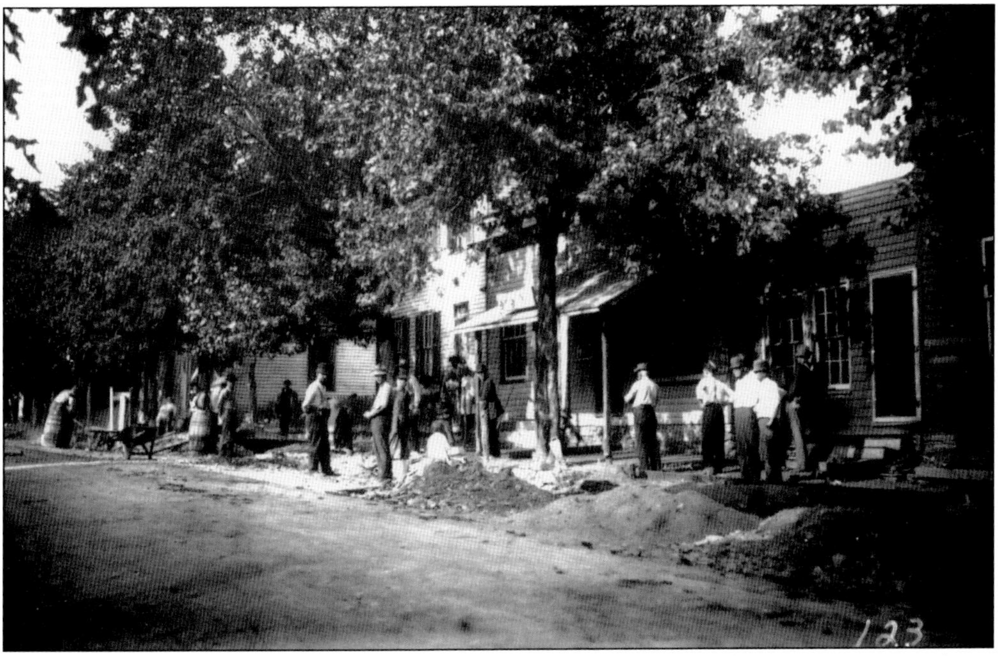

This photograph of workers and spectators gathered near the sidewalk construction site shows an urgent need for a pedestrian walkway on Main Street, Monroe. Gas lines were also installed during this construction and enabled the use of gas streetlights to illuminate the village after dark. (Courtesy of the Monroe Historical Society.)

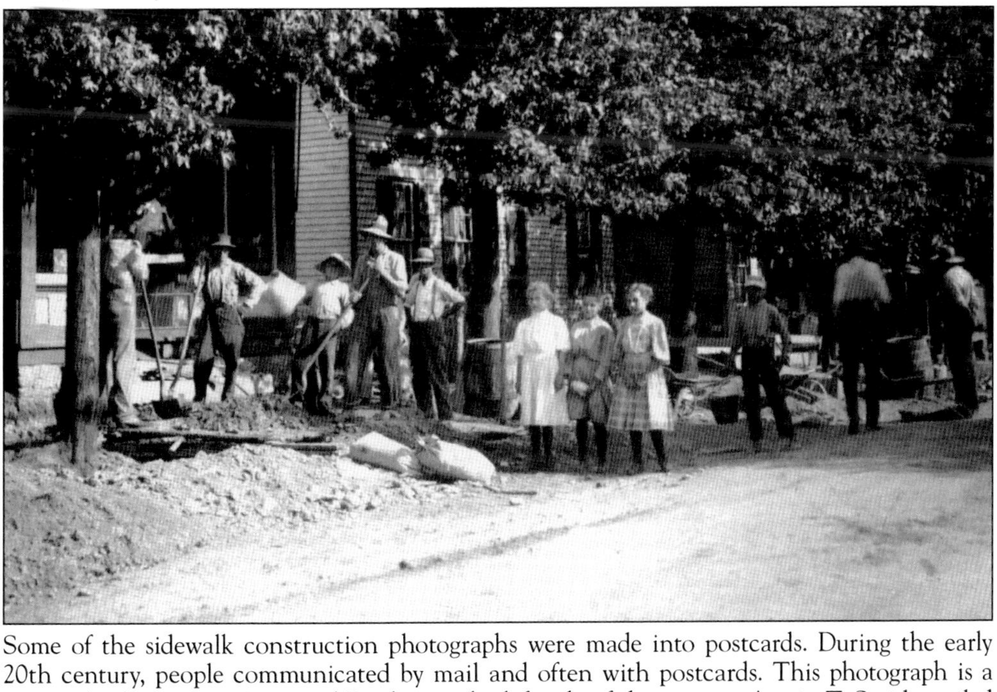

Some of the sidewalk construction photographs were made into postcards. During the early 20th century, people communicated by mail and often with postcards. This photograph is a postcard. The Monroe National Bank is at the left side of the picture. Austin T. Smith mailed this postcard to his family in Maysville, Kentucky. He was pleased with the progress of the sidewalk construction in front of the bank. (Courtesy of Boyd and Virginia Smith.)

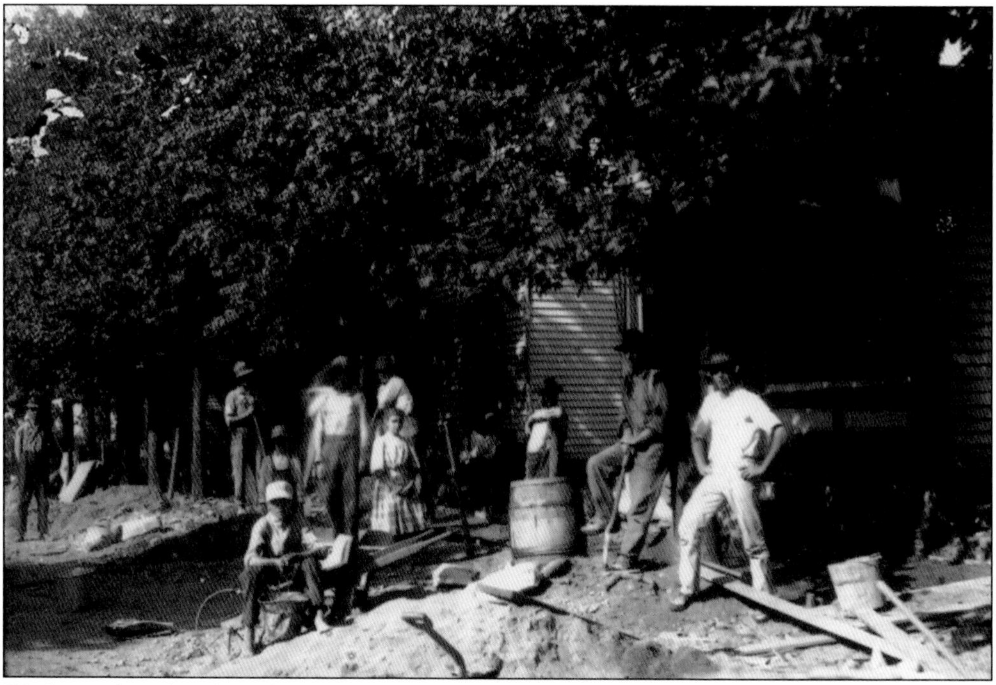

Workers take a break as they pose for this photograph taken in front of the Monroe National Bank. The sidewalk construction stirred up quite a bit of dust for Main Street residents and business, but anticipation of the new sidewalks made the temporary inconvenience of wiping dusty shelves and furniture easier to bear. This photograph was used for a postcard. (Courtesy of the Monroe Historical Society and Boyd and Virginia Smith.)

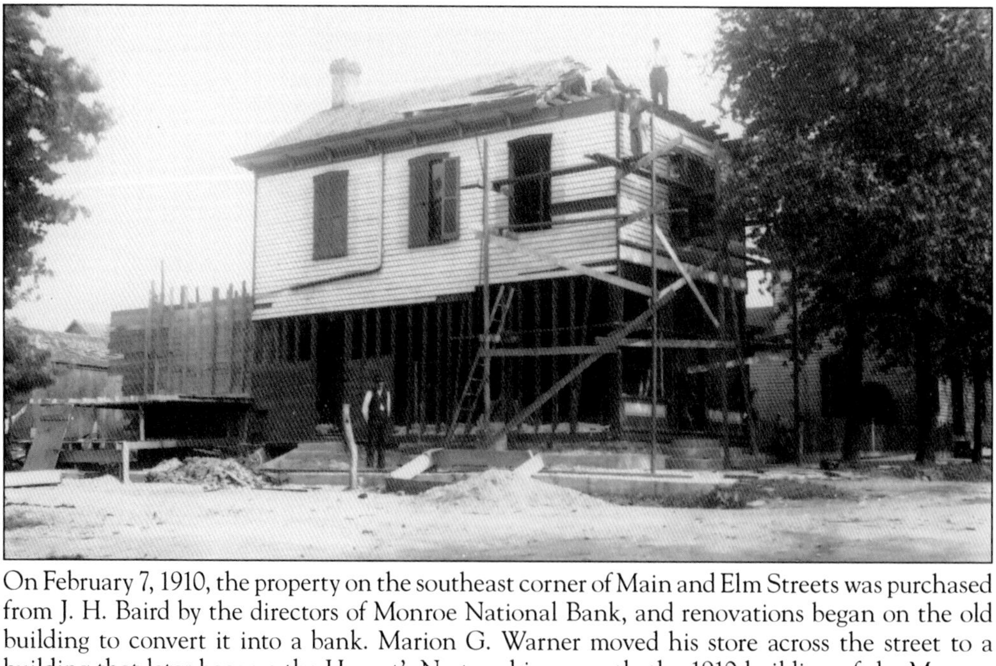

On February 7, 1910, the property on the southeast corner of Main and Elm Streets was purchased from J. H. Baird by the directors of Monroe National Bank, and renovations began on the old building to convert it into a bank. Marion G. Warner moved his store across the street to a building that later became the Hornet's Nest and is currently the 1910 building of the Monroe Historical Society. (Courtesy of the Monroe Historical Society.)

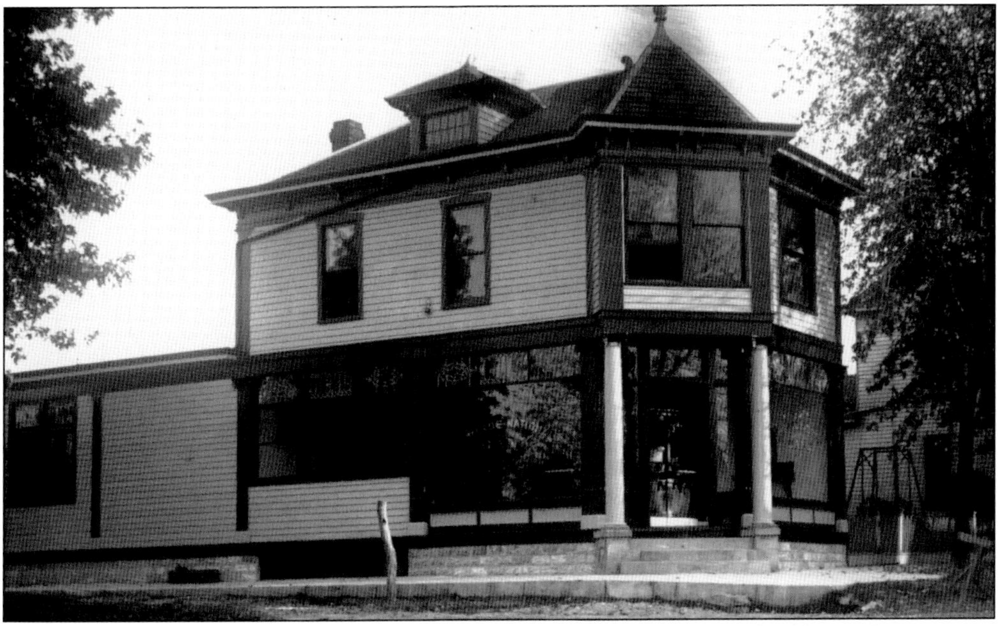

The remodeled bank building looked nothing like the old Warner store building. The entrance was moved from the front to the corner, windows were added to the side, the side and cellar entrances were removed, and an addition was added to the rear of the building. This building remained the home of Monroe National Bank until the current building was constructed in 1954. (Courtesy of Boyd and Virginia Smith.)

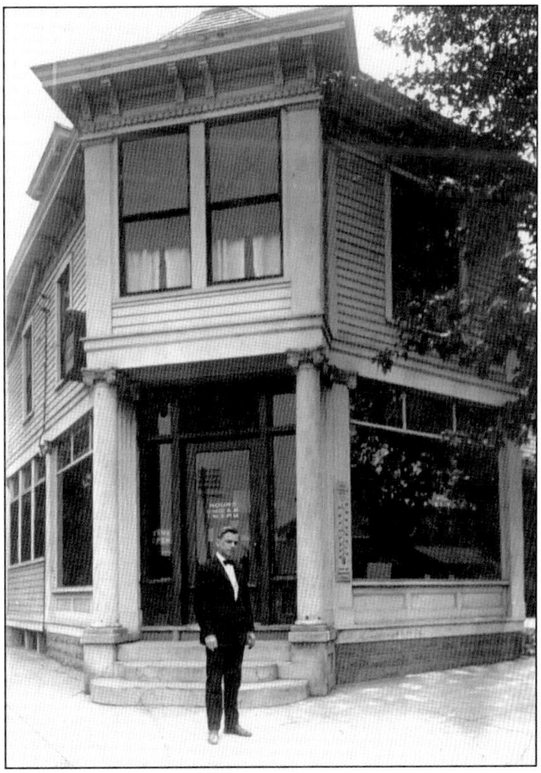

Austin T. Smith is standing in front of the new Monroe National Bank building. Monroe National Bank merged with First National Bank of Middletown in May 1953. Austin's son, Boyd, became assistant vice president and manager of the Monroe branch. First National merged with First National Bank and Trust Company of Hamilton on July 1, 1980, to become First National Bank of Southwestern Ohio. On July 19, 2002, it became First Financial Bank. (Courtesy of Boyd and Virginia Smith.)

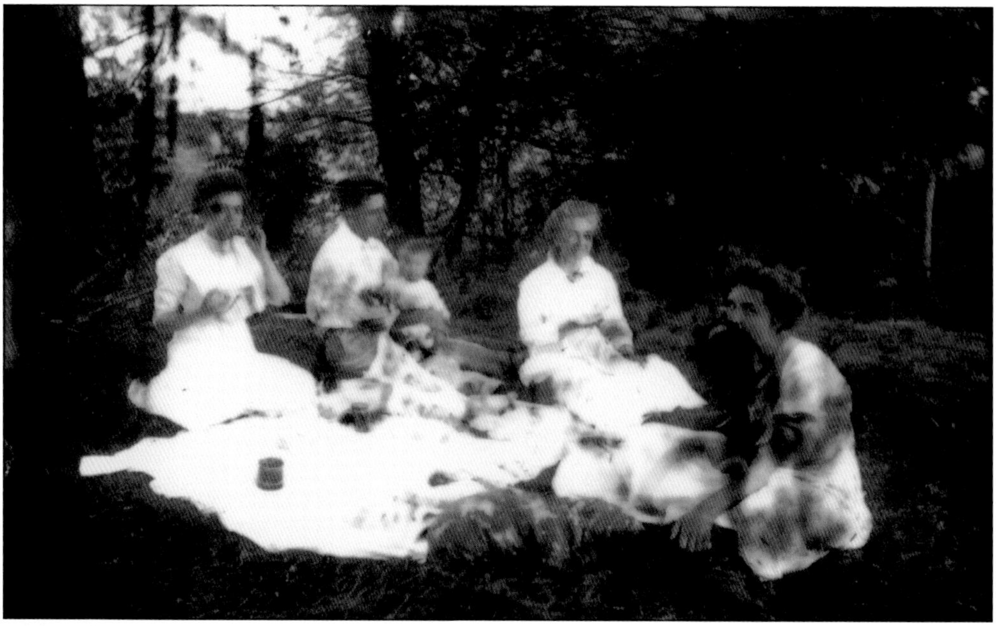

Although the Monroe citizens were hard-working, productive members of society, they also found time to relax and have fun. This June 1912 photograph shows a young family enjoying a delightful picnic lunch in the woods on a nice summer afternoon. (Courtesy of the Monroe Historical Society.)

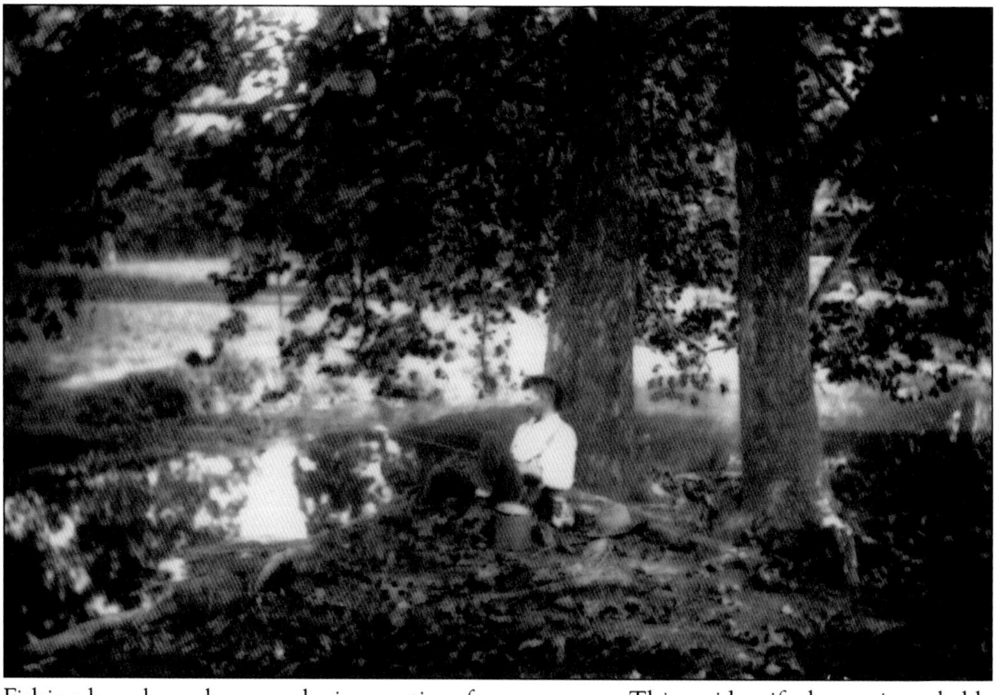

Fishing has always been a relaxing pastime for many men. This unidentified man is probably fishing on the Great Miami River. Nearby Lake Monroe has existed on Linn Road for several decades and is as a place where the family can fish together or a father can spend an enjoyable day with his son. (Courtesy of the Monroe Historical Society.)

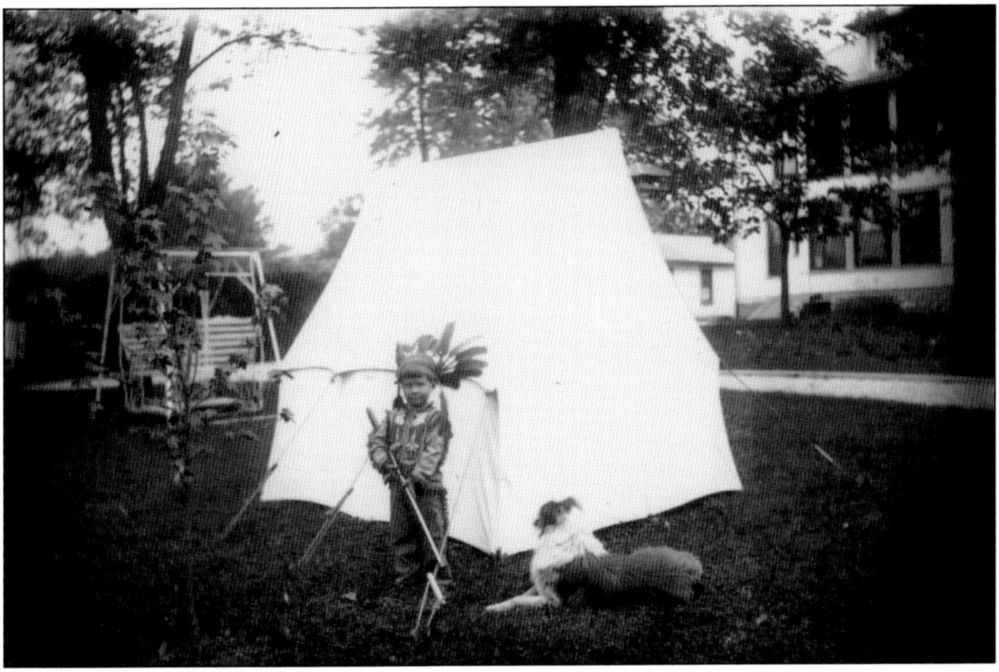

Children love to dress up and play in tents. Cowboys and Indians is a game that goes way back. Children in the 1960s played this with small plastic figurines. Other children's games that involve role-play are cops and robbers, doctor and patient, doctors and nurses, mothers and fathers, house, and shopkeeper and customer. (Courtesy of the Monroe Historical Society.)

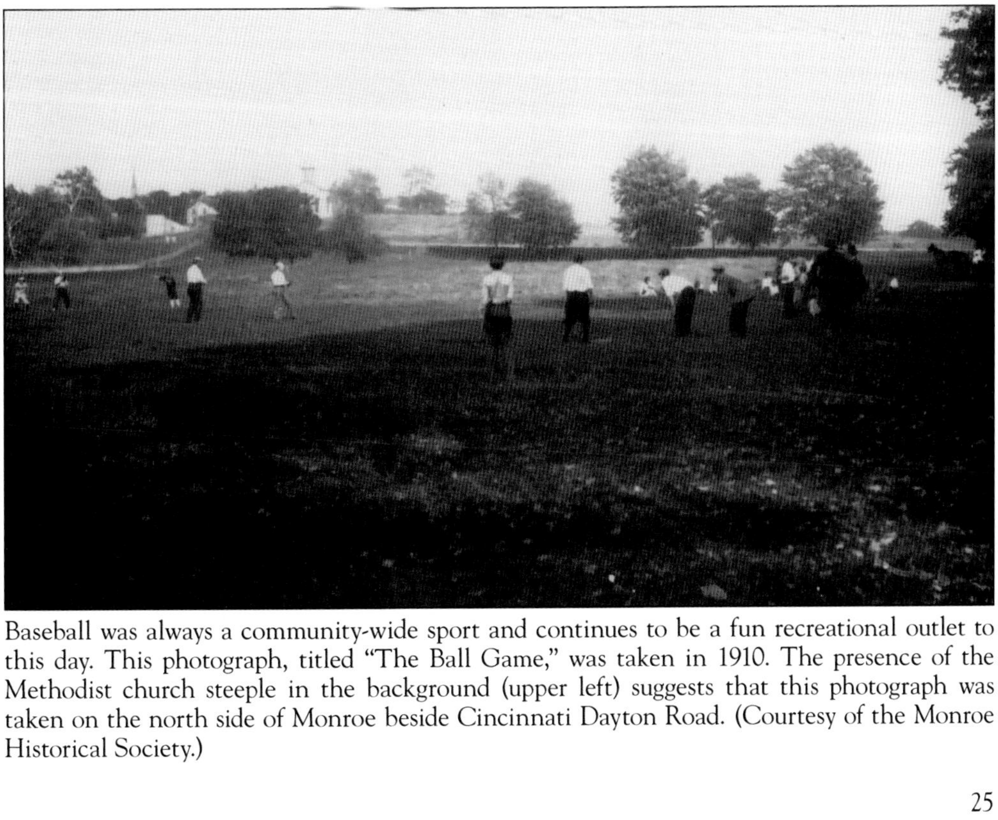

Baseball was always a community-wide sport and continues to be a fun recreational outlet to this day. This photograph, titled "The Ball Game," was taken in 1910. The presence of the Methodist church steeple in the background (upper left) suggests that this photograph was taken on the north side of Monroe beside Cincinnati Dayton Road. (Courtesy of the Monroe Historical Society.)

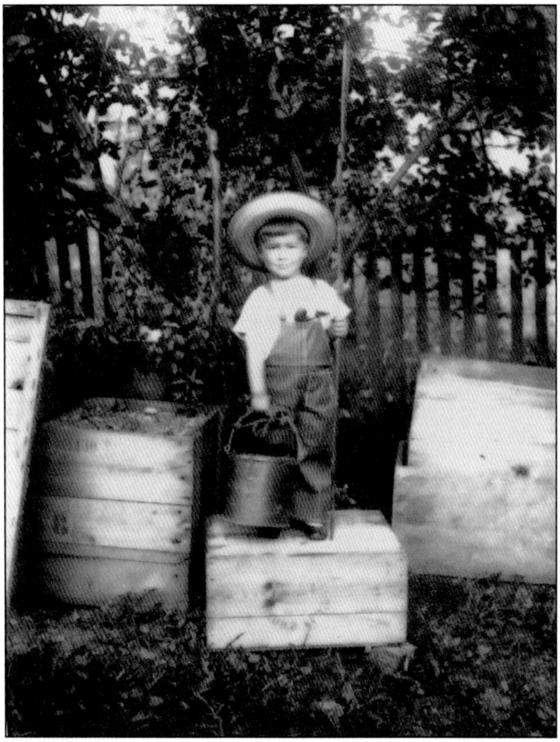

This little boy is clutching his bucket and pole and is ready for a fun-filled day of fishing. (Courtesy of the Monroe Historical Society.)

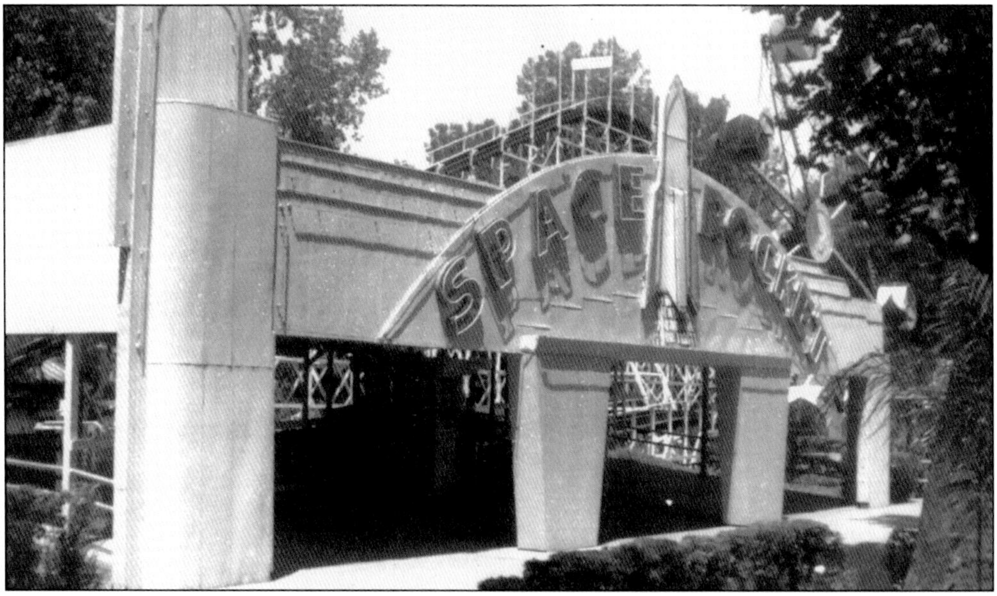

Lesourdsville Lake Amusement Park was founded in 1922 by Edgar Streifthau. The Space Rocket roller coaster was built in 1927 and was brought to Lesourdsville from an amusement park in Zanesville. It was called the Cyclone from 1938 to 1960, when the name was changed to the Space Rocket until 1978, when the name was changed to the Screechin' Eagle. Howard Berni and Frank Murru purchased the park from Streifthau in 1961. This 1963 photograph of the Space Rocket has the popular Rock-O-Planes in the background. (Courtesy of Gordon, Sylvia, and Phoebe Lindsay.)

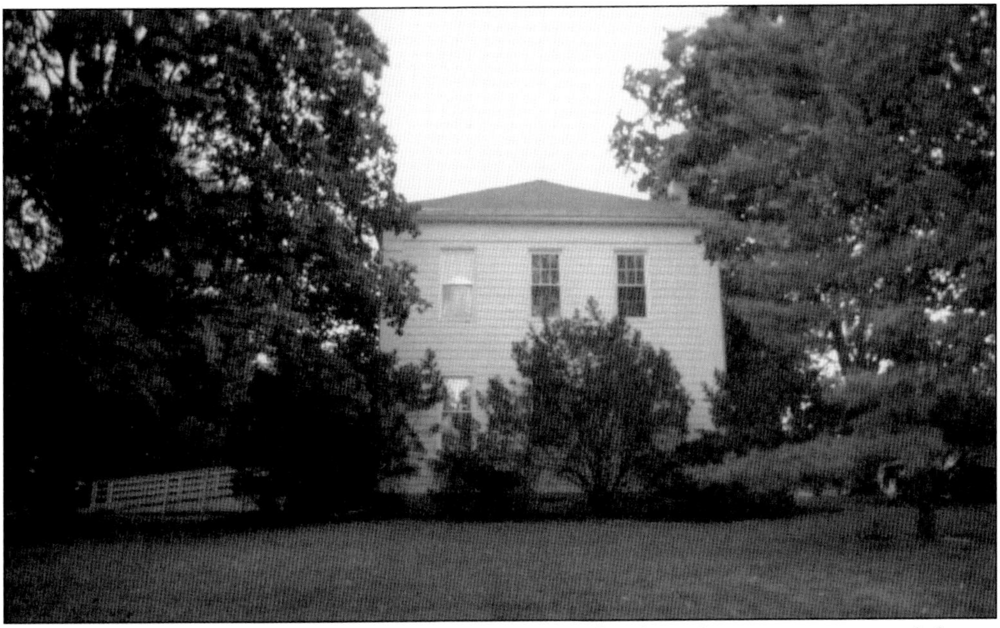

The Mount Airy farm was built in 1821 and is reported to have been a station or safe house on the Underground Railroad. There were three groups of people in Southern Ohio who did the most to further the cause: Quakers, free people of color, and Presbyterians. These hardy abolitionists risked everything, including possible death, to assist the slaves in gaining their freedom. (Courtesy of Nancy McNabb.)

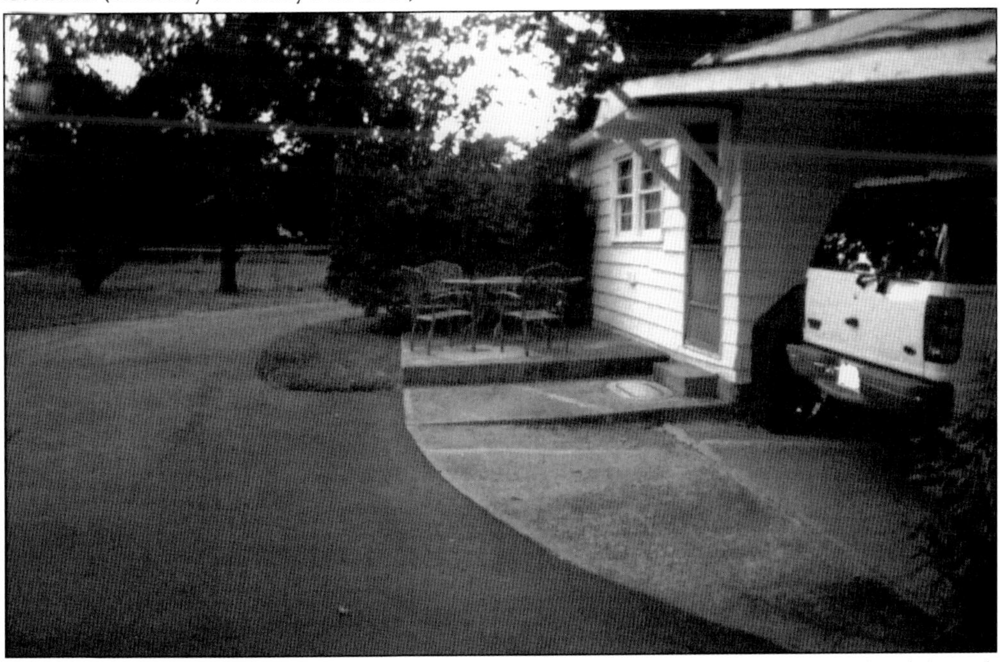

Under this patio area is where the runaway slaves were hidden, according to local legend. Current owner Melissa Giffen says there are holes in the basement wall and it appears to be hollow on the other side. She and her husband Michael purchased the house two years ago and are preparing to renovate and research its unique history. (Courtesy of Nancy McNabb.)

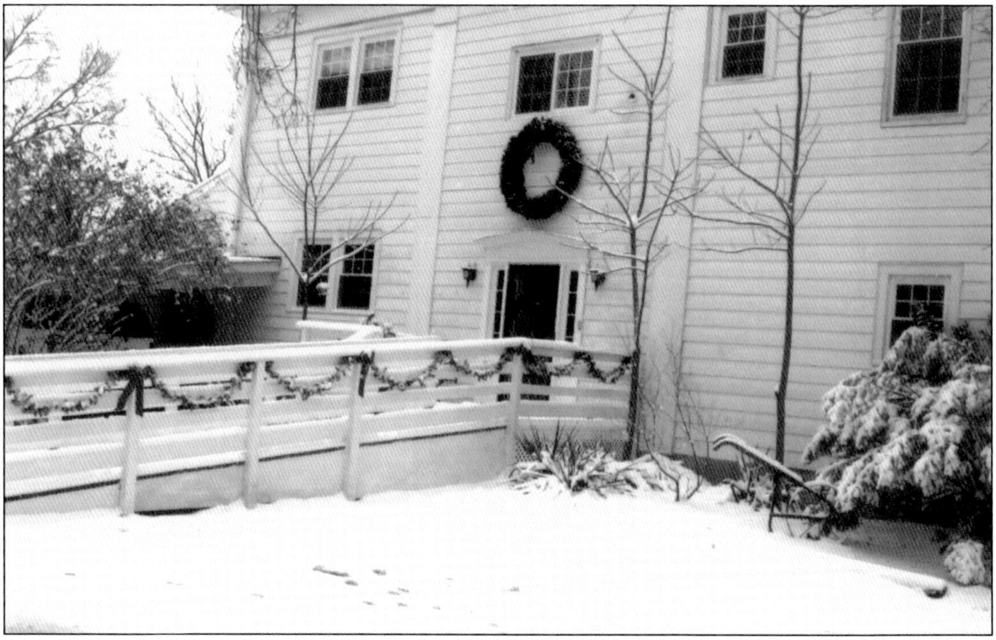

The T. J. Conover family bred hogs on the Mount Airy Farm. According to a pamphlet originally printed around 1870 and later reproduced in the sesquicentennial book, "Mr. T. J. Conover has been engaged in breeding fine hogs for thirty years." T. J. Conover was also an elder of the First Presbyterian Church, which was established in Monroe during the year 1831. The Conovers died in the 1890s and are buried in the Mound Cemetery. (Courtesy of Michael and Melissa Giffin.)

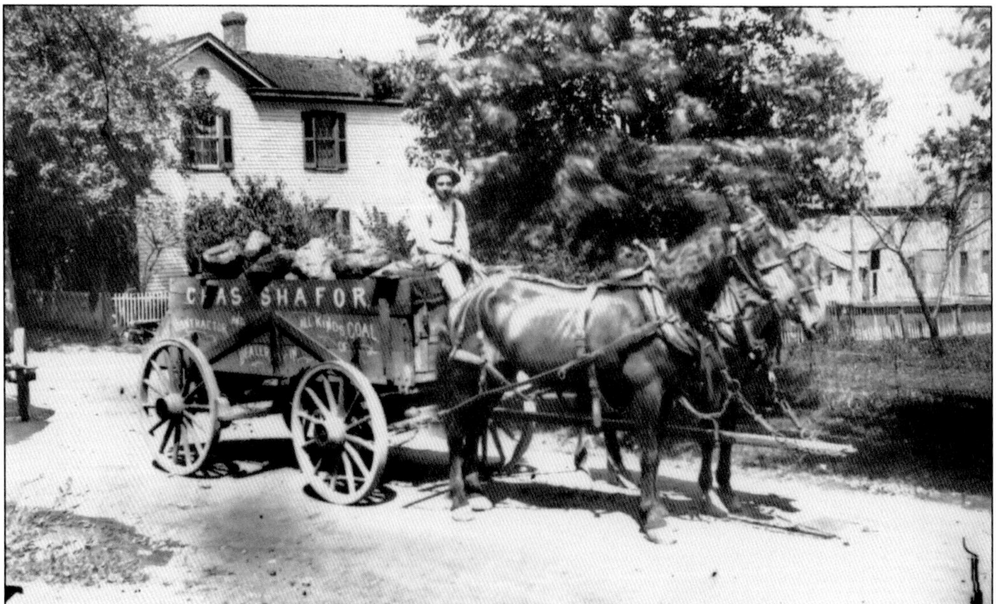

Charles Shafor pulls his cargo east on Elm Street. Another horse-drawn wagon follows behind. (Courtesy of the Monroe Historical Society.)

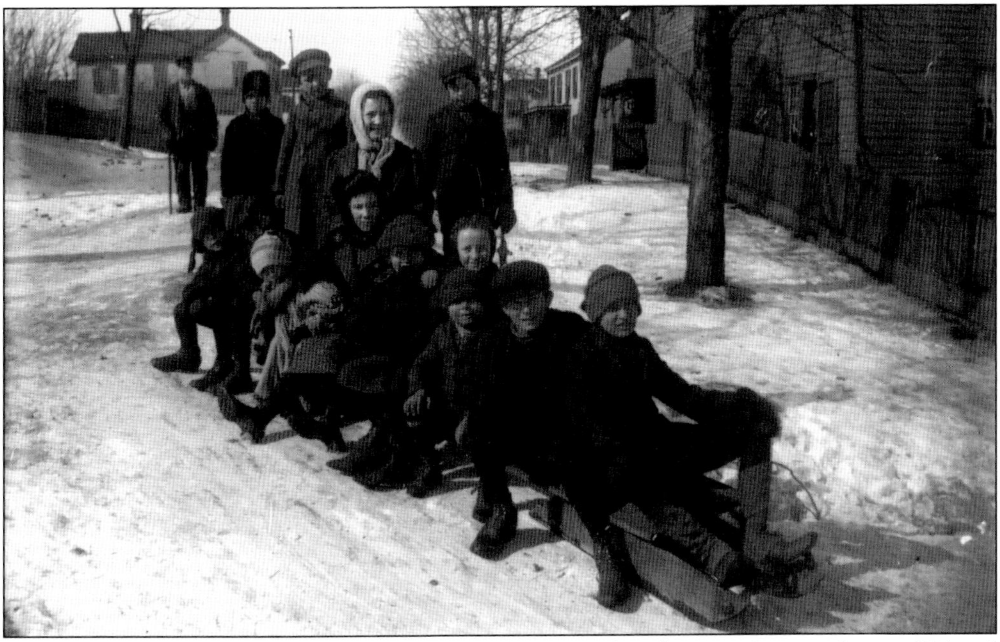

Tobogganing was a favorite winter activity for children. This photograph was taken at Old and Elm Streets in the early part of the 20th century. In the latter part of the century, the hill behind Lemon Monroe High School became popular for sledding. In the late 1960s, after a sledding accident a parent could call Dr. James Anderson, and he would open his office to stitch the wounds of an injured child, thus saving the parents from making a run to the emergency room at Middletown Hospital. (Courtesy of the Monroe Historical Society.)

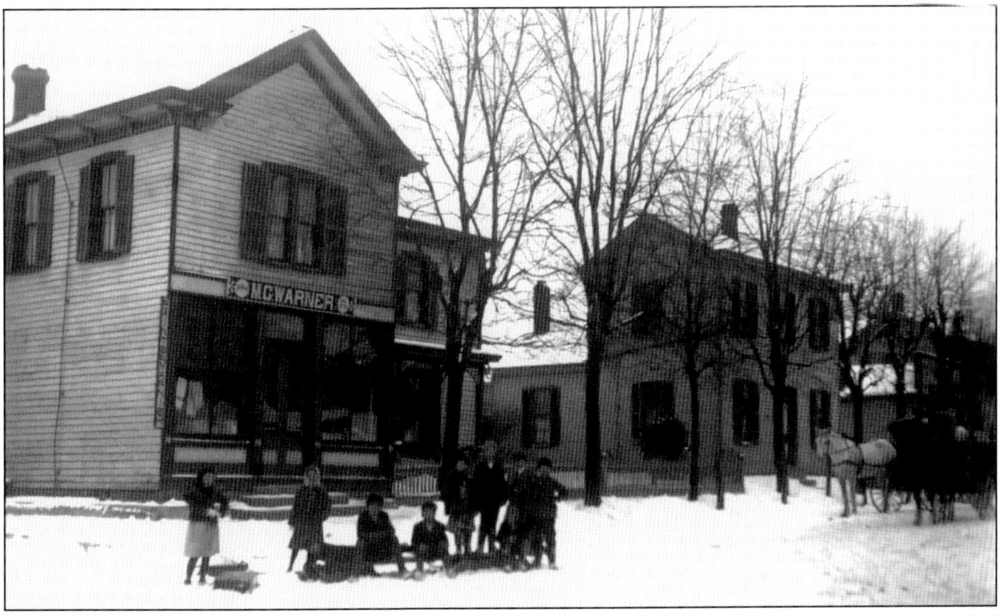

Sledding on Main Street was also a favorite pastime for the children. The main hazards for sled riders in the early 20th century were the horse and buggy or a horse-drawn sleigh, as seen in this photograph taken in front of the M. G. Warner store around 1910. (Courtesy of Boyd and Virginia Smith.)

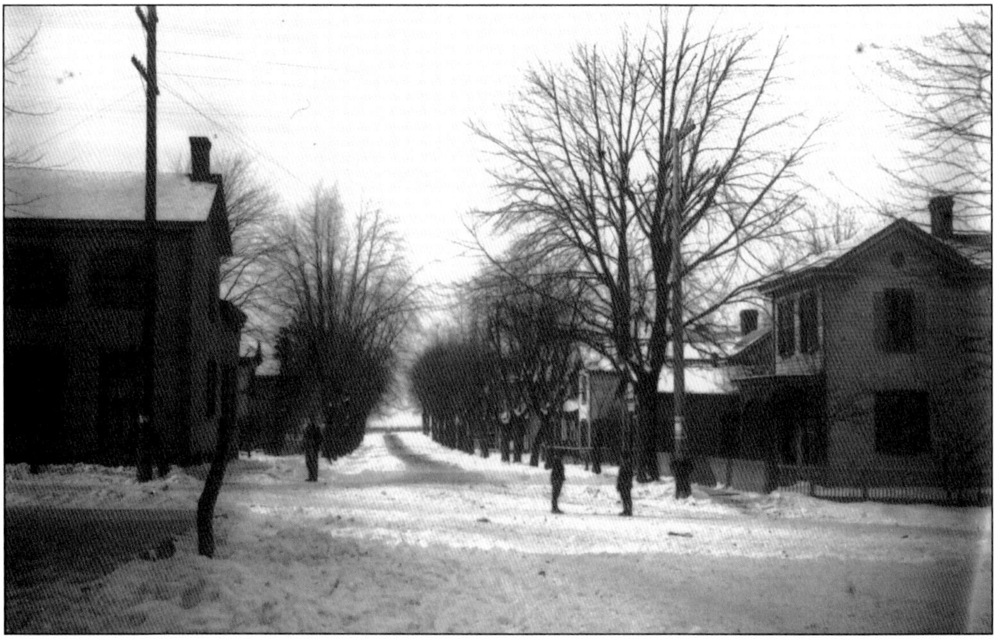

Children have always enjoyed a snowy day in Monroe, even if they are not sleigh riding. This photograph, taken at the corner of Elm and Main Streets, is looking west toward the site that would eventually become what is now the old football stadium. (Courtesy of the Monroe Historical Society.)

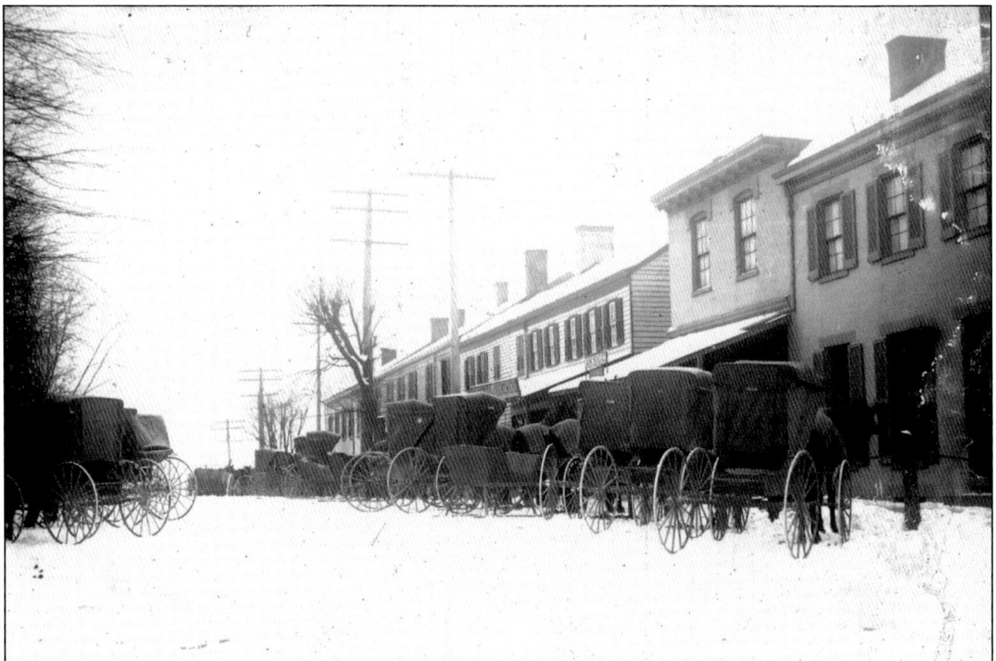

The bad weather did not keep patrons from conducting their business at the Sigg Grocery and post office on Main Street. J. H. Sigg was quite busy on this snowy day. (Courtesy of the Monroe Historical Society.)

This shivering little girl was apparently enjoying the cold snowy weather. (Courtesy of the Monroe Historical Society.)

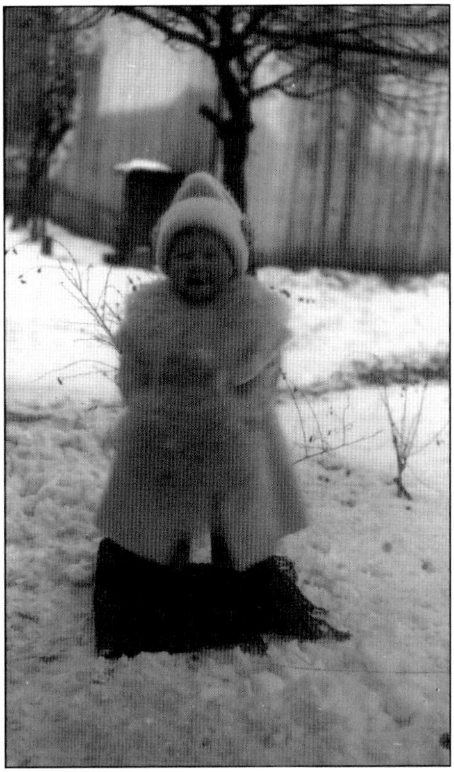

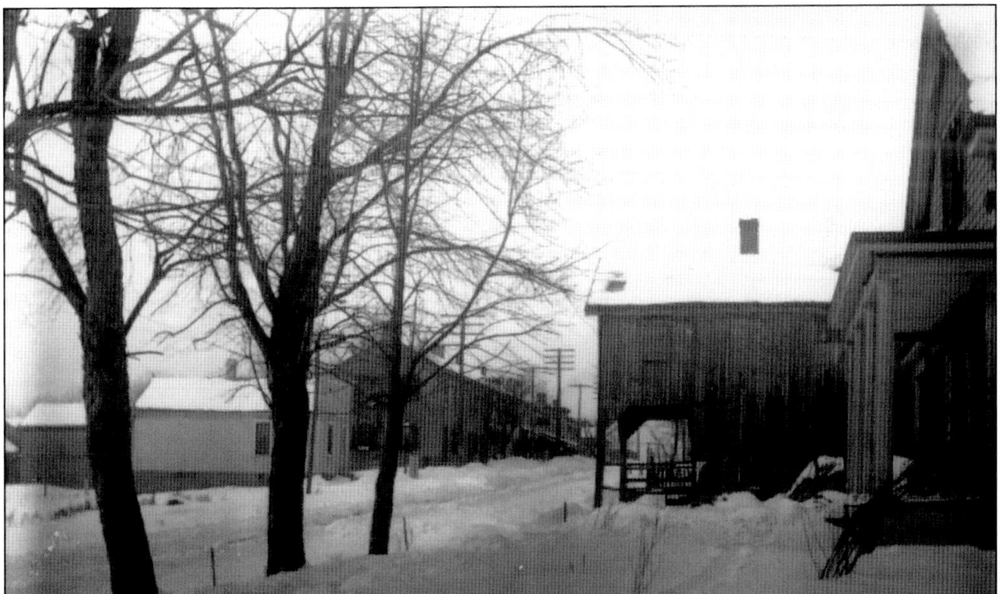

During January 1918, Monroe experienced a big snowstorm. Boone Warner was the only person in town who had a camera, and he took several shots of the snow-blanketed village. This photograph was taken at Main and Lebanon Streets and looks north toward the center of town. The city building is the small white building on the left. The International Order of Odd Fellows (IOOF) lodge is beside it. (Courtesy of the Monroe Historical Society.)

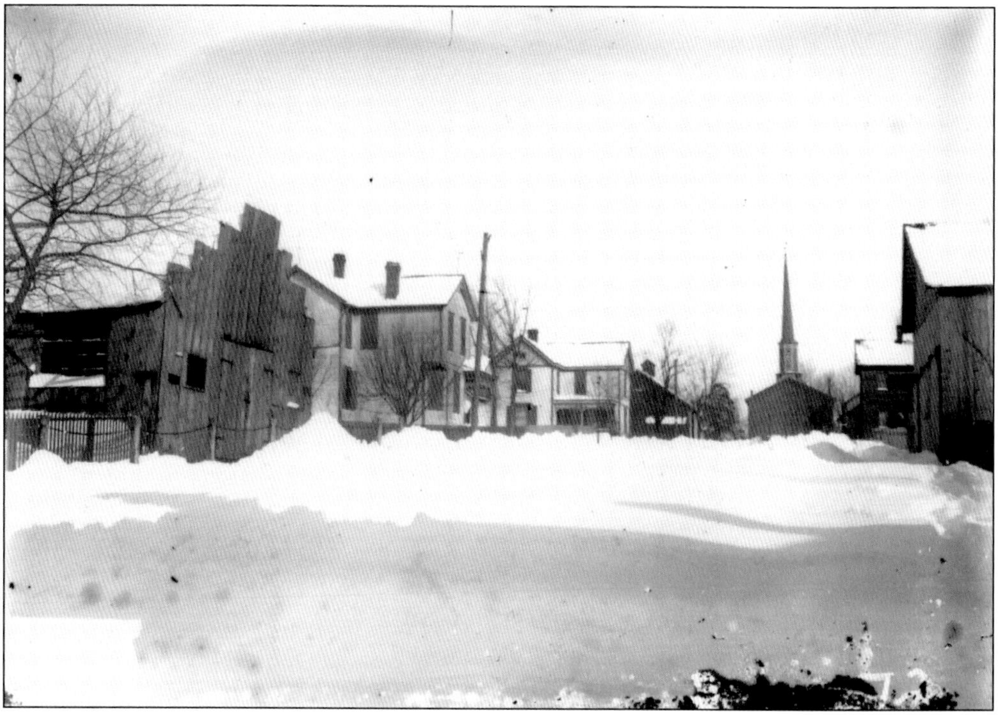

This photograph shows the corner of Church and Main Streets looking east. The Methodist church is seen in the background. Streets and sidewalks have yet to be cleared. (Courtesy of the Monroe Historical Society.)

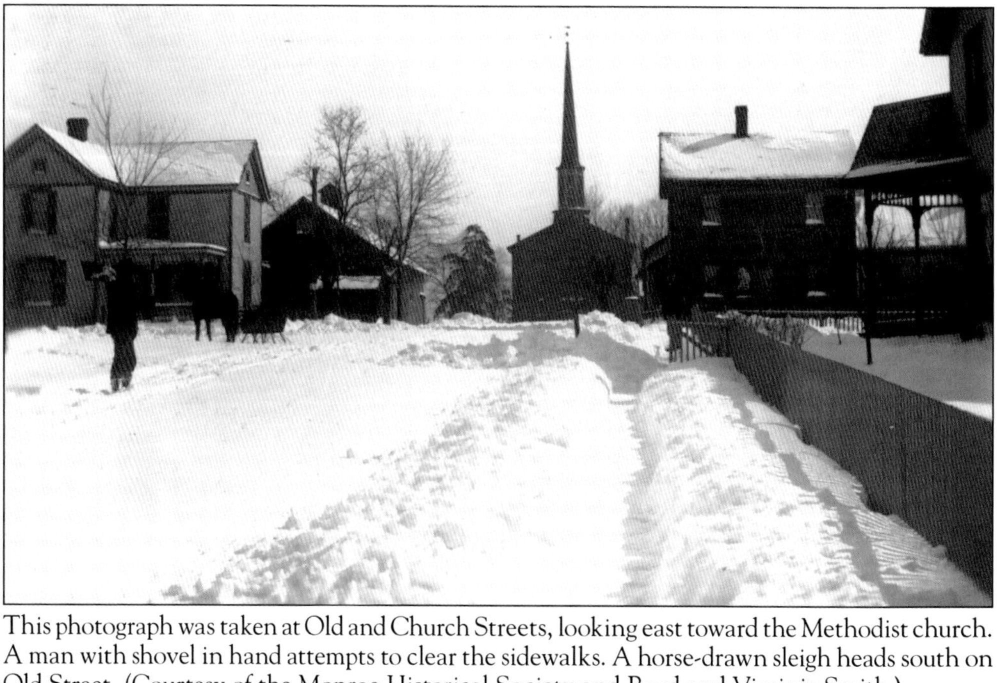

This photograph was taken at Old and Church Streets, looking east toward the Methodist church. A man with shovel in hand attempts to clear the sidewalks. A horse-drawn sleigh heads south on Old Street. (Courtesy of the Monroe Historical Society and Boyd and Virginia Smith.)

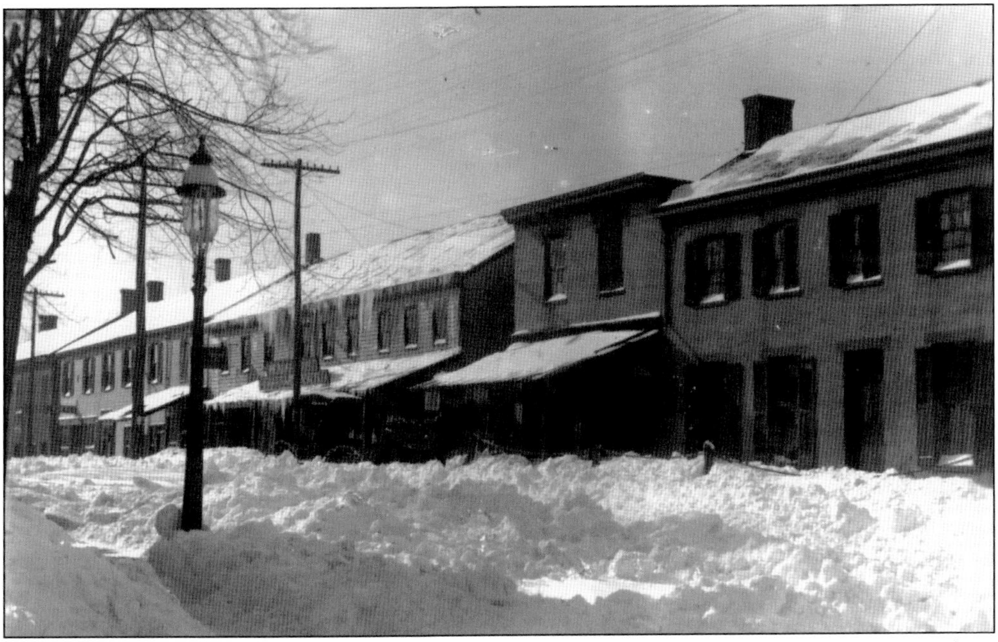

This lone horse and buggy is parked on the street where several usually gather. Peter Neu's place and the C. M. Robinson grocery and hardware were pretty well snowed in after the storm of 1918. This photograph has long been the subject of an artist's conception of early Monroe with an oil painting created in its likeness. (Courtesy of Boyd and Virginia Smith.)

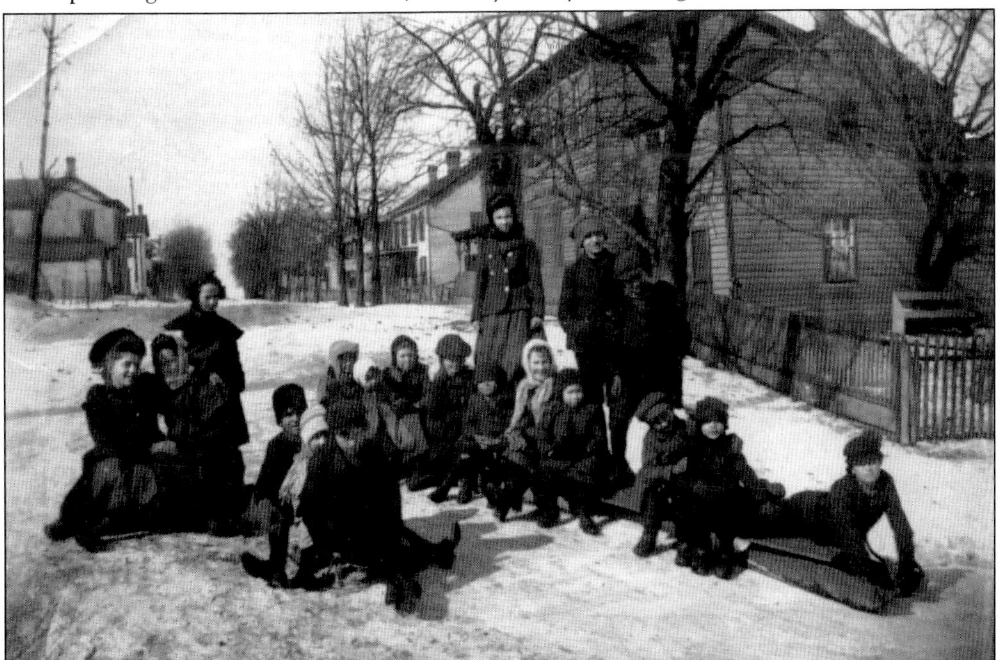

After the streets have been cleared and the snow packed down, children have fun with their sleds. Beulah Boyd (far left) is having a nice time with her friends on this frosty day. (Courtesy of Boyd and Virginia Smith.)

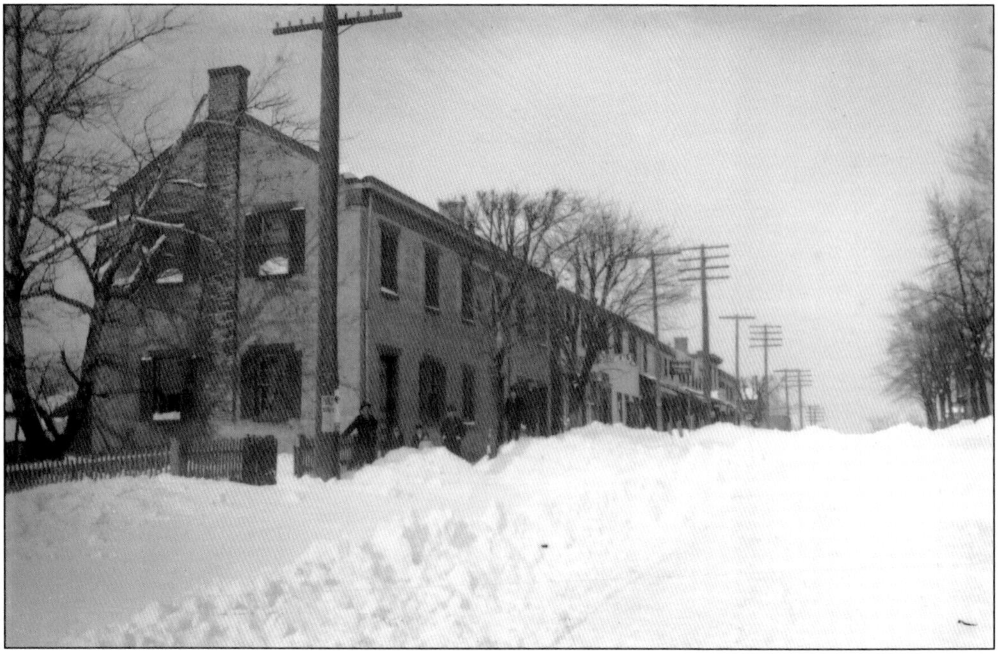

The IOOF lodge (left) is seen in this photograph looking north on Main Street in the aftermath of the 1918 big snow. Notice that there are no horse-drawn sleighs or horse and buggies in this photograph. Peter Neu's shop is in the third building to the north. All is deserted, except for a few pedestrians in front of the snowbank. (Courtesy of the Monroe Historical Society.)

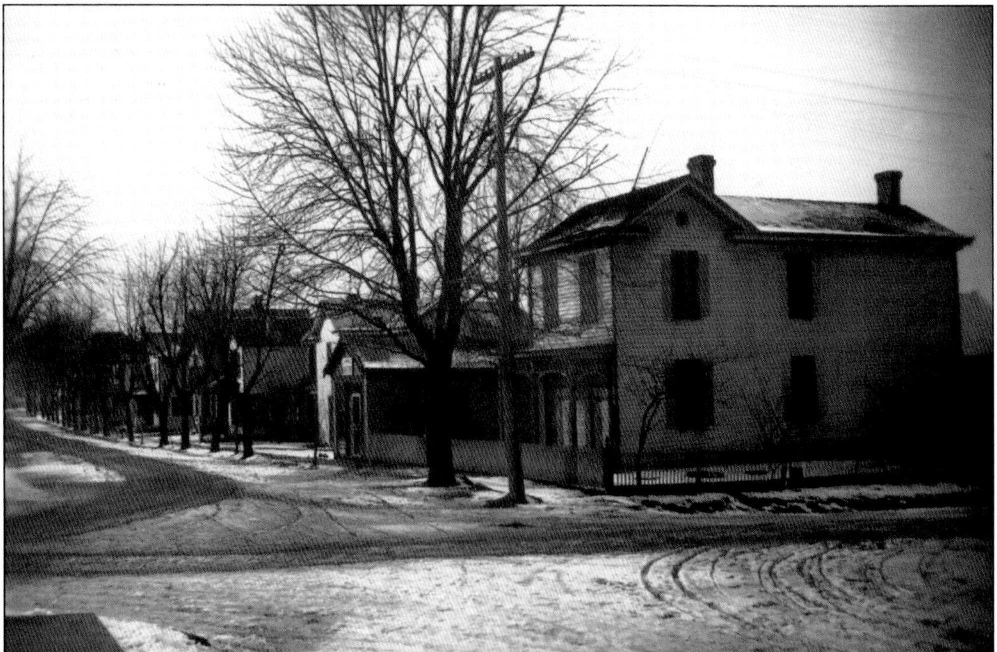

This shot was taken at the corner of Main and Elm Streets looking west. Note the buggy tracks in the snow. The bakery is the second structure on the right. The corner house is currently home to Kelly Myers Insurance. (Courtesy of Boyd and Virginia Smith.)

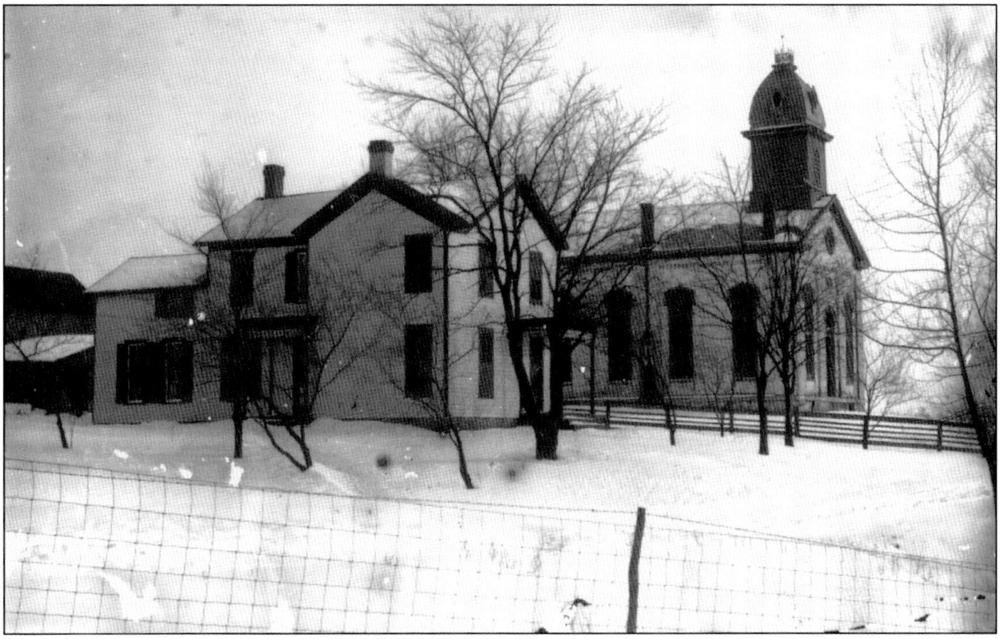

The Fitzwater house (left) and the Presbyterian Academy (right) sat below Lebanon Street near Cincinnati Dayton Road and were affiliated with the First Presbyterian Church, organized in 1831 as the Harmony Church. The first-known school in Monroe was a one-room school that sat at the corner of East Elm Street and East Avenue. That was for elementary-age children. The academy pictured above was reportedly used for a high school or may have held all the classes. Judge Todhunter went from the academy to college. (Courtesy of the Monroe Historical Society.)

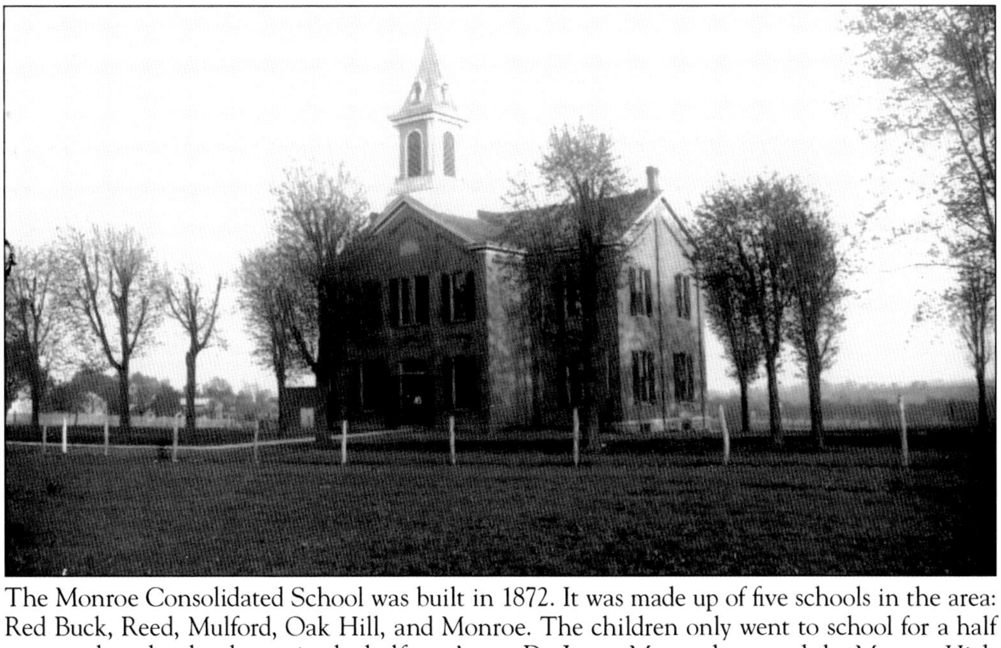

The Monroe Consolidated School was built in 1872. It was made up of five schools in the area: Red Buck, Reed, Mulford, Oak Hill, and Monroe. The children only went to school for a half year, as the school only received a half year's tax. Dr. James Macready started the Monroe High School in 1881. It was held in the same building as the lower grades. (Courtesy of the Monroe Historical Society.)

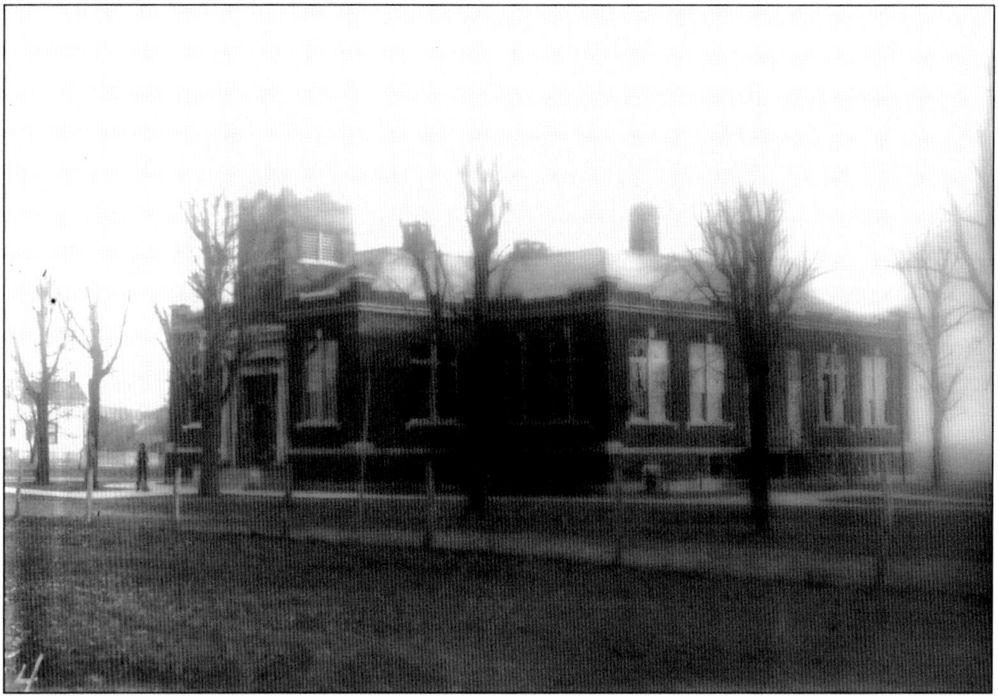

The old consolidated school building was razed in 1912, and a new one was built. This school sat on the current site of the old Lemon Monroe High School building. It soon became too small, and a south wing was added in 1948. The 1912 building eventually became part of the Middletown school system and was demolished in 1967. (Courtesy of the Monroe Historical Society.)

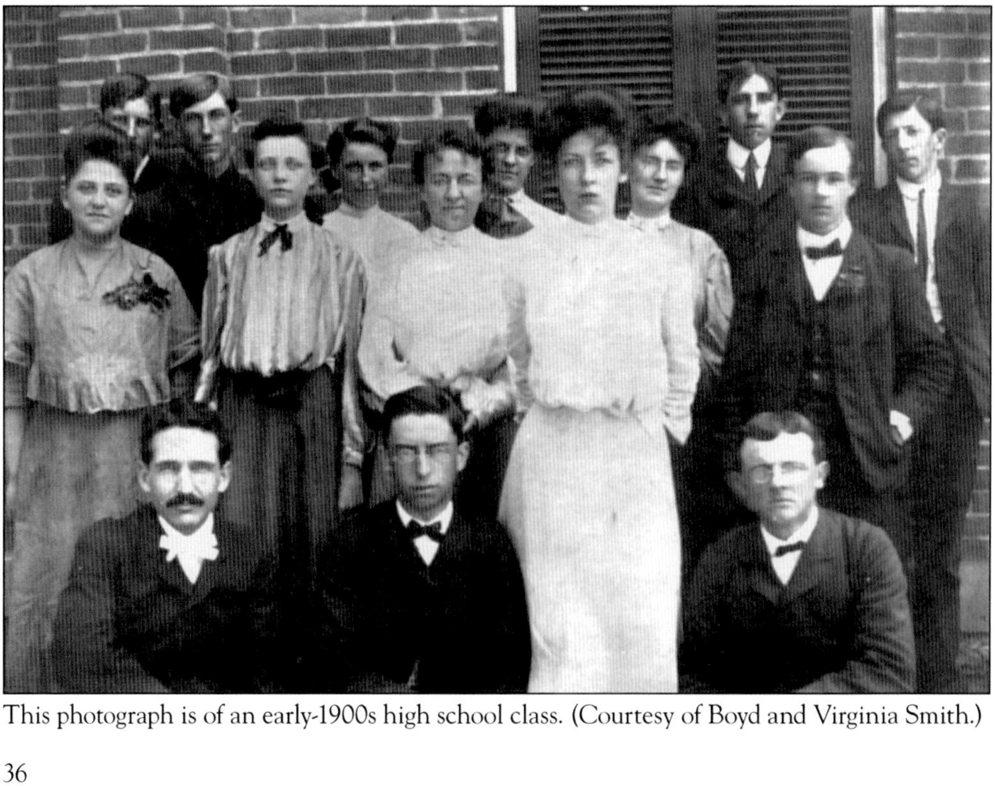

This photograph is of an early-1900s high school class. (Courtesy of Boyd and Virginia Smith.)

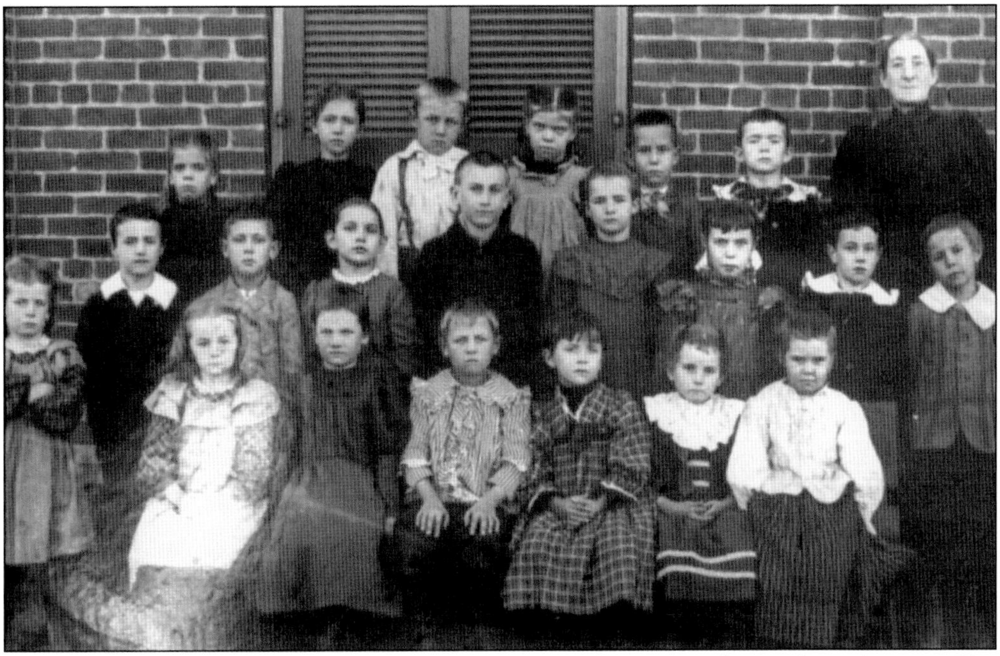

This photograph of an elementary class at Monroe School was taken during the early 1900s. The class probably attended the new 1912 building. (Courtesy of Boyd and Virginia Smith.)

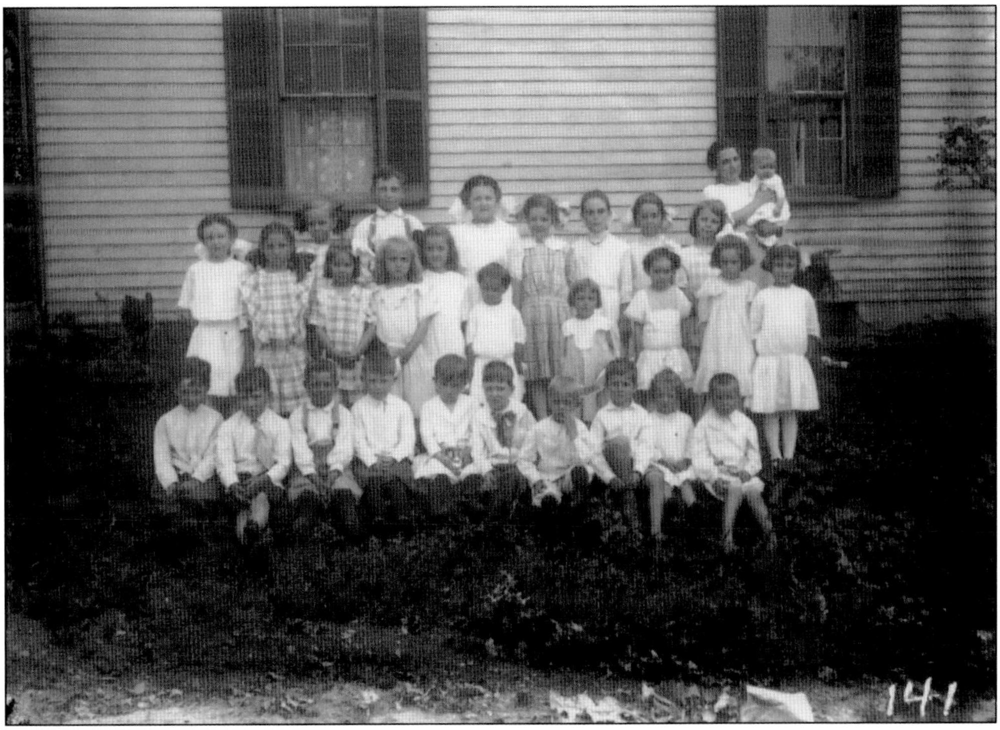

A Monroe elementary school class posed for this early-1900s photograph. The classes eventually became separated into the respective elementary grade levels, kindergarten through grade six, as the school continued to grow. (Courtesy of the Monroe Historical Society.)

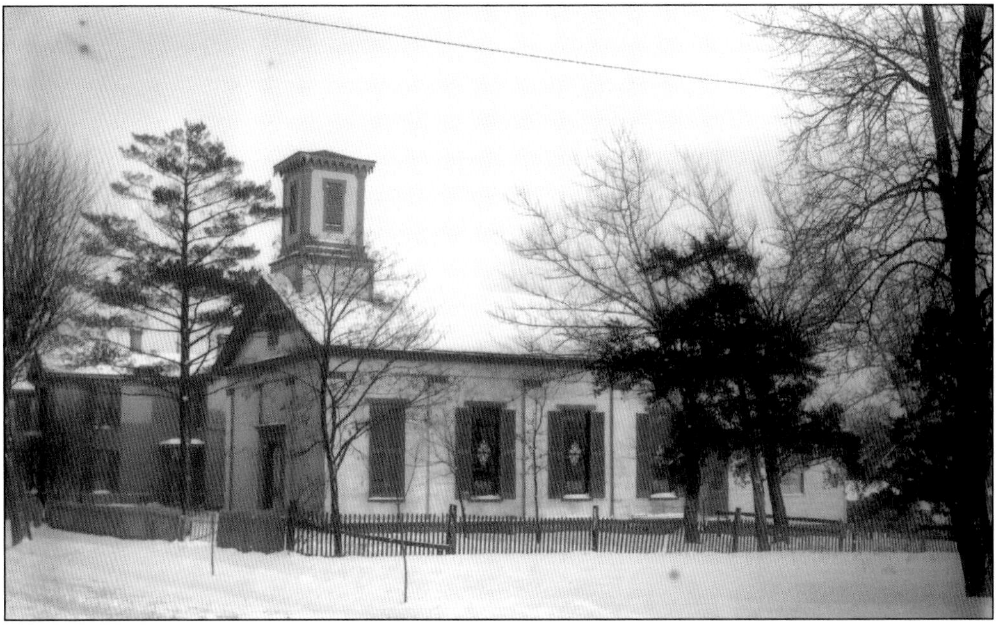

The Monroe Presbyterian Church was first organized in Kentucky in 1792 and came to Monroe around 1802. It was called the Swamp Creek Congregation from 1804 until 1807, when the name was changed to Mount Pleasant Associate Reformed Church. The Associate Presbytery and the Reformed Presbytery separated from the Church of Scotland. These two branches of the Presbyterian Church eventually came to the United States and were united in 1782 to become the Associate Reformed Presbyterian Church. (Courtesy of the Monroe Historical Society.)

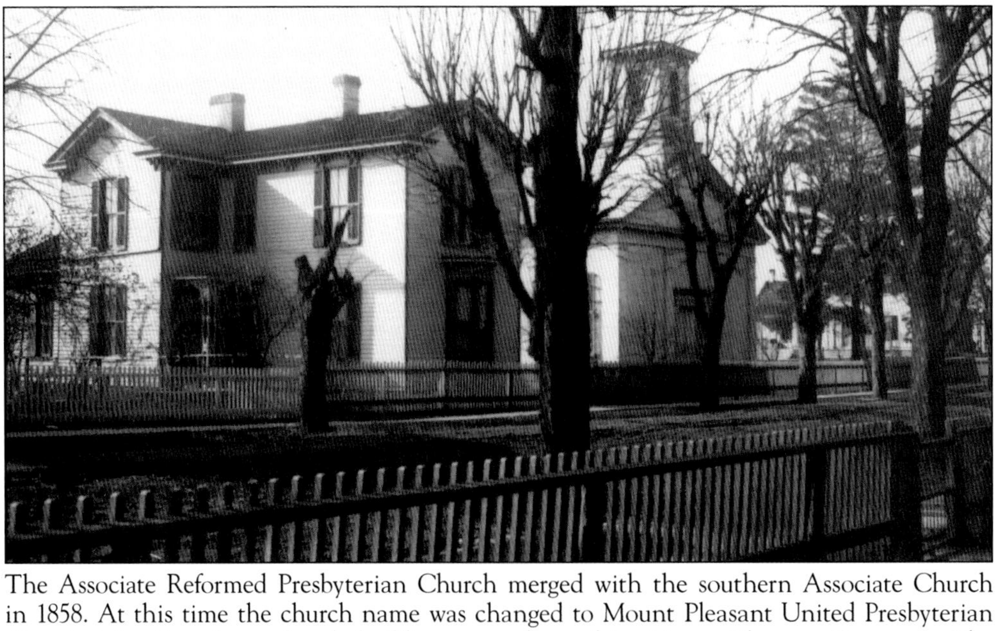

The Associate Reformed Presbyterian Church merged with the southern Associate Church in 1858. At this time the church name was changed to Mount Pleasant United Presbyterian Church. The first three church buildings were located in Mount Pleasant Cemetery. The sanctuary featured in this photograph was built in 1854 and served the congregation until 1956, when the current church was built. The name was later changed to the Monroe Presbyterian Church. (Courtesy of the Monroe Historical Society.)

In addition to platting and naming the village of Monroe, Nathaniel Sackett Jr. was also a local Methodist preacher. He purchased a double log house from John Baker, and this house was often used for worship. This brick church building was erected in 1860. The 1860 church lost the steeple during the tornado of 1969. (Courtesy of the Monroe Historical Society.)

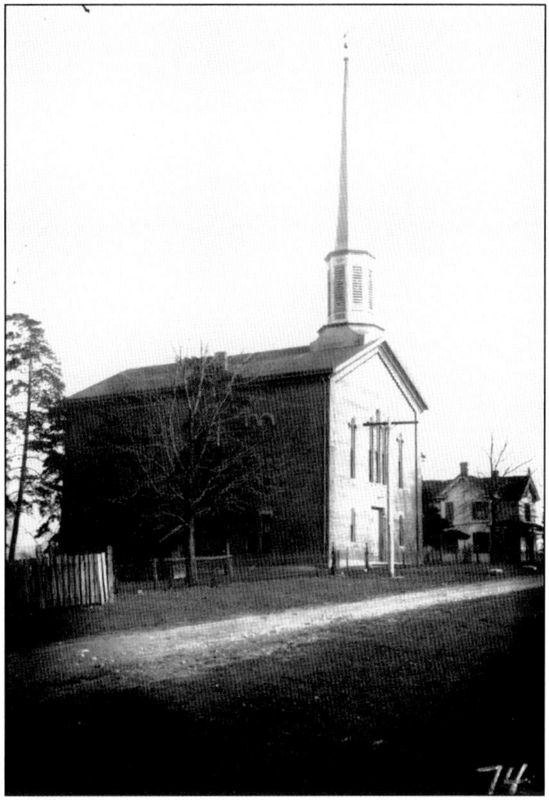

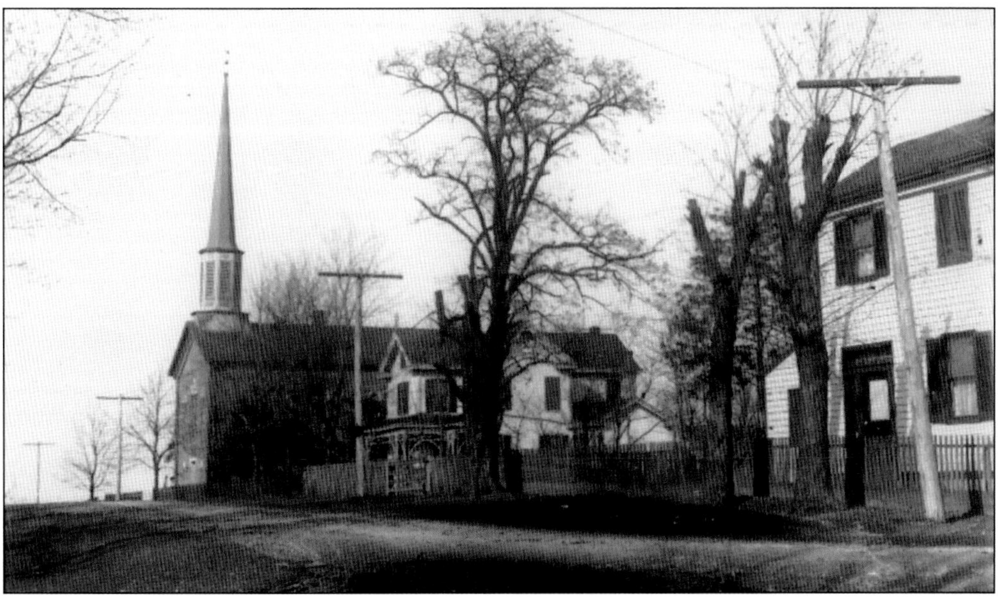

The parsonage sat beside the Methodist church as was built in 1868. Some notable ministers who served the congregation after 1860 were Rev. Jonathan Verity, who was the father of George M. Verity, founder of Armco Steel Corporation; Rev. W. B. Moler, grandfather of author Merle Constiner; and Rev. C. Wones, who was the father of Mary Warner. (Courtesy of the Monroe Historical Society.)

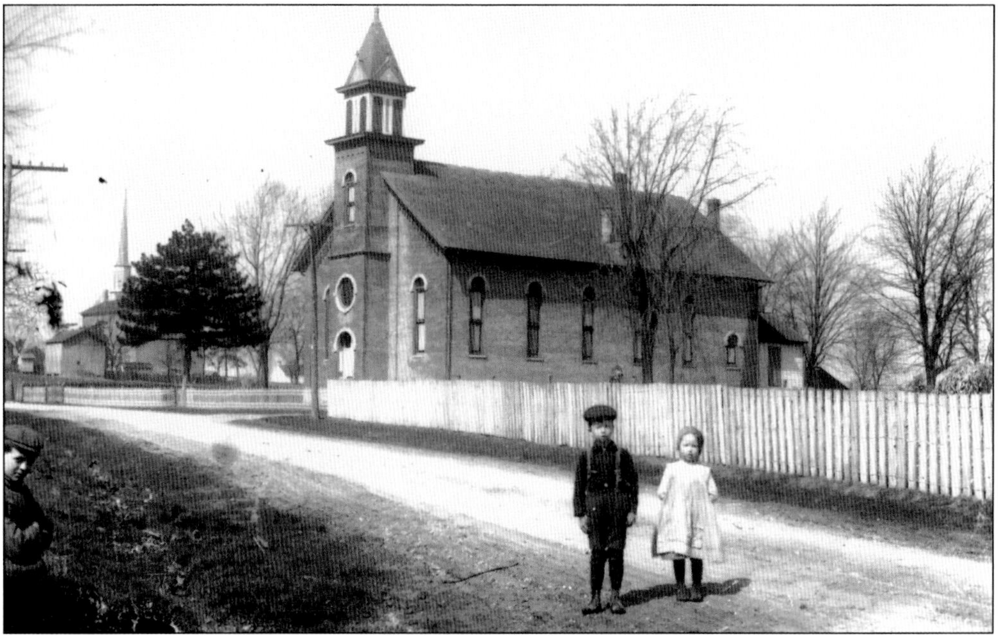

St. Stephen Church in Hamilton was the mother parish of Holy Trinity Church in Middletown. Holy Trinity was founded in April 1852 due to the increasing number of Irish immigrants. Gradually the Catholic population in the area became more numerous and diversified with Germans, Slovaks, and Italians. This created a need for more parishes. Five churches were organized from Holy Trinity, and the Seven Dolors Church pictured here was one. (Courtesy of the Monroe Historical Society.)

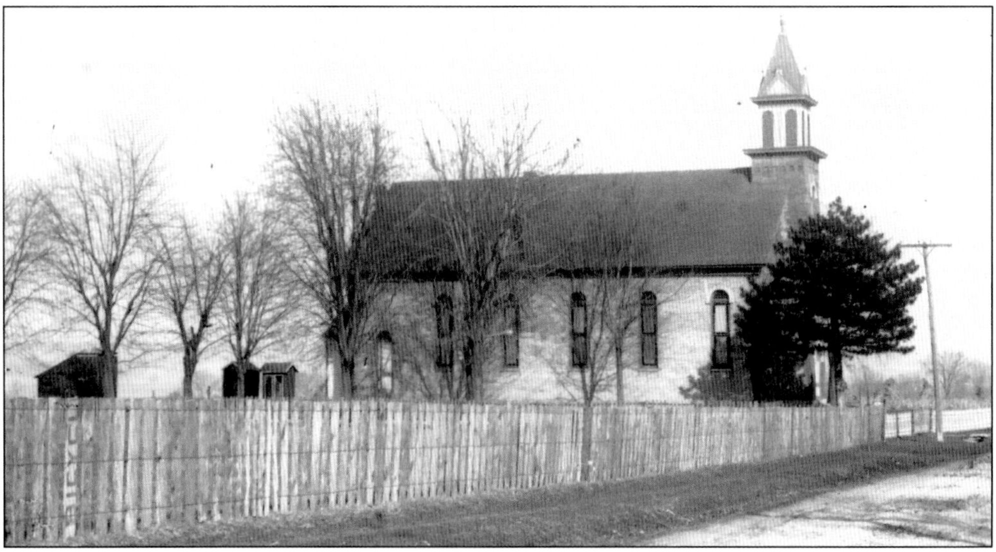

Our Lady of Sorrows Parish was founded in 1883 as Seven Dolors. Seven Dolors means seven sorrows and it honors the Mother of Christ and refers to her sorrows due to the suffering of Christ. The parish is located on Lebanon Street behind the Methodist church. The Catholic, Methodist, and Presbyterian churches have often combined efforts within the community for various events: vacation Bible school, the sesquicentennial ecumenical service, and religious films shown at the school yard in 1923. (Courtesy of the Monroe Historical Society.)

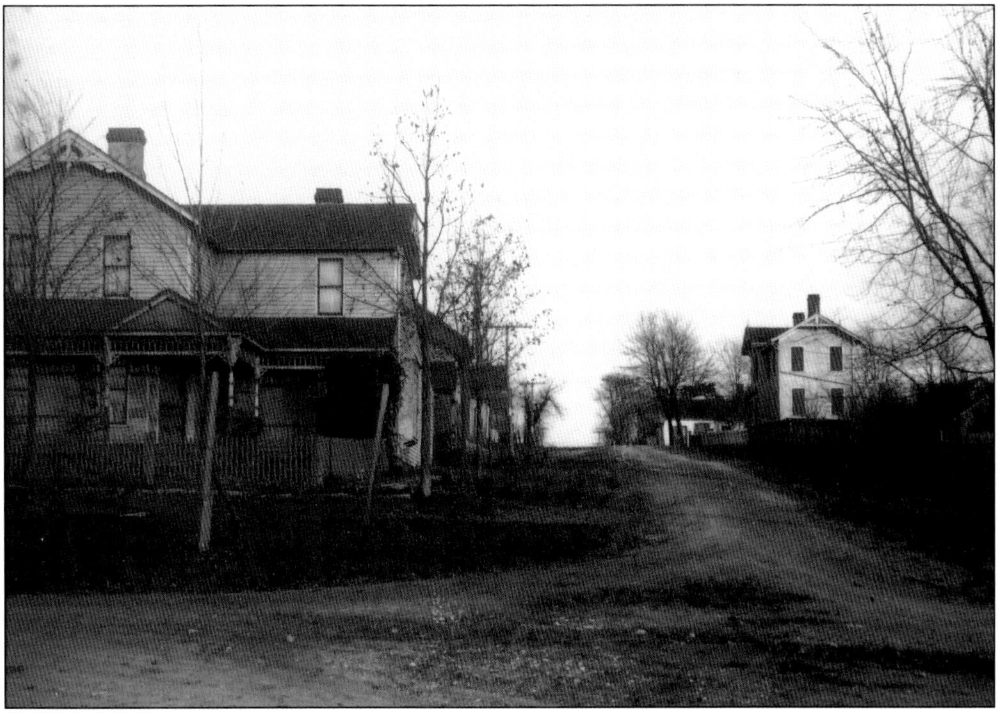

This photograph was taken at South Main Street looking east on Lebanon Street toward the Catholic church and Methodist church. The Thompson house is located on the left. (Courtesy of the Monroe Historical Society.)

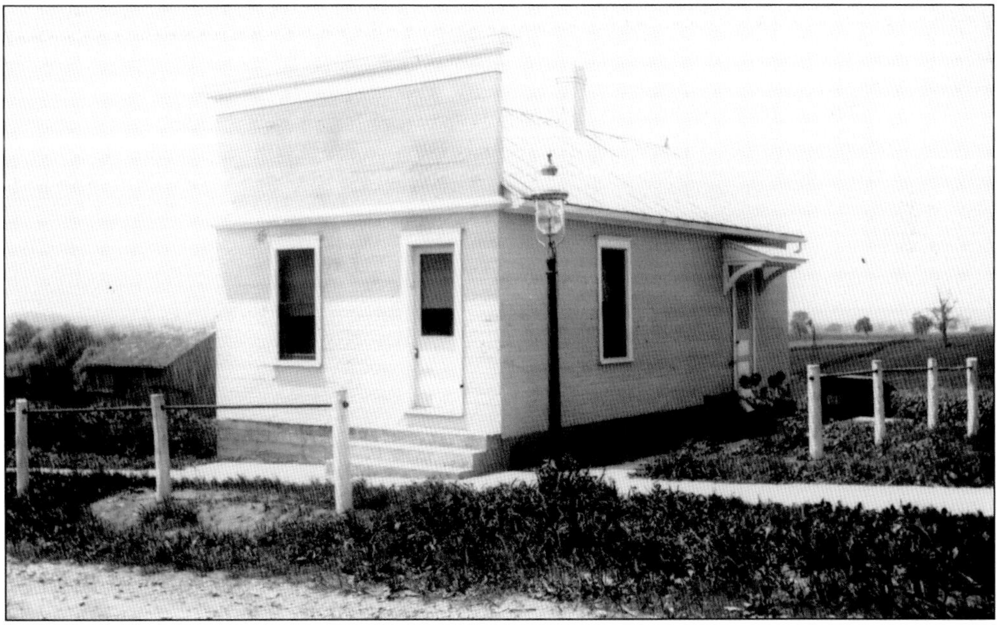

The new village hall, seen here in this *c.* 1912 photograph, was located on approximately the same place on South Main Street as the current city hall building. Note the newly completed sidewalks and gas lamp to illuminate the street and building at night. (Courtesy of the Monroe Historical Society.)

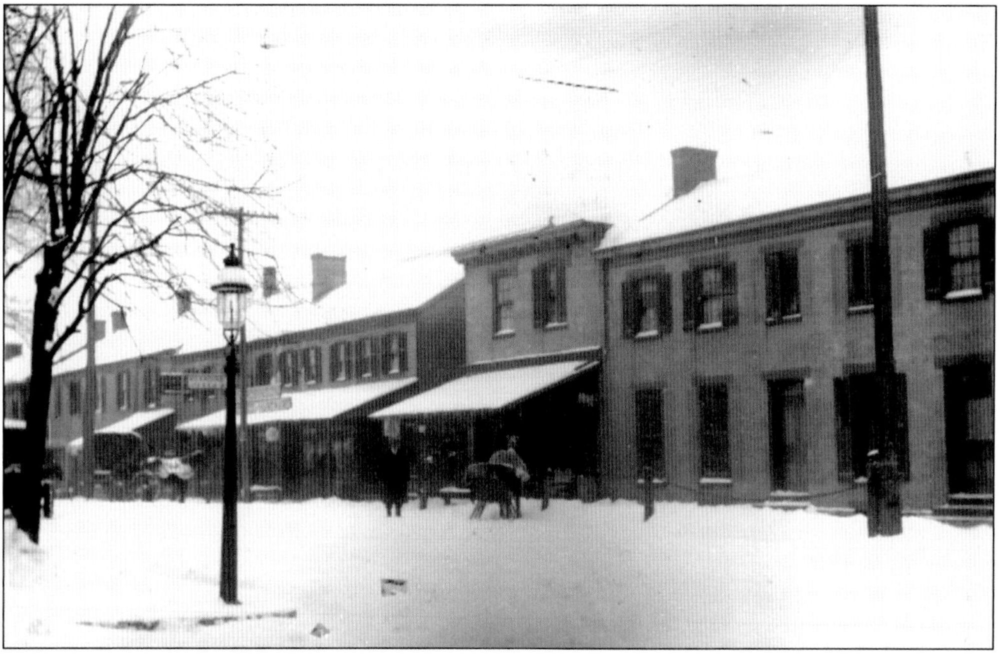

The advent of the horseless carriage changed Monroe. Many were resistant to the change and held onto their old ways with the belief that the horse and buggy was a more reliable mode of transportation. This photograph illustrates the transition showing an automobile (left), a horse and buggy (left center), and a horse-drawn sleigh (center). (Courtesy of the Monroe Historical Society.)

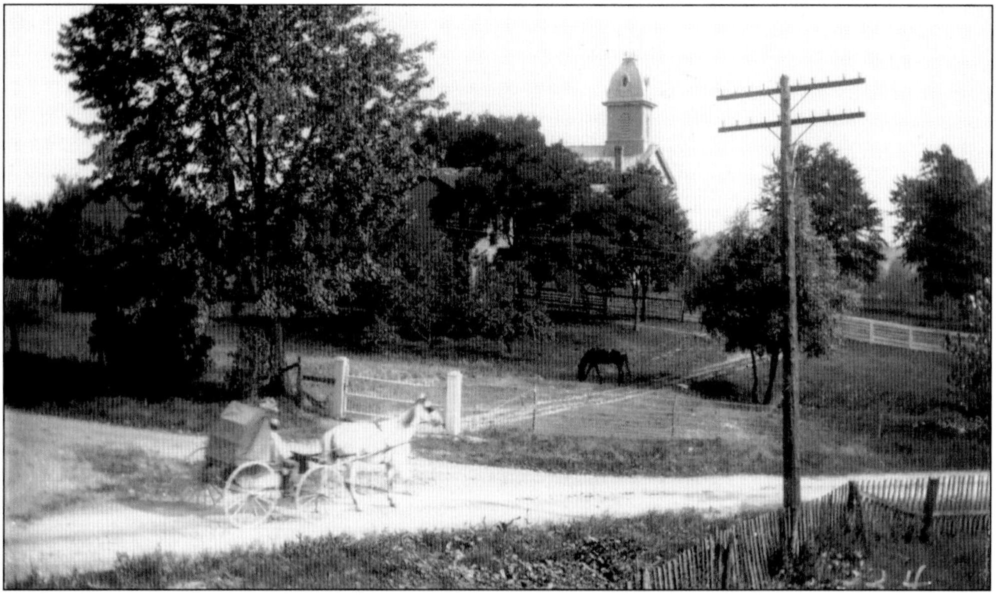

This photograph captures a horse and buggy in motion, heading south on Main Street toward Liberty Township. The horse and buggy was the primary mode of travel during the early 20th century, despite the manufacture of the first Ford Model T in 1908. By the middle of the century, the automobile had replaced the horse and buggy as the primary means of transportation, with the exception of Amish communities who still use the horse and buggy today. (Courtesy of the Monroe Historical Society.)

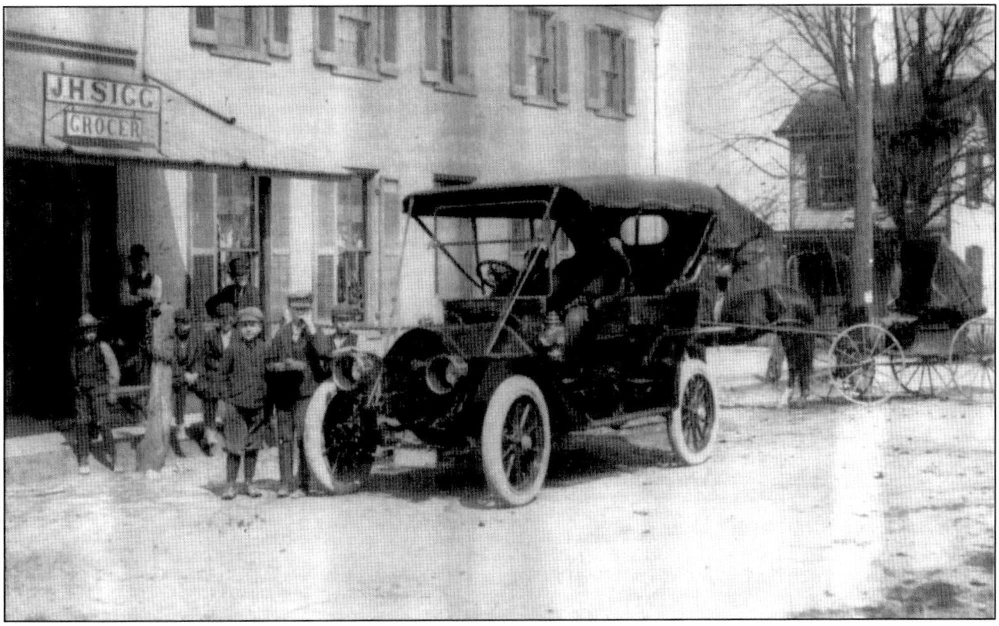

In the early years, the automobile was a novelty and attracted an audience whenever it came into town. This pre–World War I brass-era automobile sits in front of the J. H. Sigg Grocer at the corner of Main and Elm Streets around 1912. Although the horse and buggy shown in the background would create excitement today, at the time of this photograph it was virtually shunned, like a rusted used car. (Courtesy of Boyd and Virginia Smith.)

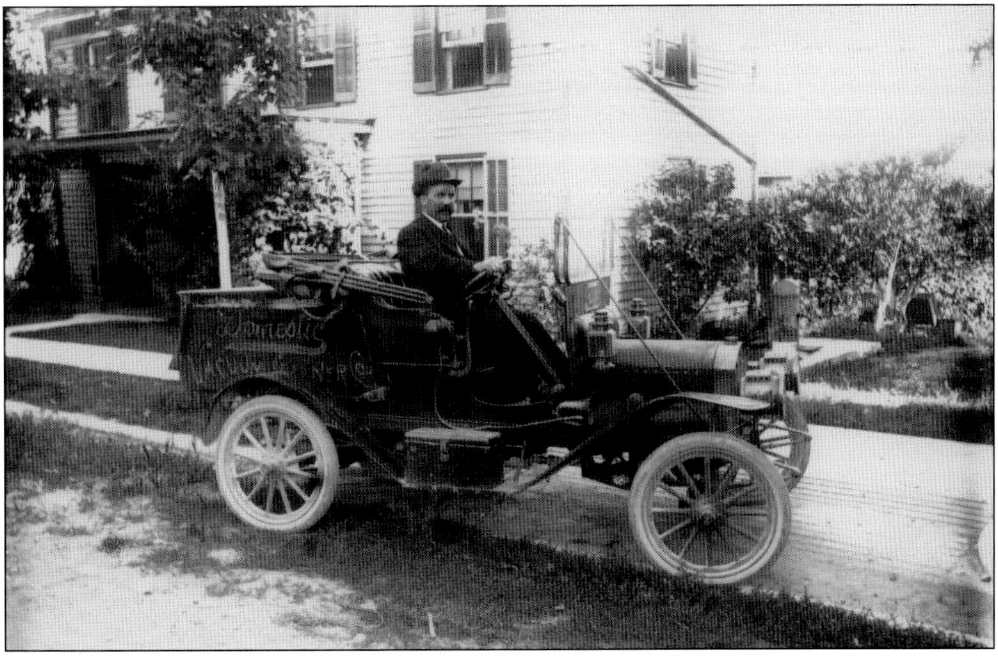
The automobile brought many changes in the way people conducted their business and brought new employment opportunity. The blacksmith shops evolved into auto mechanic garages. This photograph of the Domestic Vacuum Cleaner Company vehicle was taken July 28, 1913. The automobile appears to be a *c.* 1908 Maxwell. (Courtesy of the Monroe Historical Society.)

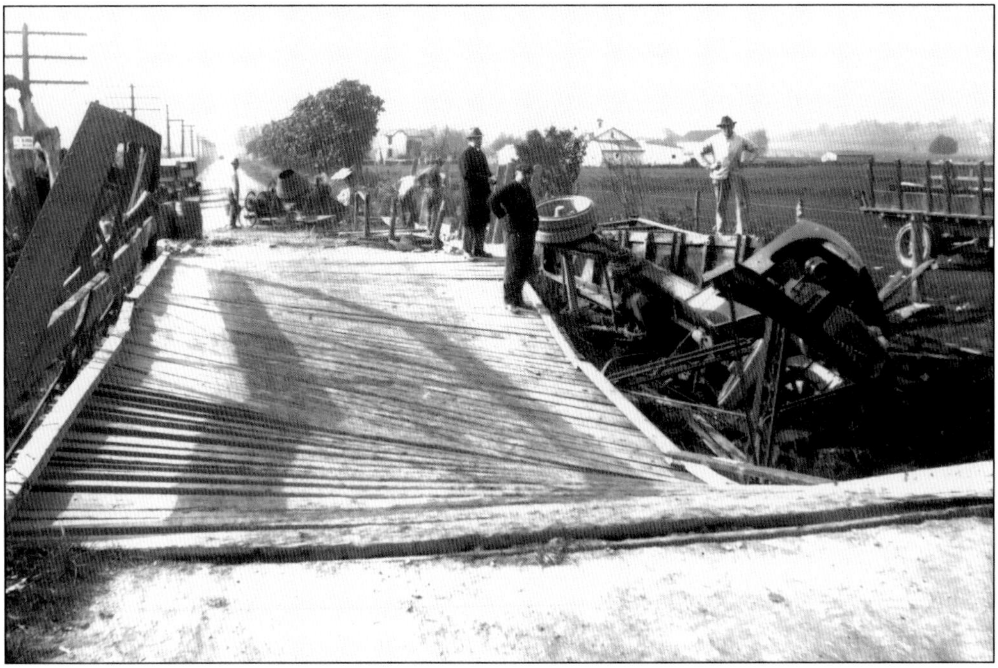

As the automobile grew in popularity, so did potential hazards. This wreck at a nearby bridge shows the twisted metal of an early vehicle that provided little safety protection to its occupants, caused a traffic jam, and left the bridge virtually impassible. (Courtesy of the Monroe Historical Society.)

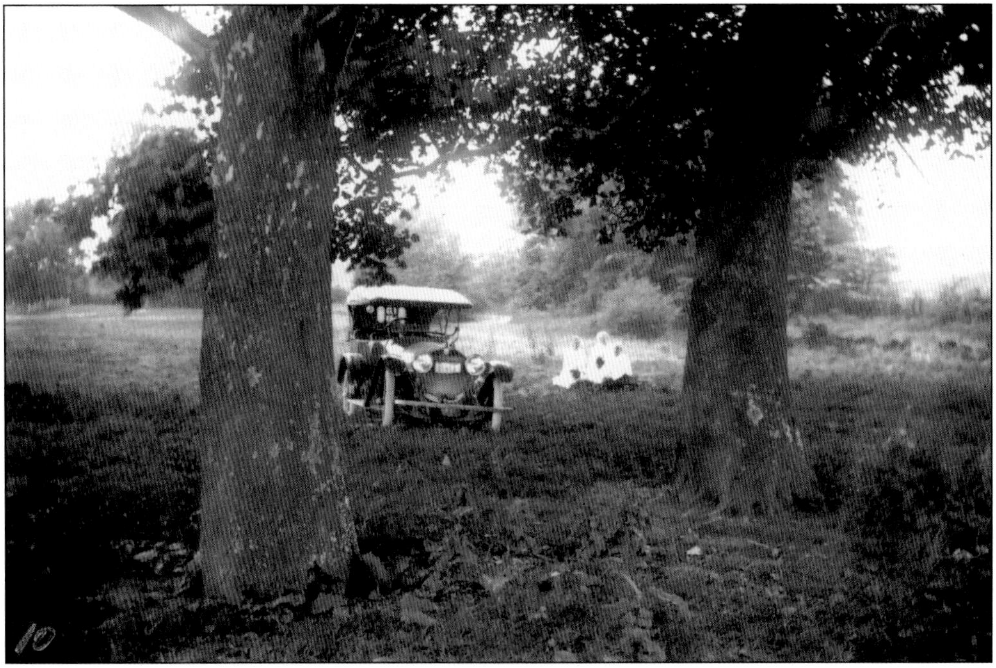

The new automobiles were not always dangerous. This July 1916 photograph shows people enjoying a picnic lunch under a tree next to their automobile. Leisurely Sunday drives were all the rage and continued to be well into the mid-20th century. (Courtesy of the Monroe Historical Society.)

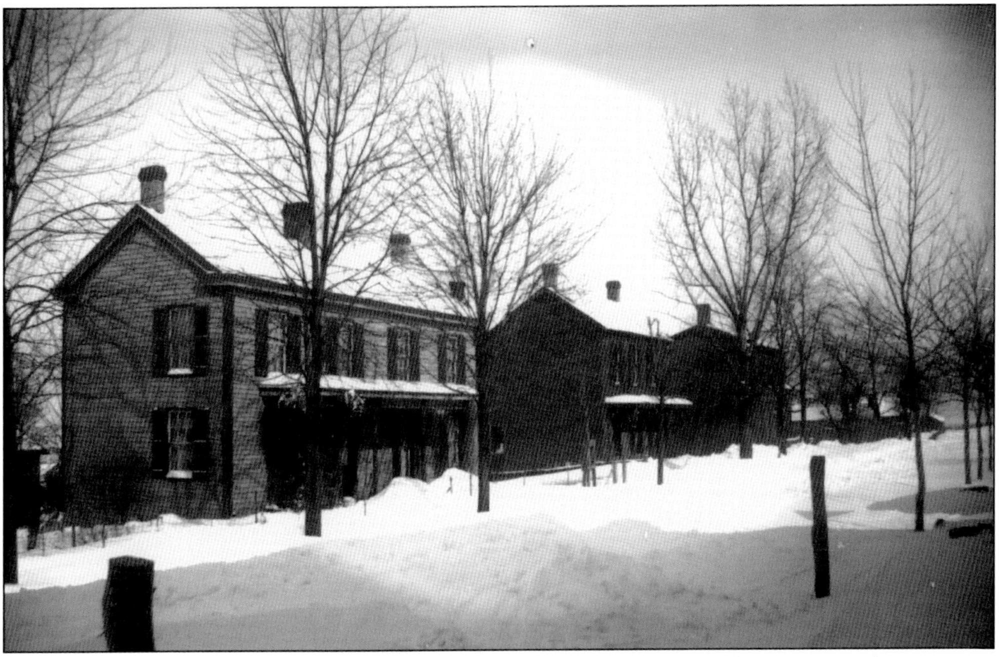

Seen here from left to right, the Marion G. Warner, John Boyd, and James Linn homes were located across from the Monroe National Bank on East Elm Street. At that time, Elm Street was called Maple Avenue, according to the 1920 U.S. census for Butler County. James F. Linn died September 14, 1928. (Courtesy of the Monroe Historical Society.)

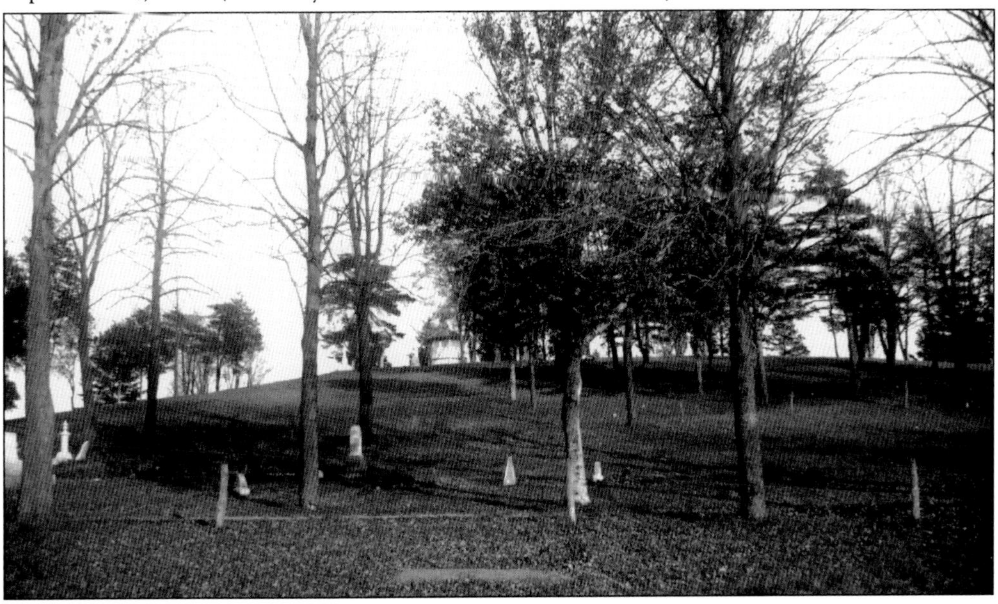

Marion G. Warner and John Boyd lived next to one another during their lifetime and are both buried in the Mound Cemetery. This photograph of the Mound Cemetery was taken about 1912. It was virtually an empty cemetery at that time. Many Monroe citizens, such as Warner and Boyd, lived their entire lives here and chose to be buried in this quiet cemetery. The cemetery was originally an American Indian burial site and many of the early settlers of Monroe are buried there, including Nathaniel Sackett Jr. (Courtesy of the Monroe Historical Society.)

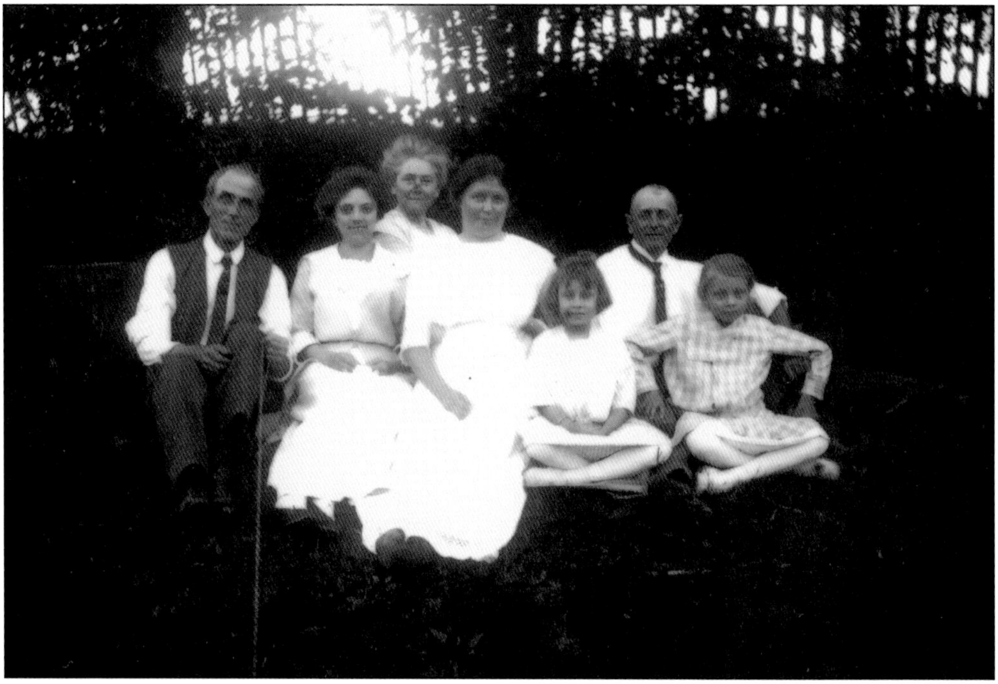

This photograph of a local family was taken by Marion G. Warner in 1914. (Courtesy of the Monroe Historical Society.)

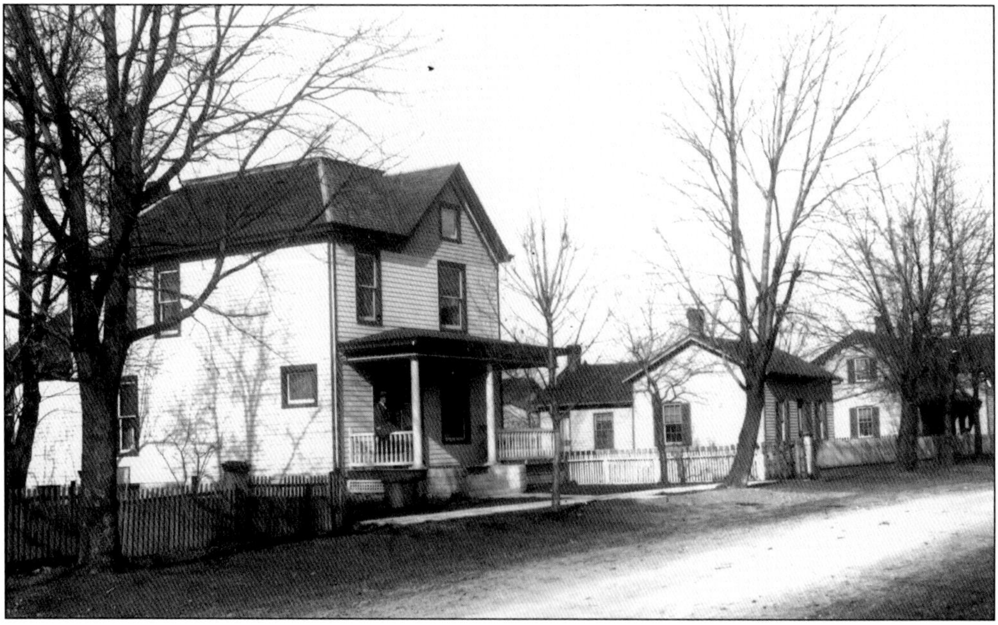

The Carpenter and Constiner homes were located on Church Street in Monroe. Francis Merle Constiner was an American pulp author and in 1932 was nominated for an O. Henry Award for his short story "Big Singing," published by *Household Magazine*. He wrote detective fiction and westerns. He also wrote stories for the *Saturday Evening Post* and published western novels. Constiner died September 24, 1979, and is buried in the Mound Cemetery. (Courtesy of the Monroe Historical Society.)

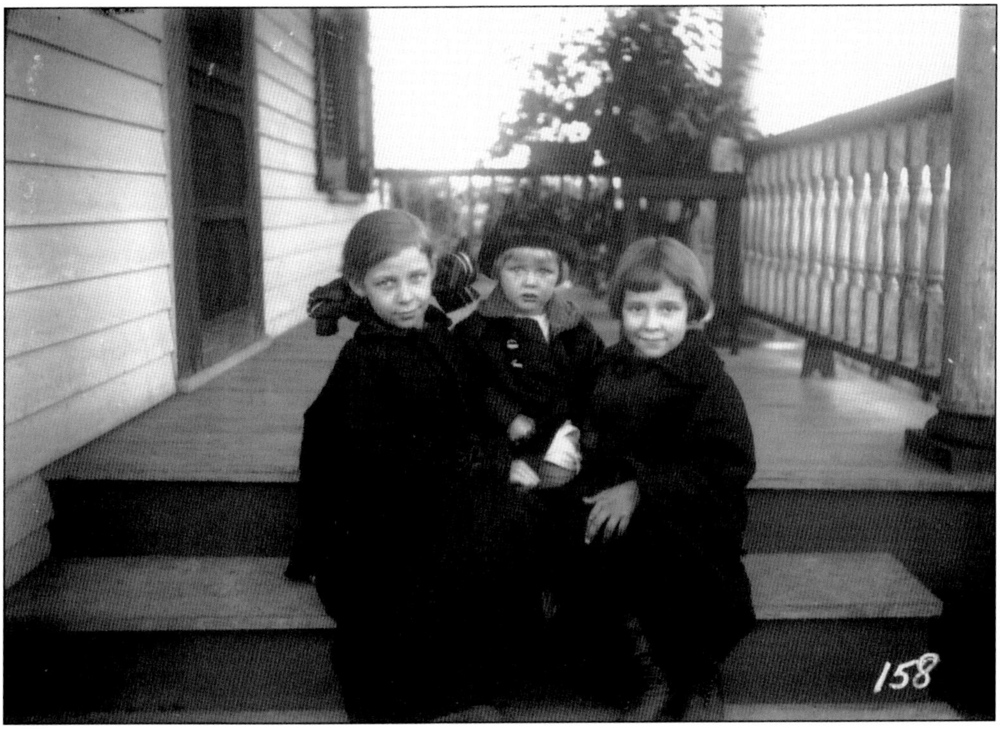

This photograph of three unknown girls seated on porch steps was taken October 11, 1914. They would have been about the same age as author Merle Constiner, and they probably attended the Monroe School with him. (Courtesy of the Monroe Historical Society.)

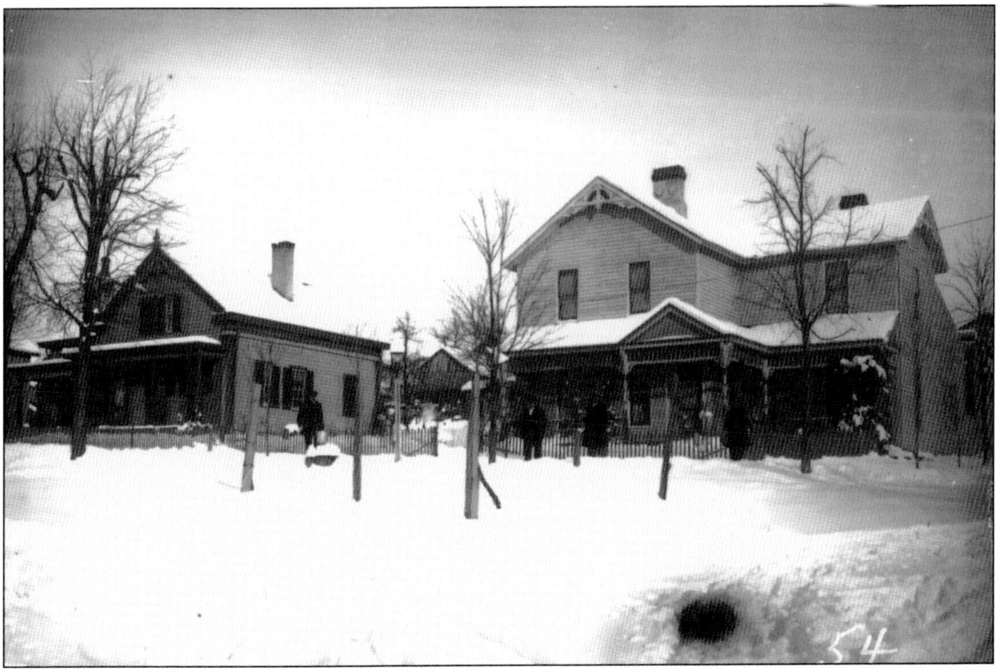

The east side of Main Street around 1910 was partly residential. (Courtesy of the Monroe Historical Society.)

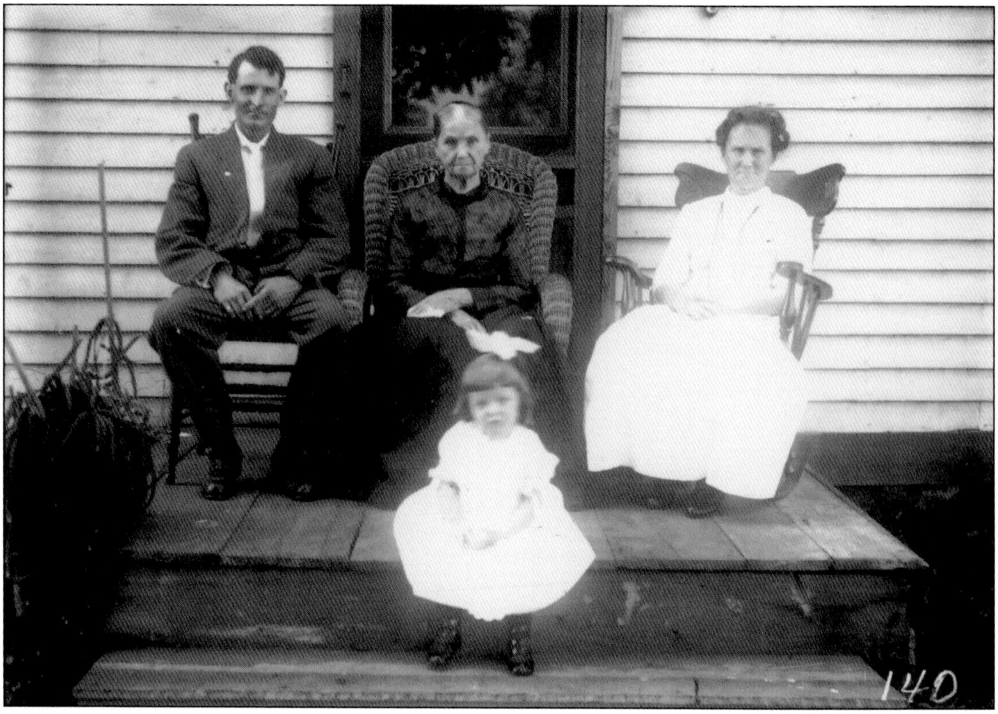

A Monroe family gathers for their photograph on September 15, 1912. (Courtesy of the Monroe Historical Society.)

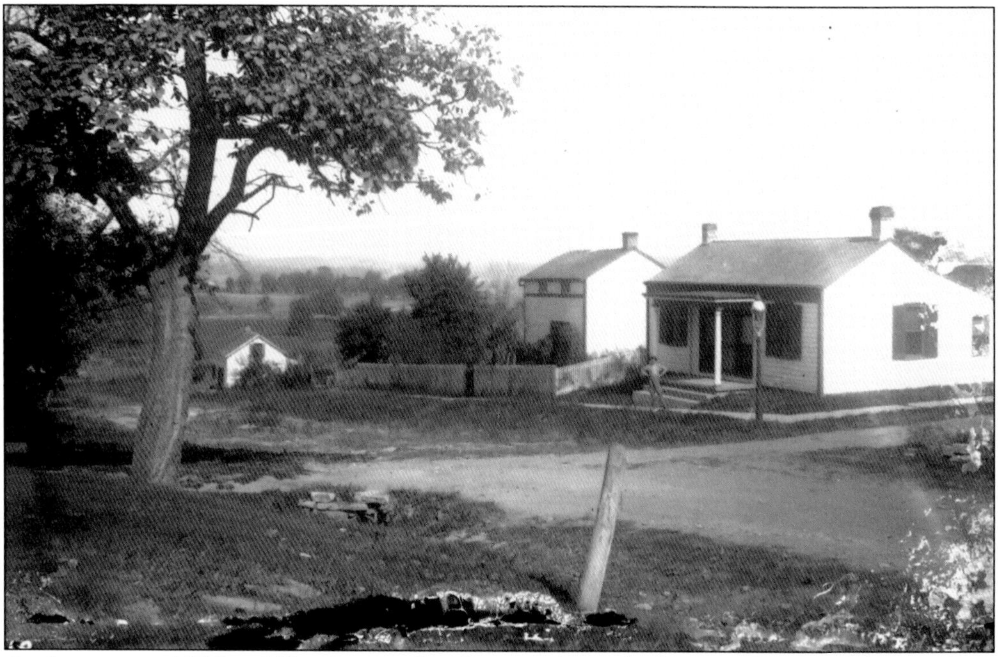

At the corner of Old and Elm Streets, the photographer is looking south toward the northern end of town. The Boyd blacksmith shop sat on this section of Old Street in the early 1900s. Today the Old Street Saloon quietly graces this location and offers excellent entertainment for those with alternative lifestyles. (Courtesy of the Monroe Historical Society.)

This August 1915 photograph is of a multigenerational Monroe family. The oldest man (upper right) is 93 years old. (Courtesy of the Monroe Historical Society.)

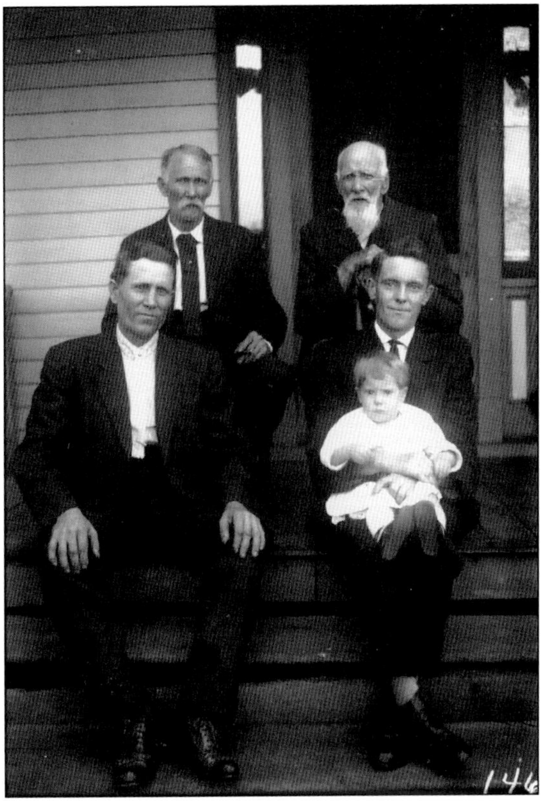

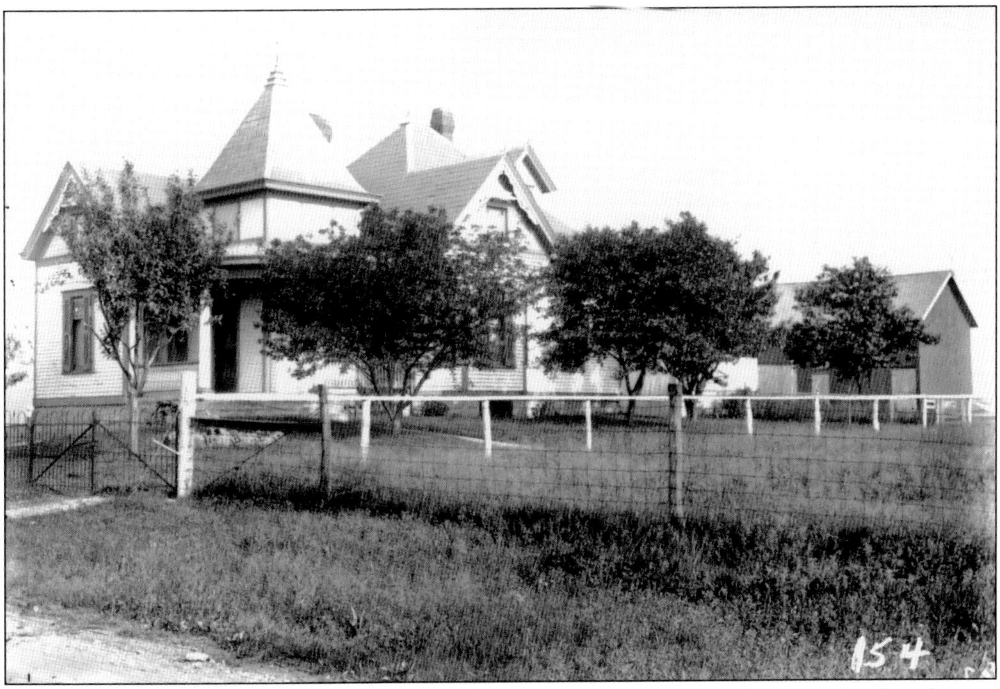

This Victorian farmhouse with a barn in the rear is the typical architectural style of many Monroe homes of the Victorian era. (Courtesy of the Monroe Historical Society.)

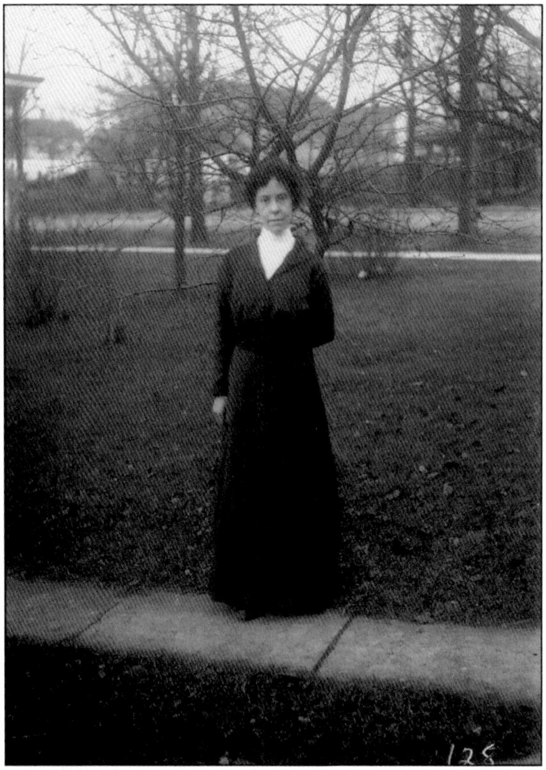

The woman in this photograph is wearing a dress typical of the early 20th century. (Courtesy of the Monroe Historical Society.)

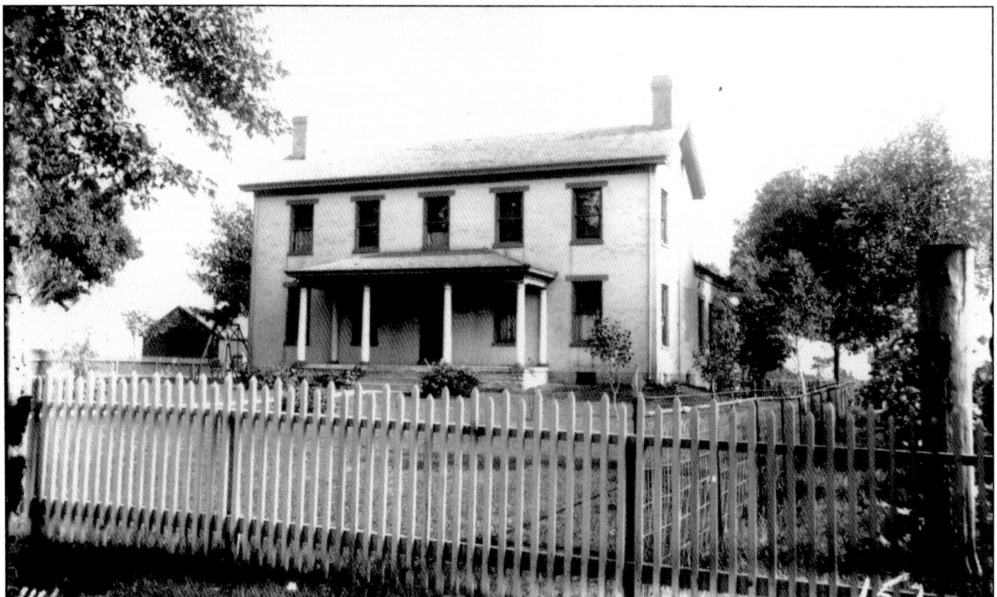

The Brocks' house sits on Macready Avenue past the Highview subdivision and close to the new Kroger grocery store. It dates back to the 1820s and had operated as a farm for several generations. The last Brock descendants to own the house were Tom and Vickie Brock. The old Brock farmland is now being developed into a new subdivision. (Courtesy of the Monroe Historical Society.)

This grandmother in her neatly pressed dress poses for the photograph sitting in her rocking chair. Women did not have an easy life in those days, and many would die after giving birth. This photograph was taken around 1910–1915, before women had the right to vote. It is possible that this woman never had the chance to cast her ballot. Today women in Monroe are elected to and serve on the city council. (Courtesy of the Monroe Historical Society.)

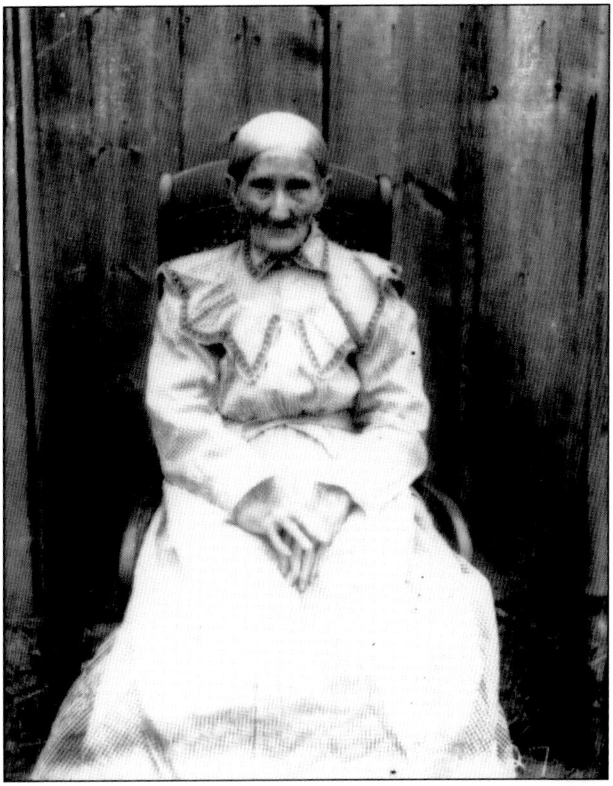

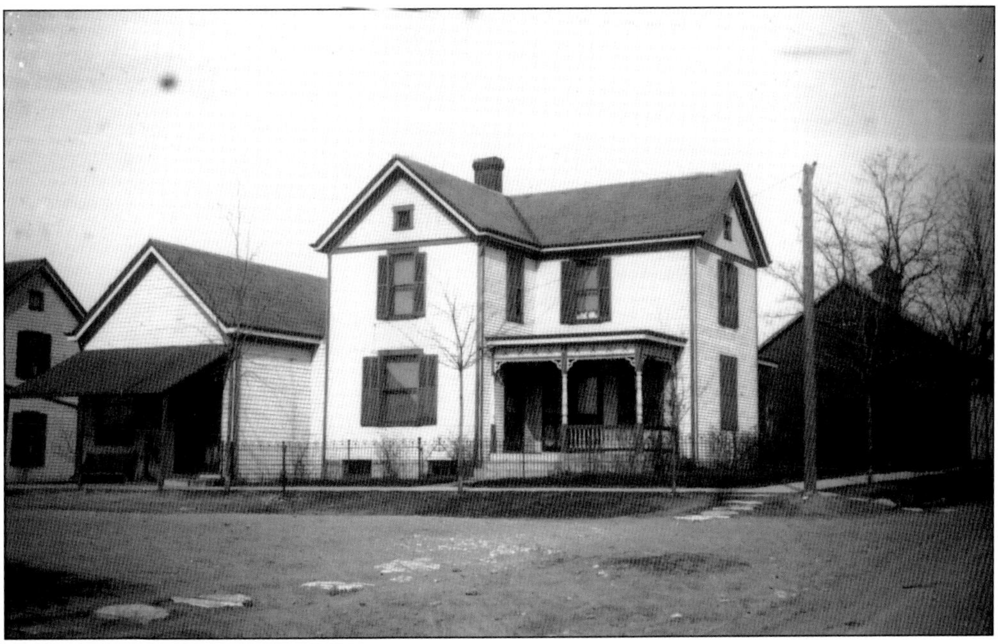

Homes at the corner of Old and Church Streets had stepping-stones entering the dirt street for pedestrian use in crossing the street while walking downtown or to the Catholic and Methodist churches. Note the water pump on the porch of the small house (left). (Courtesy of the Monroe Historical Society.)

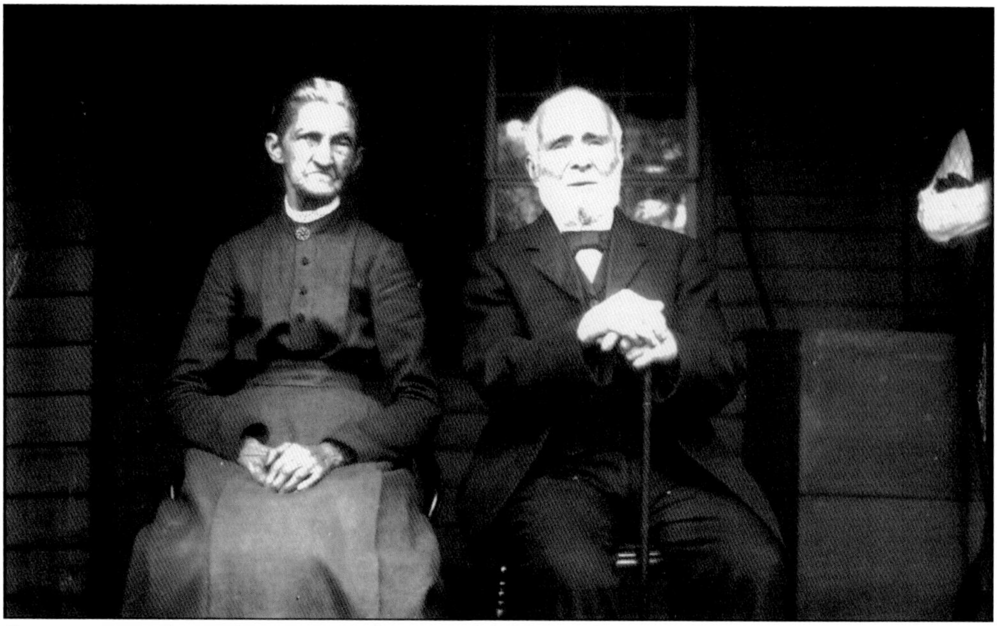

Senior citizens have always enjoyed a peaceful life in the quiet village of Monroe, as shown in this photograph taken October 4, 1916. Although the village has now grown into a city, it continues to remain a haven for seniors as well as to attract new young families. (Courtesy of the Monroe Historical Society.)

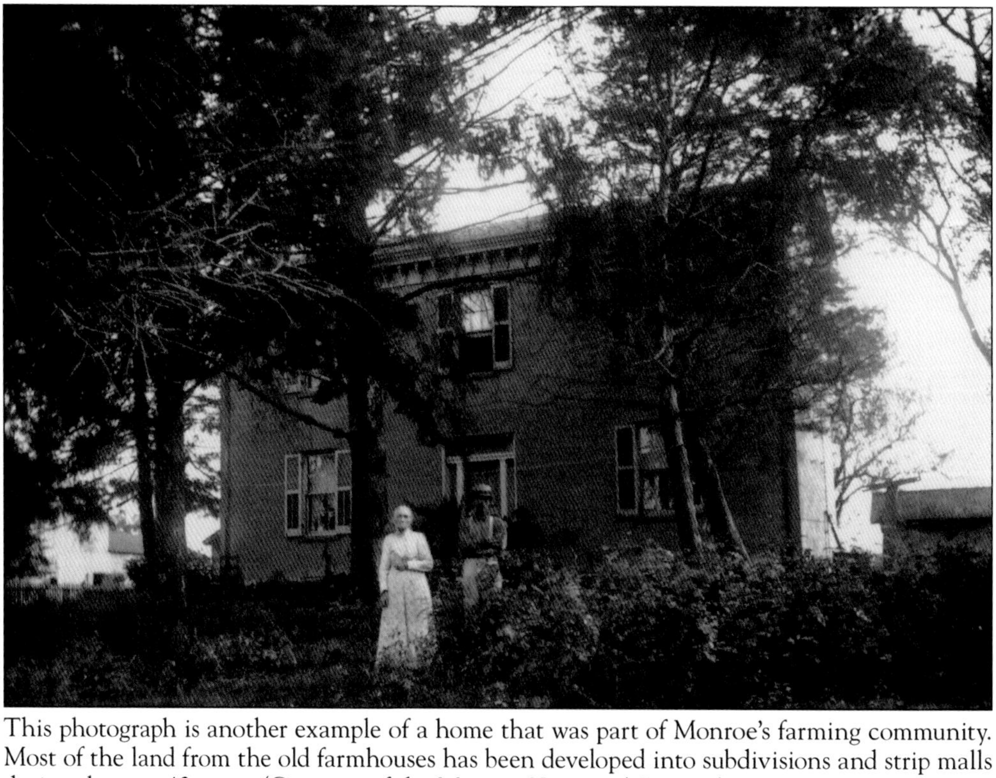

This photograph is another example of a home that was part of Monroe's farming community. Most of the land from the old farmhouses has been developed into subdivisions and strip malls during the past 40 years. (Courtesy of the Monroe Historical Society.)

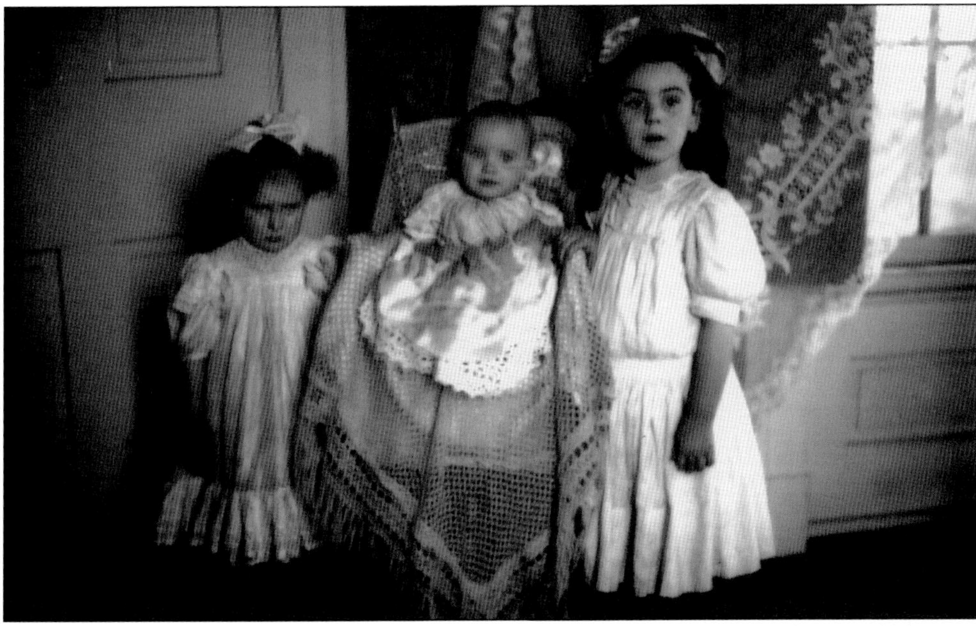

These three little girls do not appear to enjoy posing for the photographer. They would become the first generation of women voters in Monroe and would see many changes in their lifetimes. (Courtesy of the Monroe Historical Society.)

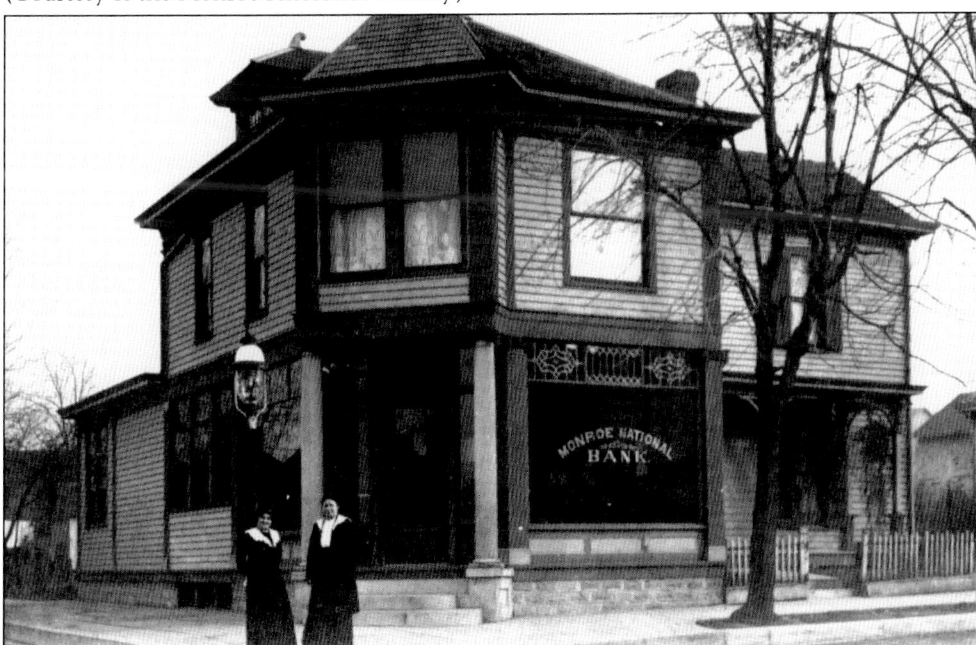

Patrons pose for this photograph outside of the newly remodeled Monroe National Bank. According to the Monroe sesquicentennial book, there were only two attempted robberies of this bank up to 1967. The first was March 28, 1928. This robbery was botched when the perpetrator was shot and killed. The second was on January 4, 1931, by two men and a woman. Shots were fired. The trio fled and was captured north of the village. (Courtesy of Boyd and Virginia Smith.)

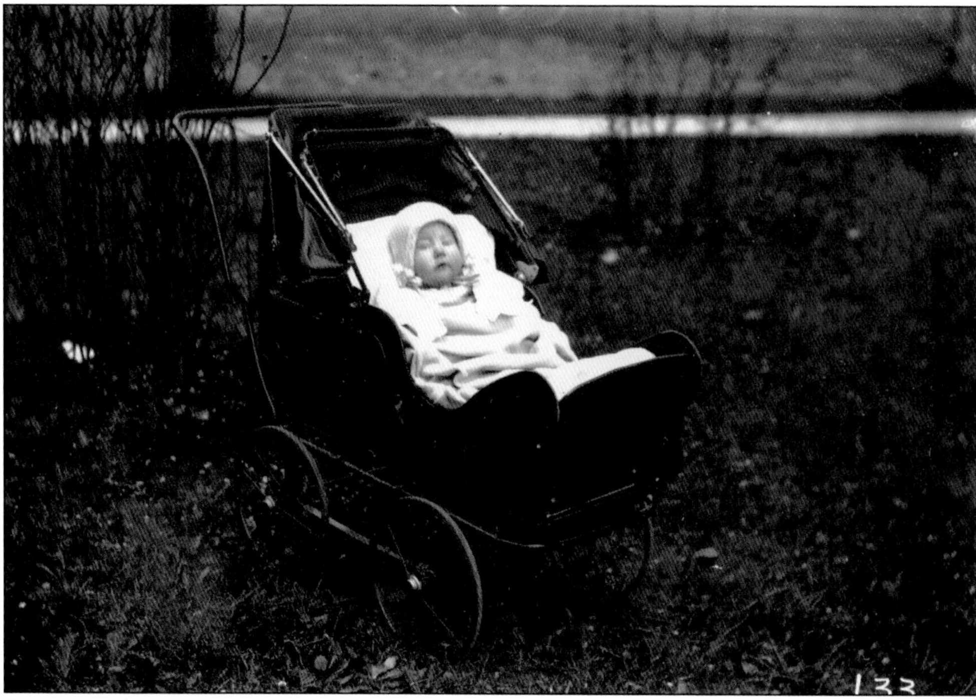

Young families have always found Monroe to be a safe community for rearing children. This photograph of an infant and his carriage was taken April 24, 1918. (Courtesy of the Monroe Historical Society.)

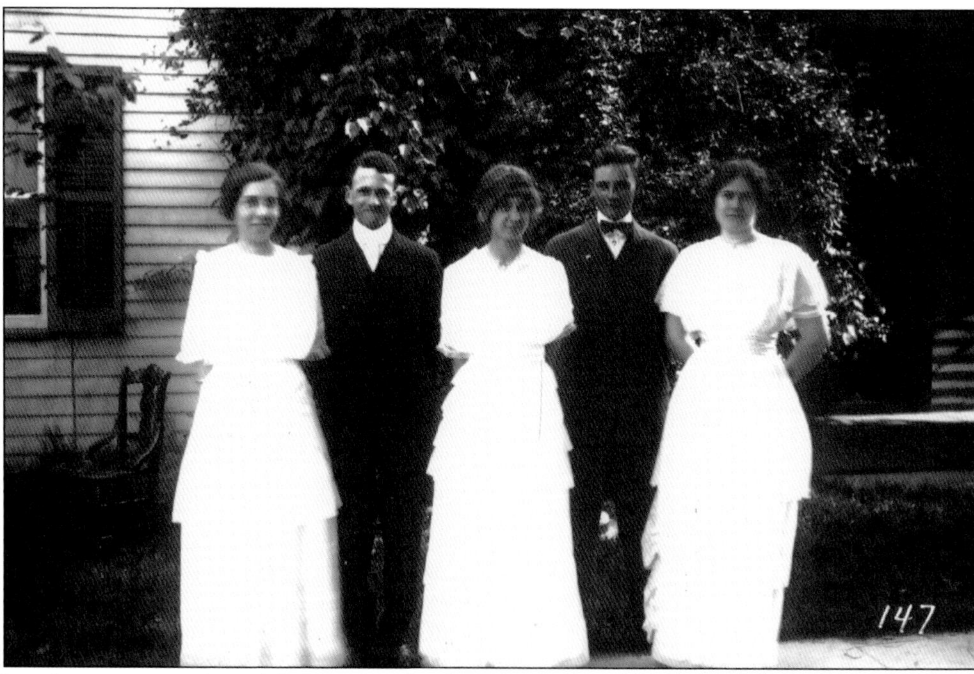

Local teenagers in formal dress gather for this May 6, 1914, photograph. They could have been attending a dance at the newly built Monroe School or were preparing for a wedding. (Courtesy of the Monroe Historical Society.)

A man dressed in a suit and tie pauses on the sidewalk for this c. 1915 photograph. Although Monroe was primarily a farming community, its citizens enjoyed prosperity in the early decades of the 20th century, before the Great Depression. (Courtesy of the Monroe Historical Society.)

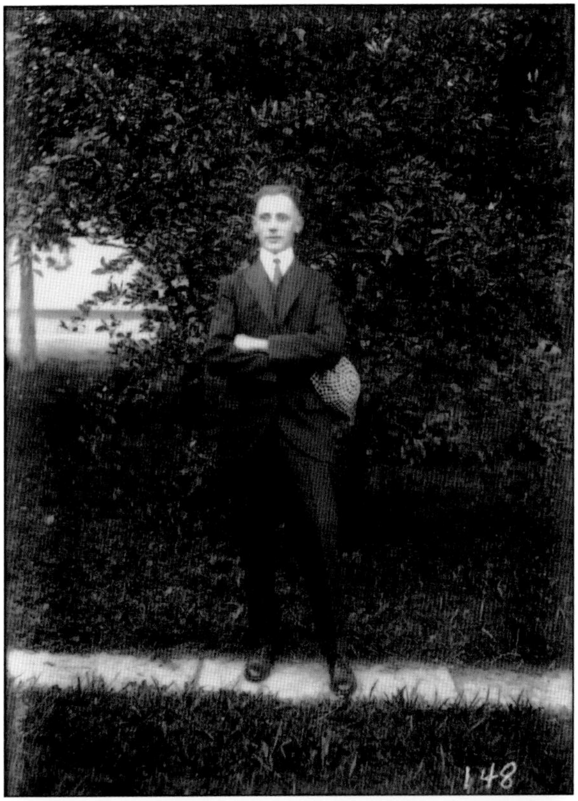

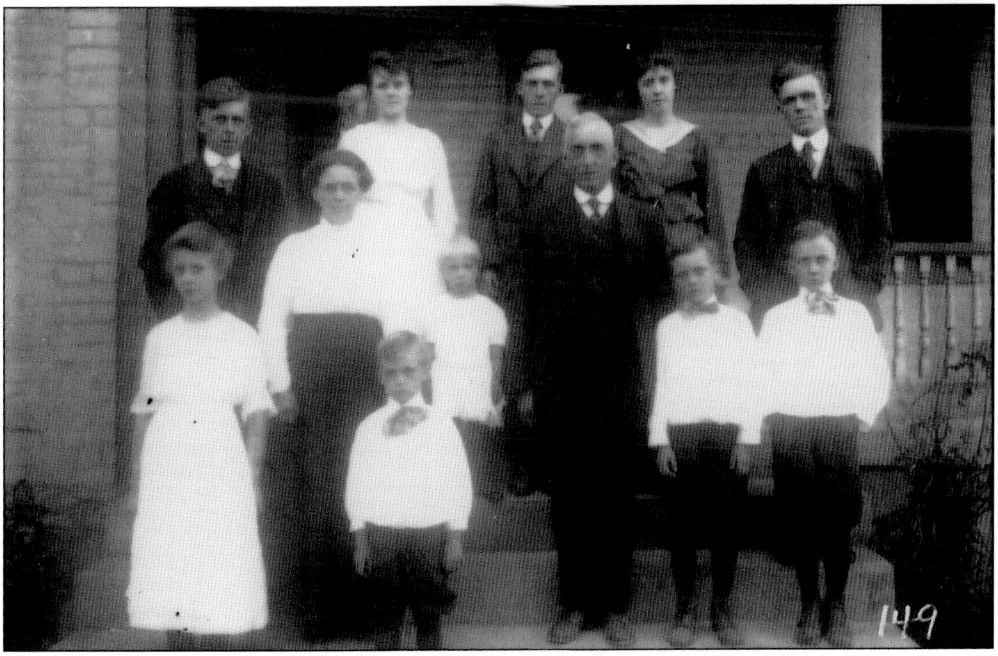

This photograph, dated October 1, 1916, portrays a family that resided in the growing village of Monroe at that time. Many of Monroe's citizens were born and lived their entire lives here, as have many of the city's contemporary residents. (Courtesy of the Monroe Historical Society.)

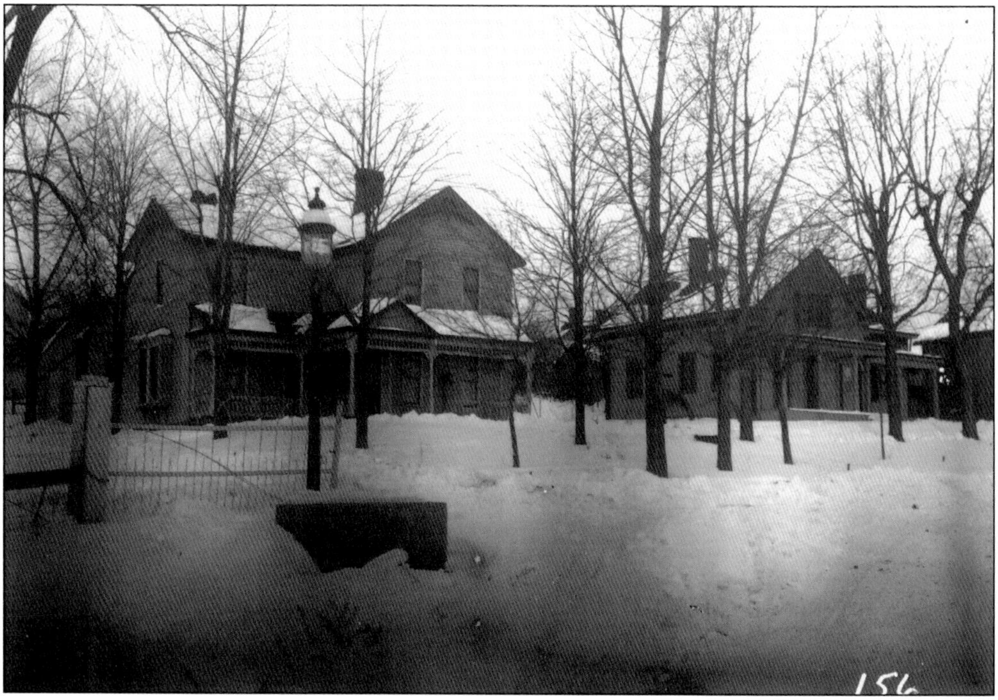

This street scene was taken during the big snow of January 1918. The new street gas lamp proudly stands near the fence line. The house (left) is also sporting a new bay window. (Courtesy of the Monroe Historical Society.)

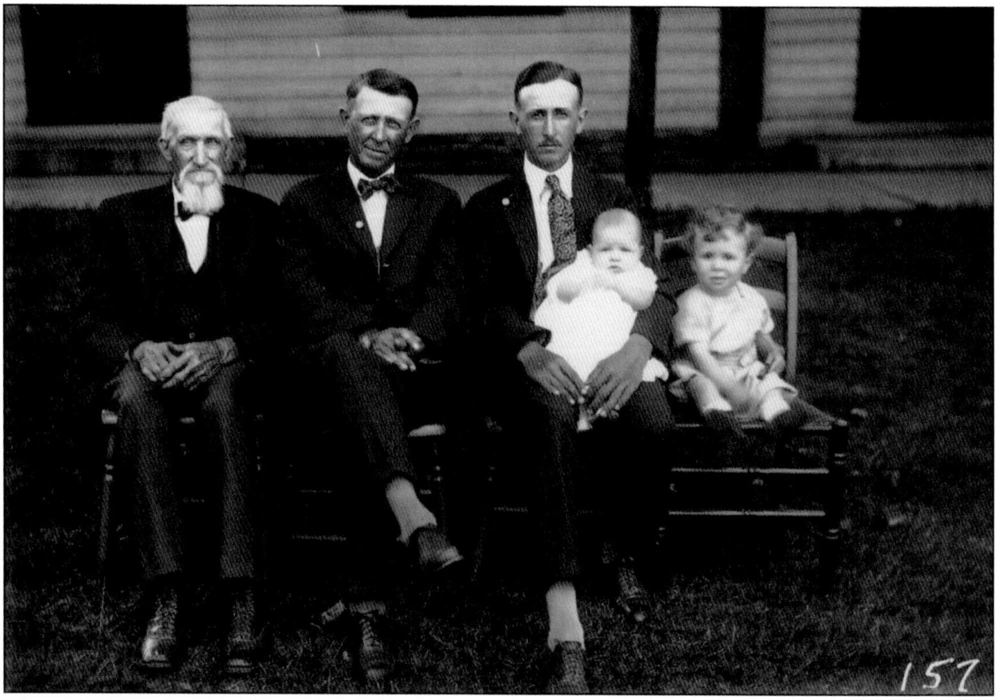

This photograph was taken on July 14, 1918, of a multigenerational family. It also mirrors the prosperity within the community at that time. (Courtesy of the Monroe Historical Society.)

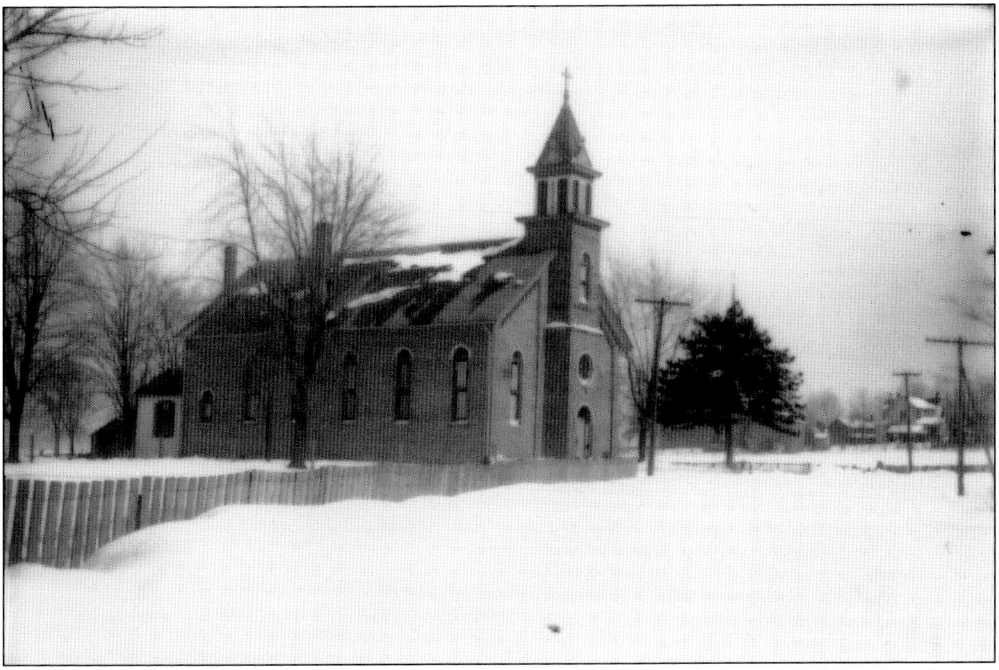

The Catholic church braves the January 1918 snowstorm. The drifts are halfway to the top of the picket fence. Lebanon Street was virtually impassible. (Courtesy of the Monroe Historical Society.)

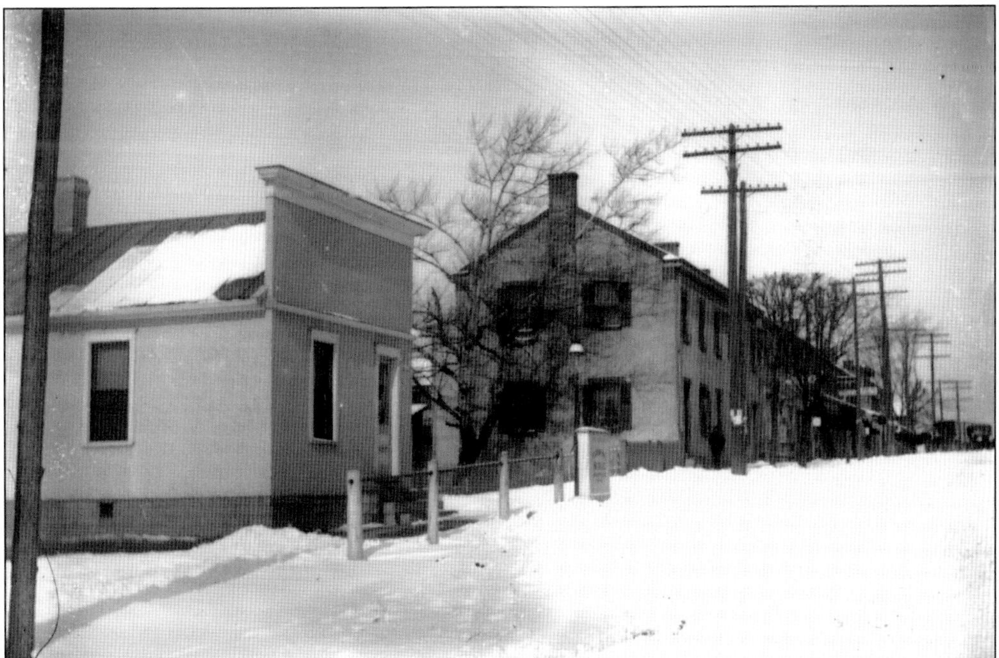

Village hall and the west side of Main Street are seen here after the sidewalks had been cleared of snow. A lone horse and buggy and automobile are visible (right) near the intersection of Main and Elm Streets. (Courtesy of the Monroe Historical Society.)

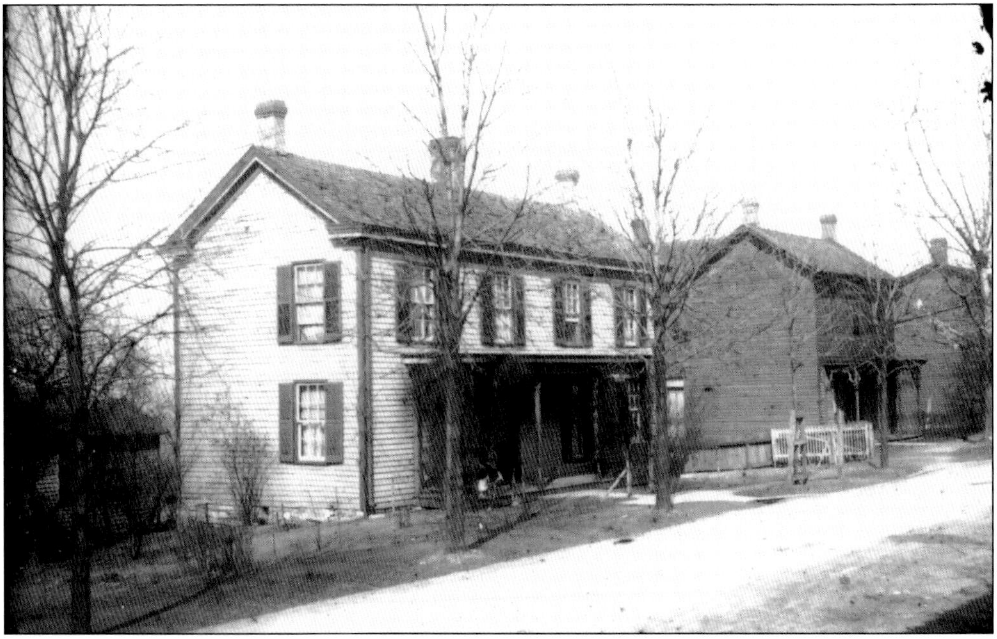

Marion G. Warner's house sat near his store, which was located on the corner of Elm and Main Streets. This photograph was taken when Elm Street was a dirt road and had no sidewalks. The Warner store was owned by Jim Price and is now occupied and used as a museum by the Monroe Historical Society. In 1999, a new building was built on the property and the museum opened in 2000. (Courtesy of the Monroe Historical Society.)

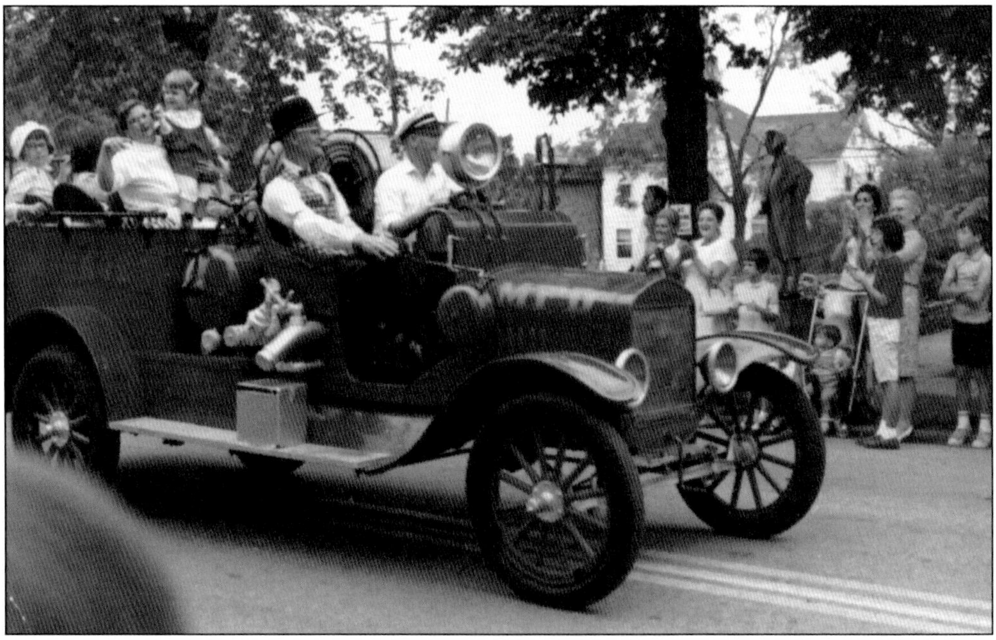

The 1924 Model T pictured here was the first motorized firefighting apparatus in Monroe. It was in use for many years until replaced in the late 1940s. After retirement, it was used primarily in parades. The old Model T is currently owned by the Monroe Fire Department. (Courtesy of the Monroe Fire Department.)

Two

Post–World War II Development

Following the Great Depression and World War II, America experienced a baby boom that peaked during the mid-1950s and ended about 1964. The marriage rate greatly increased during the 1950s, and many couples chose Monroe as a place to raise their young families. Monroe experienced tremendous growth between 1950 and 1960, and the village underwent a metamorphosis to accommodate the needs of its new citizens. New subdivisions sprang up. A community park and also a private swim club were constructed. The existing service clubs had a strong presence, and their presence greatly benefited the growing village. Religion remained at the heart of the community, and new churches were organized. Businesses were attracted to Monroe. During all the growth and change, in 1967 Monroe paused to celebrate the sesquicentennial of its 1817 founding. After the baby boom, children came of age and many left the village during the 1970s and 1980s. Although several baby boomers continue to make Monroe their home, the village did not experience much growth from 1980 to 1990.

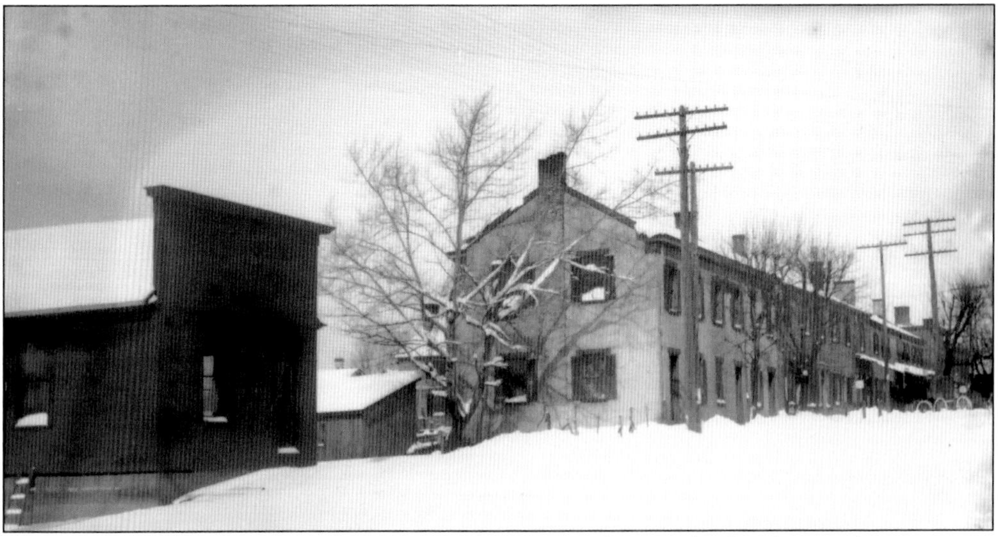

The IOOF in Monroe was organized on August 10, 1847. This was the first fraternal organization in Monroe. They first met on the fourth floor of the tavern called Half Way House, which was locally known as the Red Onion Hotel. The IOOF built its temple (center) in 1850 on Main Street. After the tornado damaged its Main Street temple, the lodge relocated to Britton Lane, where the temple still remains today. (Courtesy of the Monroe Historical Society.)

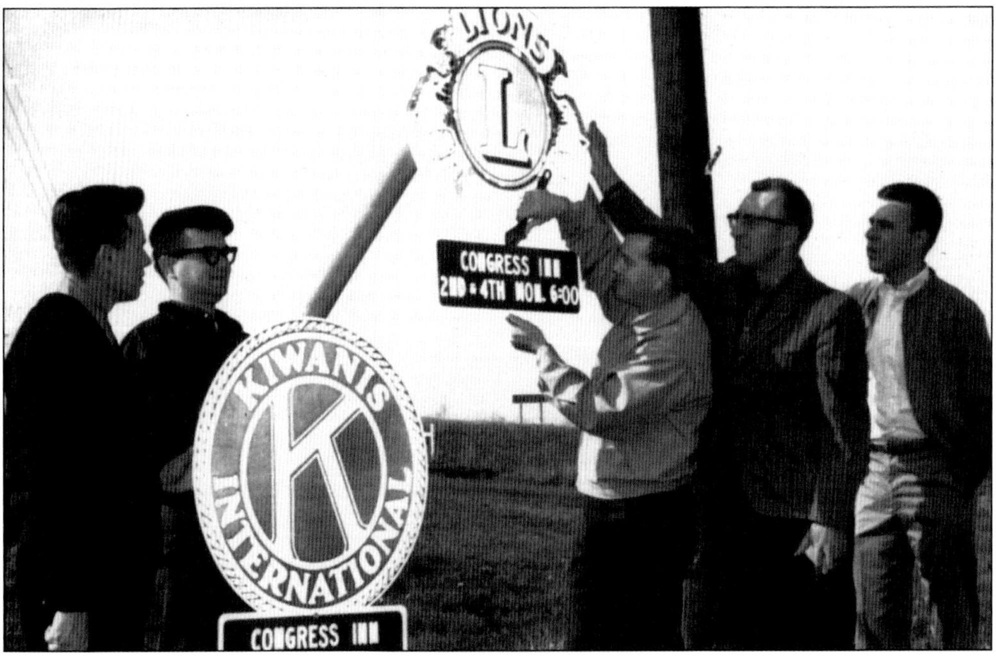

The Monroe Lions Club was organized on April 10, 1946. The club met in the IOOF hall and had distinguished speakers such as William Verity and George Hook for its July 1946 town meeting. In January 1947, the club sponsored a Christmas tree burning in the yard of Monroe High School, which became a tradition that continued into the early 1960s. In December 1967, Lions and Kiwanis erected new road signs at the entrances to the village. Seen here from left to right are Bert and Charles Lerch, Tom Reed, Al Brooks, and Joe Ponder. (Courtesy of the Monroe Lions Club. Reprinted with permission from the Middletown Journal.)

The old gaslight system had been eliminated by 1948. Lions Club members started the movement to secure electric streetlights. On July 26, 1948, at 9:00 p.m., a ceremony and celebration was held and the electric streetlights were turned on. In March 1966, Tom Leeds (top), William Lubberger, Gale Beatty, and Seth Johnson change a lightbulb on Main Street. Funds from lightbulb sales were disbursed in the community for vision needs. (Courtesy of the Monroe Lions Club. Reprinted with permission from the Middletown Journal.)

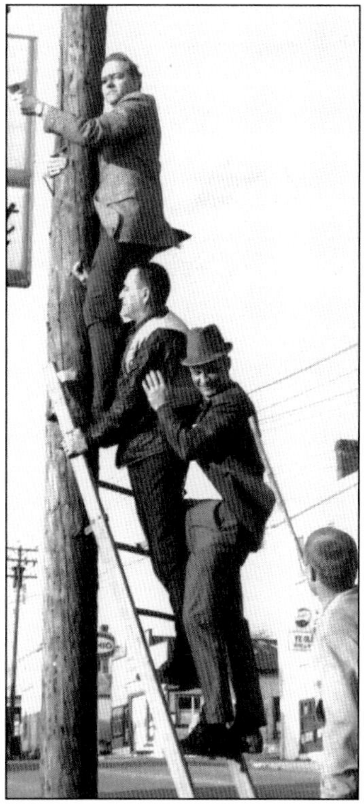

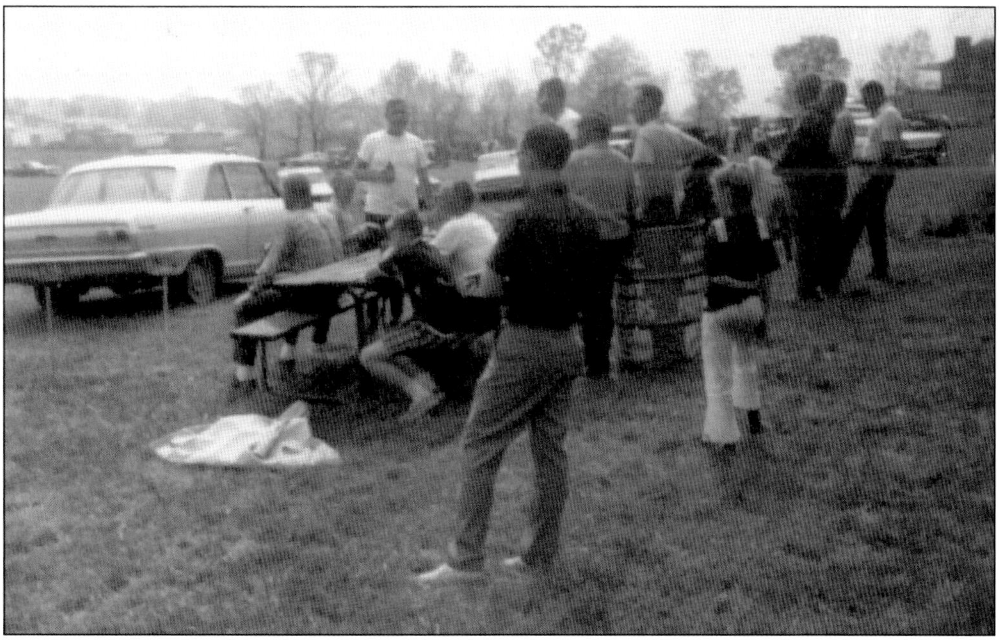

In January 1958, the Monroe Park Association was formed in the community. It purchased 16 acres of land adjacent to Mound Cemetery that would be developed into a picnic and recreation area for area families and would also be used for celebrations and vocational and civic activities of the village. The groundbreaking took place in May 1958. Picnic tables, fireplaces, and playground equipment were installed. (Courtesy of the Monroe Lions Club.)

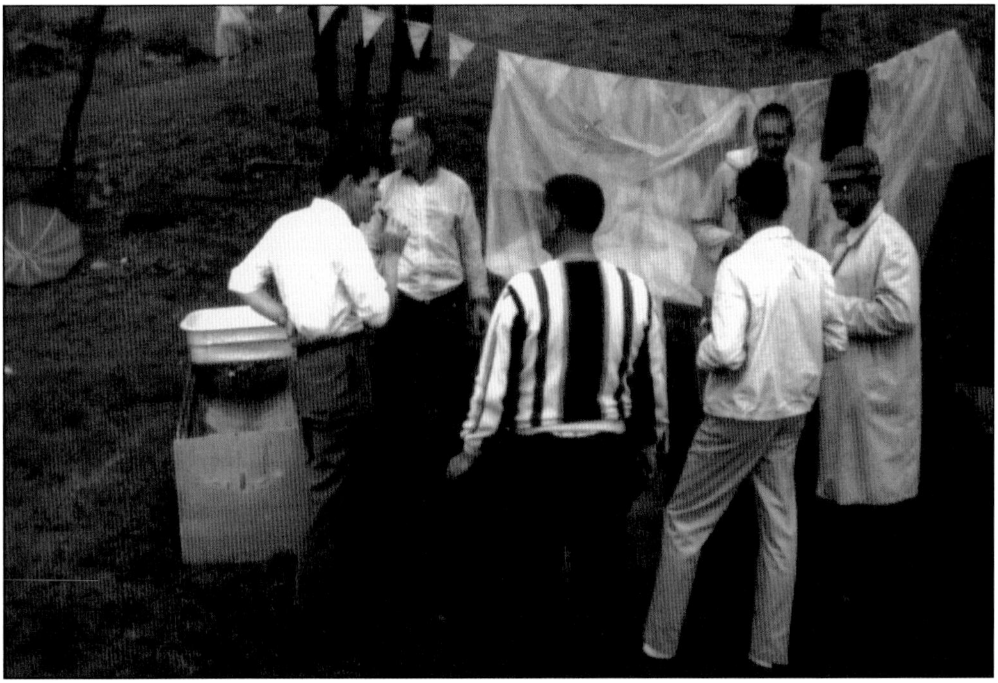

The Monroe Park Association was made up of people from most of the churches, clubs, and civic organizations in the village: Methodist church, Presbyterian church, Catholic church, Rebekah's, IOOF, Lions Club, firemen, Boy Scouts, Girl Scouts, planning commission, village council, and board of public affairs. It was a nonprofit organization set up to develop the park. These men were probably members of the association. (Courtesy of the Monroe Lions Club.)

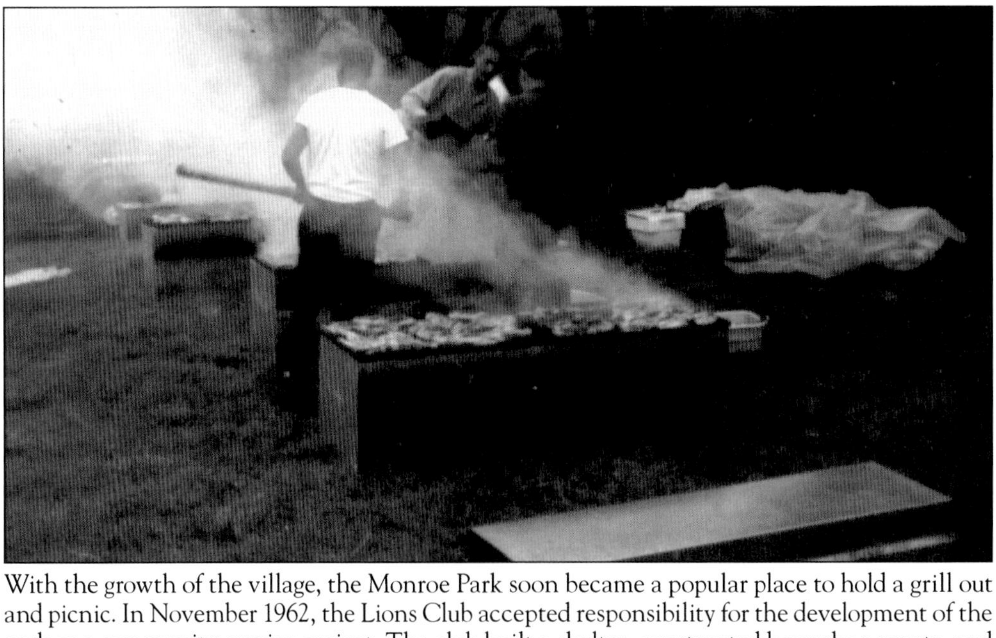

With the growth of the village, the Monroe Park soon became a popular place to hold a grill out and picnic. In November 1962, the Lions Club accepted responsibility for the development of the park as a community-service project. The club built a shelter, constructed horseshoe courts, and planted trees. The park was used for the Easter egg hunt, turkey shoots, and various community outings. (Courtesy of the Monroe Lions Club.)

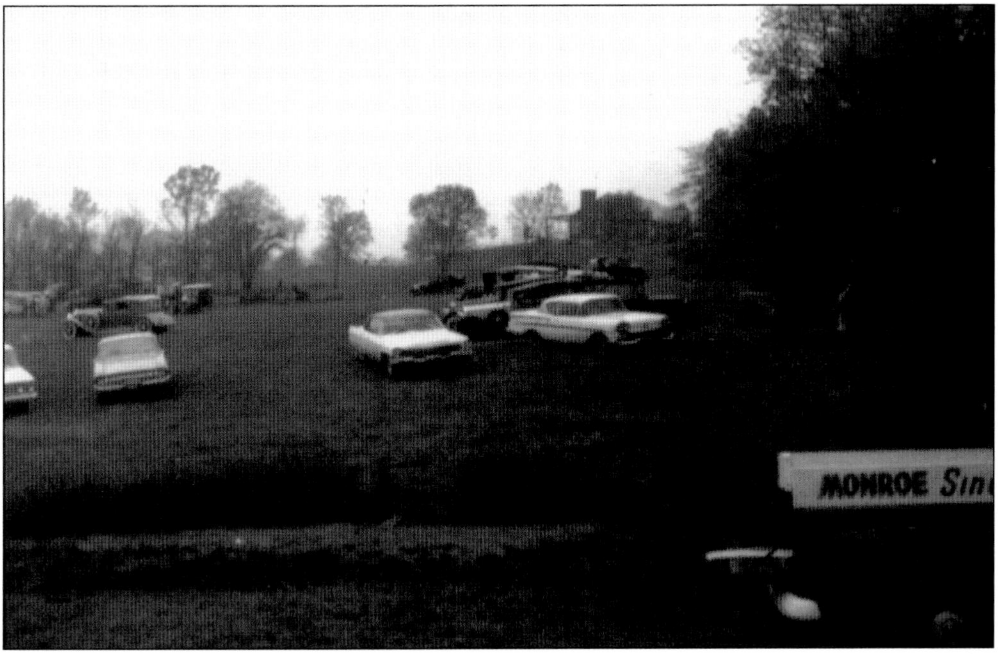

This photograph, taken at the new park, contrasts the newer automobiles with the older ones. The Monroe Sinclair truck can be seen in the foreground. (Courtesy of the Monroe Lions Club.)

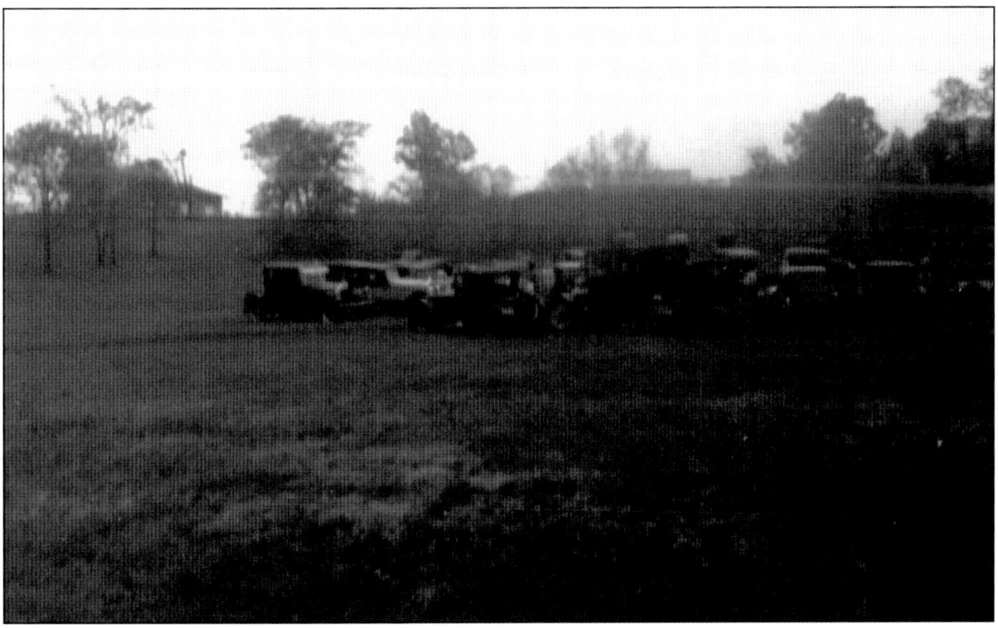

Monroe Park lies beside Mound Cemetery. In 1968, the Lions Club presented development plans to other community organizations to generate help with the responsibility of developing and maintaining the park. The Monroe Garden Club added flowers and landscaping to the park entrance, and the Monroe Historical Society rebuilt a log cabin in the wooded area of the park. In 1972, the Lions leased the park to the Village of Monroe. (Courtesy of the Monroe Lions Club.)

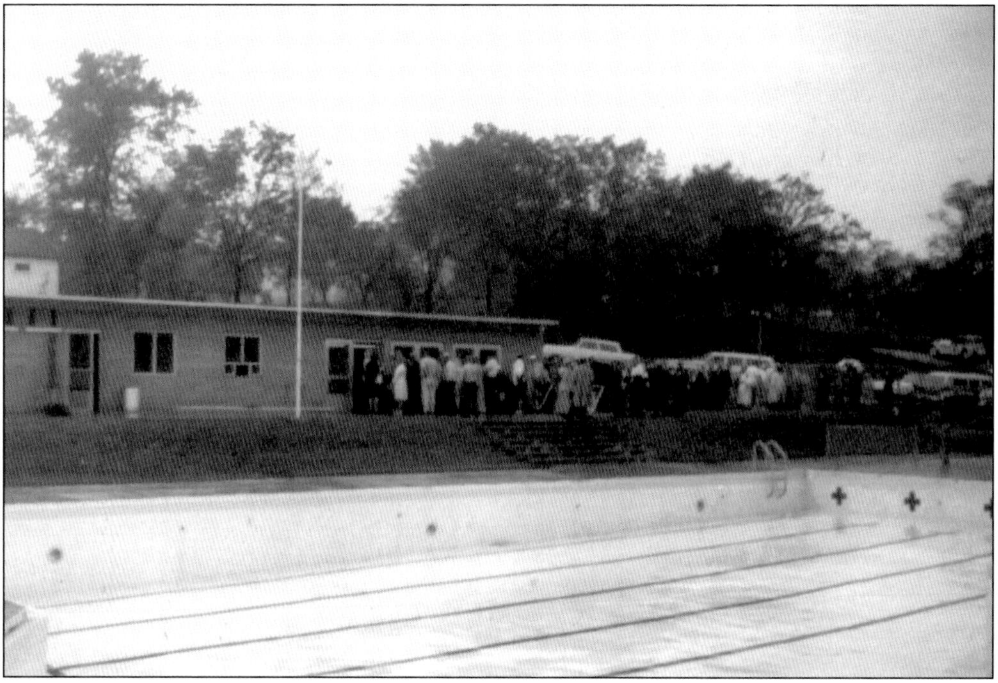

By 1962, the baby boom had nearly reached its end, and the village was experiencing tremendous growth with young families. The need for additional recreational facilities was evident. A swim club was formed and the Lions Club provided a small parcel of land for the pool site and promoted and assisted in the planning and construction of the pool. (Courtesy of the Monroe Lions Club.)

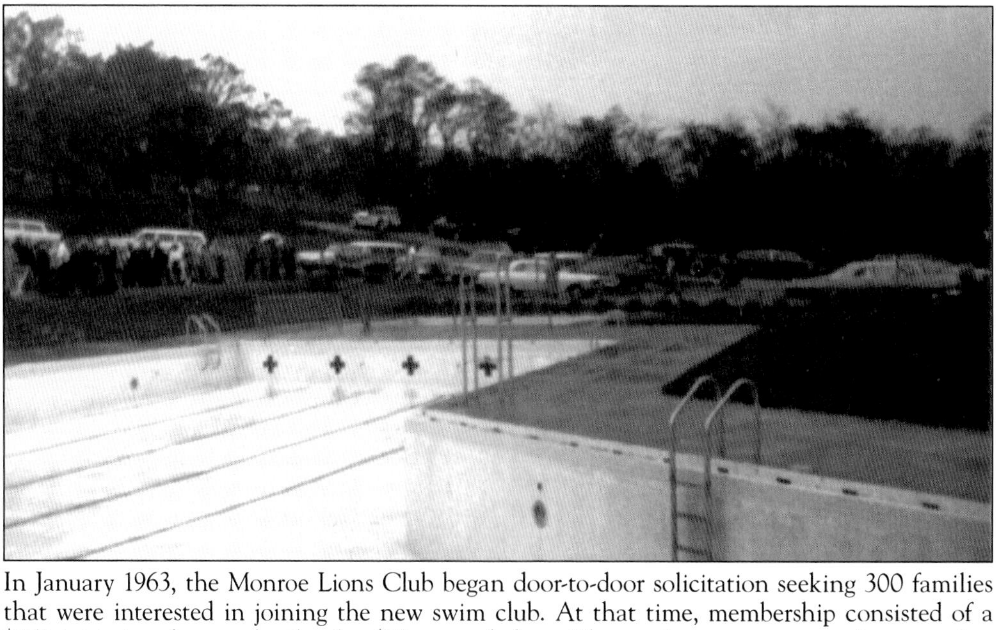

In January 1963, the Monroe Lions Club began door-to-door solicitation seeking 300 families that were interested in joining the new swim club. At that time, membership consisted of a $250 initiation fee per family plus $25 annual dues. The pool was patterned after one that had been completed in Hamilton not long before the Monroe pool construction began. Local contractors contributed free labor to help build the pool. (Courtesy of the Monroe Lions Club.)

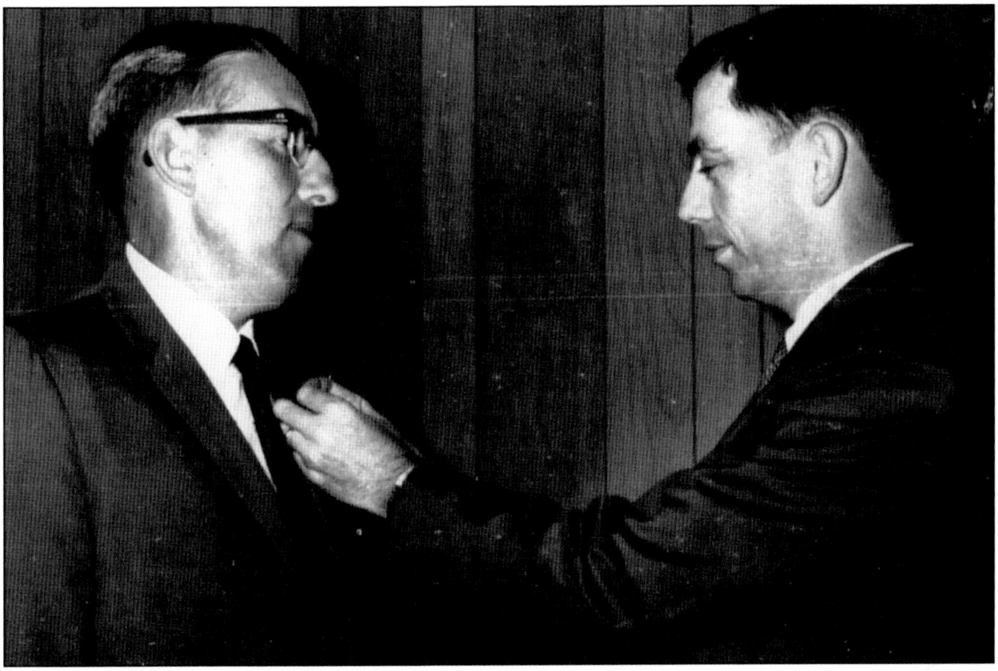

In July 1967, Ed MacDonald (left) was installed as the new Lions Club president. Boyd Smith (right) congratulates him. Both men attended Muskingum College in New Concord during the early 1950s. (Courtesy of the Monroe Lions Club. Reprinted with permission from the Middletown Journal.)

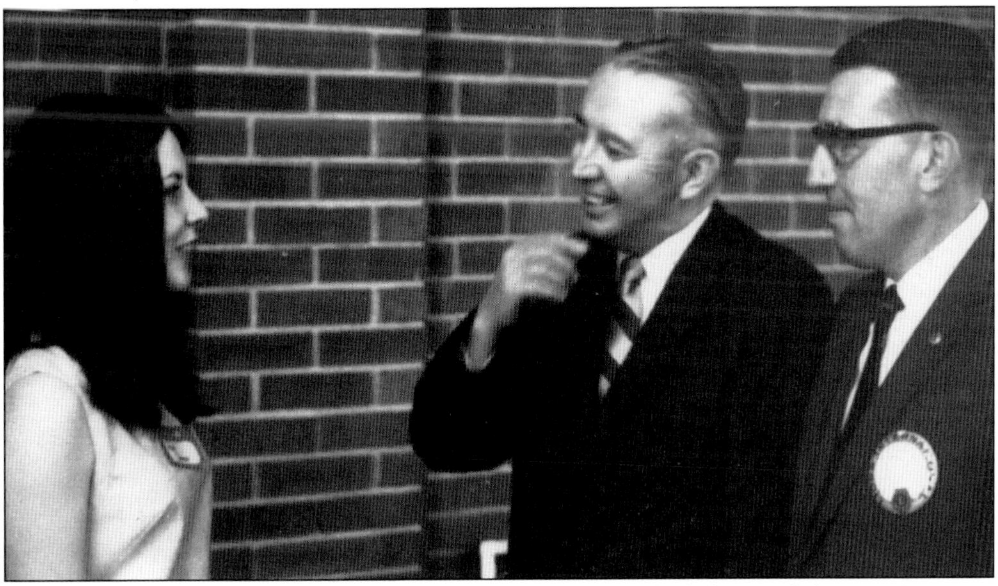

The Monroe Lions Club held annual scholarship banquets, which honored the top 10 percent of the Lemon Monroe High School senior class. Posing for the *Middletown Journal* in this 1968 photograph are, from left to right, student Jane Owens, state auditor Roger Cloud, and Ed MacDonald. Cloud was the speaker at the banquet. He had served five terms as speaker of the Ohio House of Representatives and lived in DeGraff. (Courtesy of the Monroe Lions Club. Reprinted with permission from the Middletown Journal.)

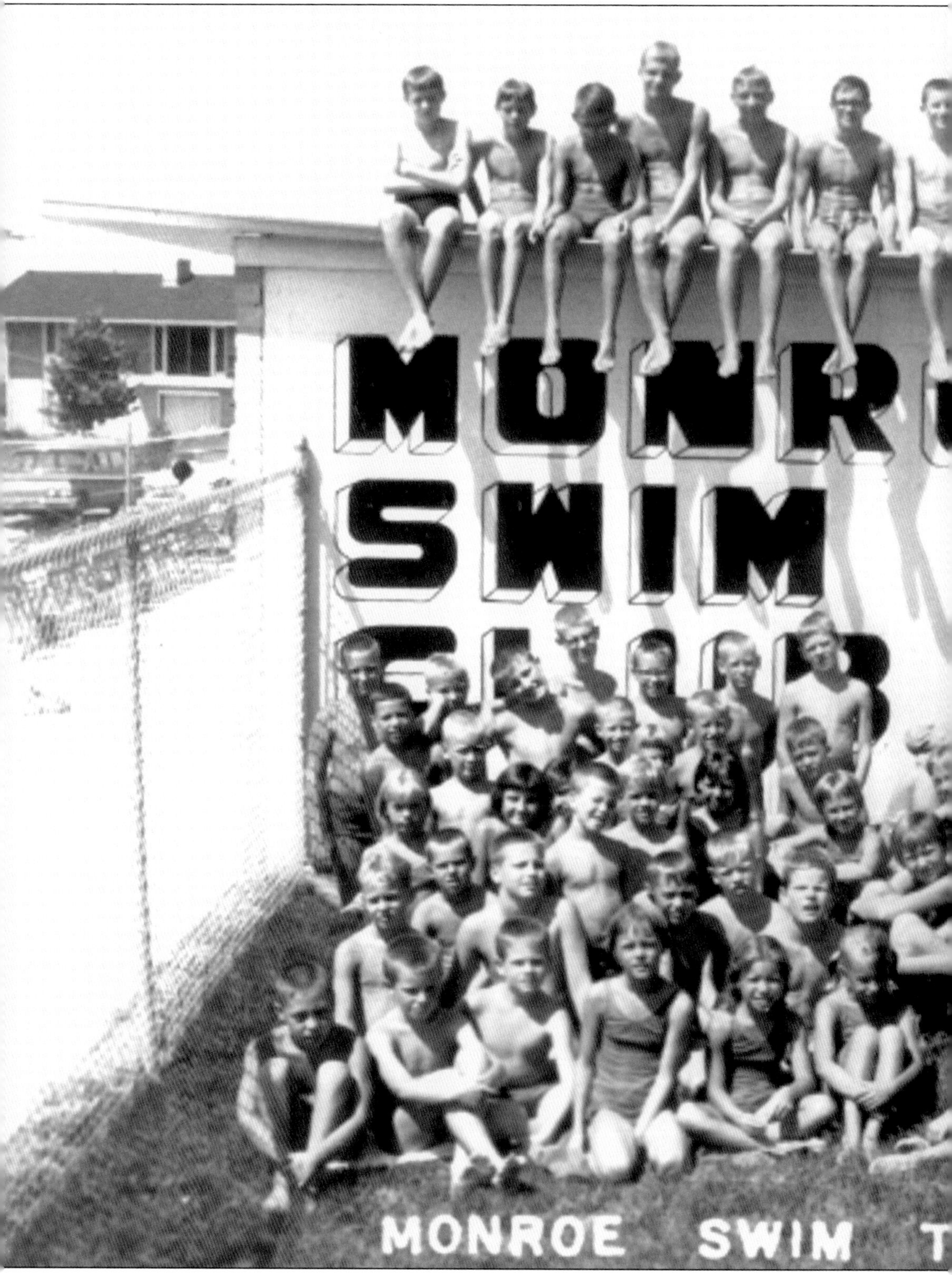
MONR
SWIM
MONROE SWIM T

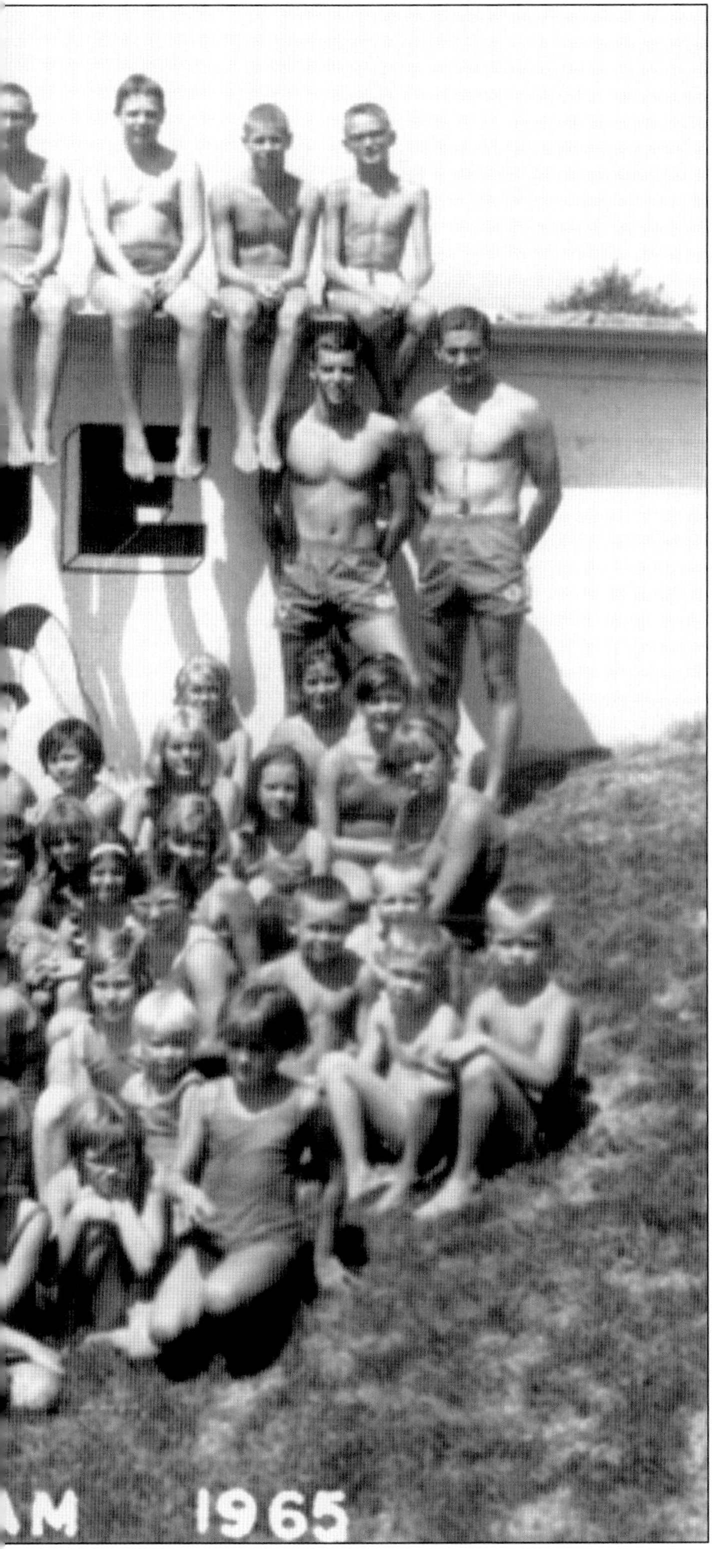

The 1965 Monroe swim team poses for this photograph at the new Monroe Swim Club. In the top row are Dean Constiner, Steve Walch, Joe Beatty, Dave Bussell, John Routson, Jim Davis, Dan Bussell, Steve Miltenberger, and Mike Monroe. The coaches are Rick Haiges and Larry Henry. The members kneeling include Mark Tannreuther, John Singleton, Sam Johnston, Glenn ?, and Randy Monroe. Those seated on the left side include Stene Hollon, Bill Hendrickson, Erick Barnes, Ben Constiner, Scott Young, Cindy Whitenack, Patty Foreman, Karen Bussell, Pam Majors, Brian Young, Ben Raulson, Gary Walch, Ed Singleton, Ken Bussell, Todd Miltenberger, Jeff Raulson, Mike Downs, Bill Daves, Patty Tannreuther, and Cindy Hollon. Those seated on the right side include Christen Steigerwald, Brenda Jones, Patty Reedy, Sandy Young, Lori Whitnack, Mary Routson, Holly Young, Kayla Miltenberger, Pam Beatty, Candy Cain, ? Chamberlin, Teddy Whitenack, Molly Chlendorff, ? Ridenour, John Schrock, Jana Durham, Kay Frazee, Susan Monroe, and Mary Barnes. Also on the swim team were Ruthie Pierce, Sue Brower, and Jason and Jim Blount. (Courtesy of Mary Jo Russell. Reprinted with permission from Herb Davis and the Monroe Swim Club.)

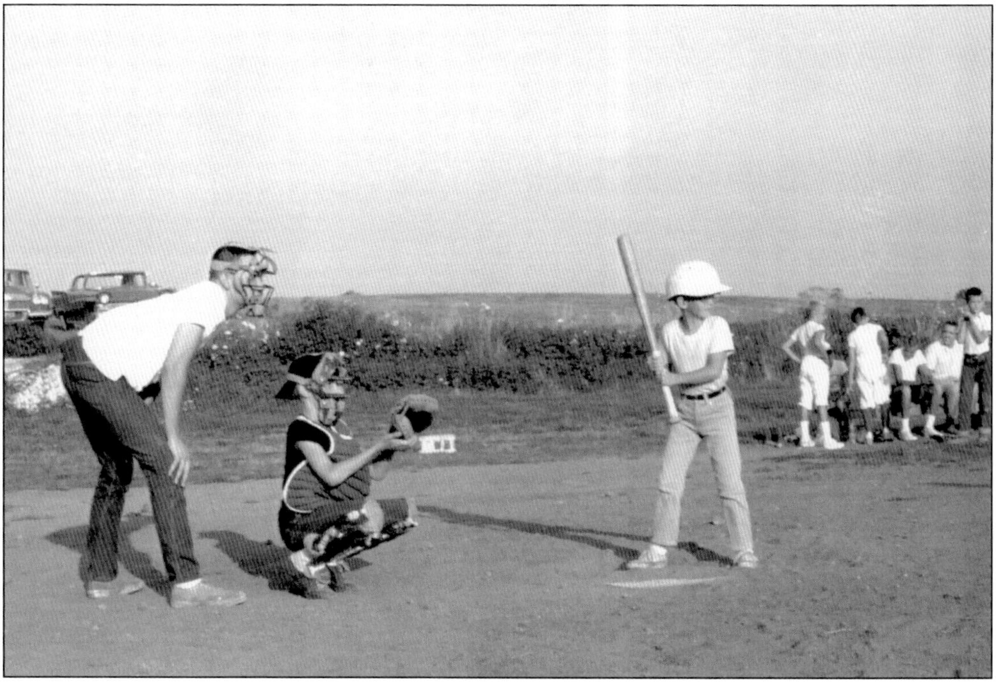

Monte Miltenberger is at bat during this local baseball game. The *c.* 1963 photograph was taken when he was eight years old. Monte is the son of Richard and Gloria Miltenberger. His widow, Gina, and two sons Alex and Ryan still live in Monroe. (Courtesy of Gloria Miltenberger.)

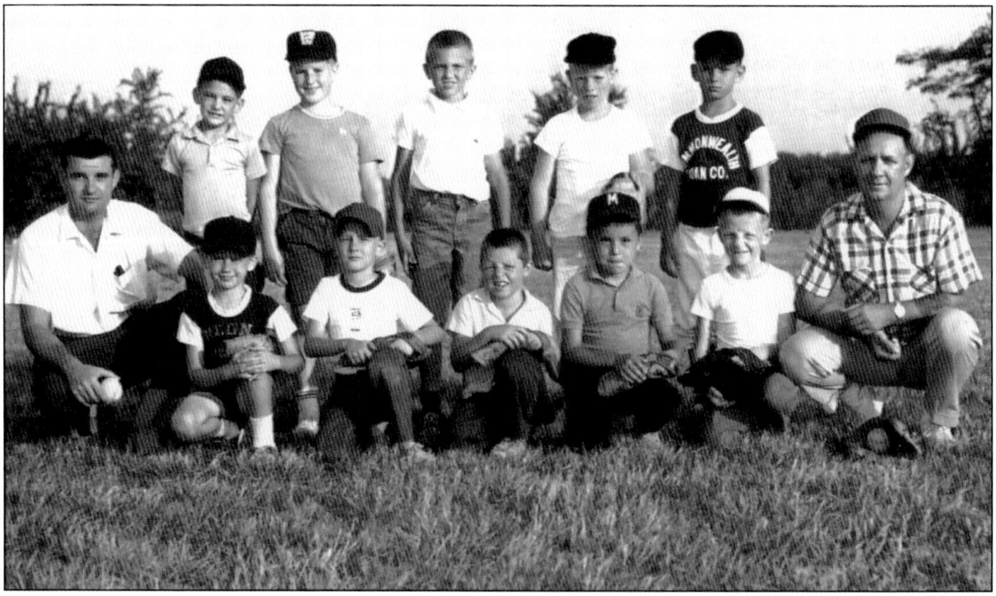

This photograph of a baseball team was taken around 1964. The children are around 50 years of age now and most are still in the Monroe area. In the early 1960s, teams did not wear uniforms or need sponsors. From left to right are (first row) coach Dean Johnson, Brent Goodwin, Tom Tolson, Rick Propps, Jim White, Basil Fleming II, and coach Basil Fleming; (second row) Billy Combs, Mike Johnson, Kim Goodwin, Todd Miltenberger, and John Deisenroth. (Courtesy of Gloria Miltenberger.)

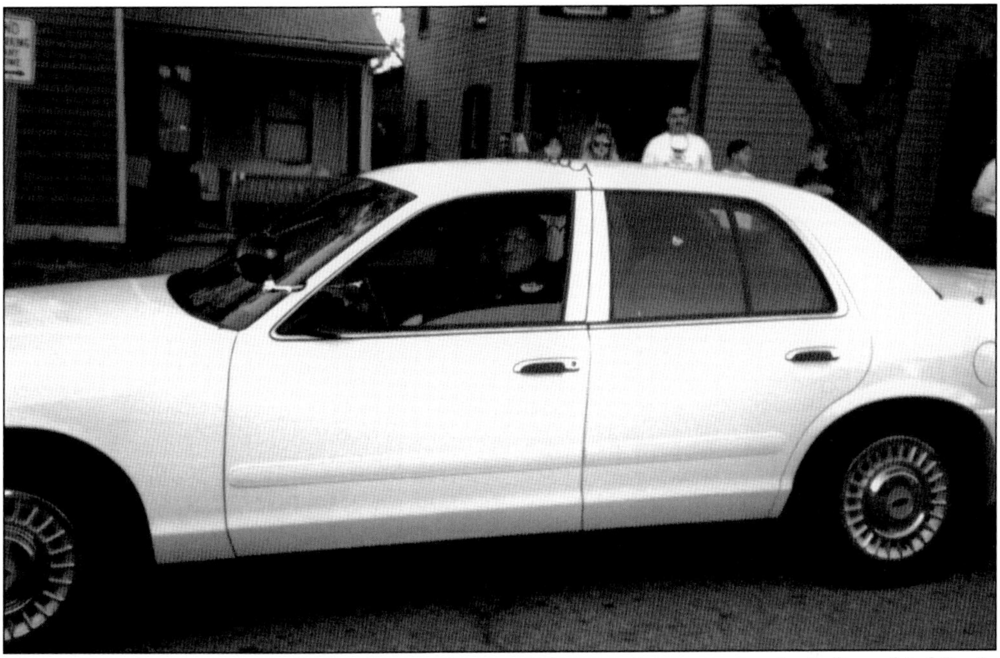

The police department works hard to make sure Monroe citizens are safe. Police chief Ernie Howard is pictured monitoring a parade in 2002. Howard retired a few years later and is a member of the Lions Club. The current police chief of Monroe is Gregory Homer. (Courtesy of Ed and Marge MacDonald.)

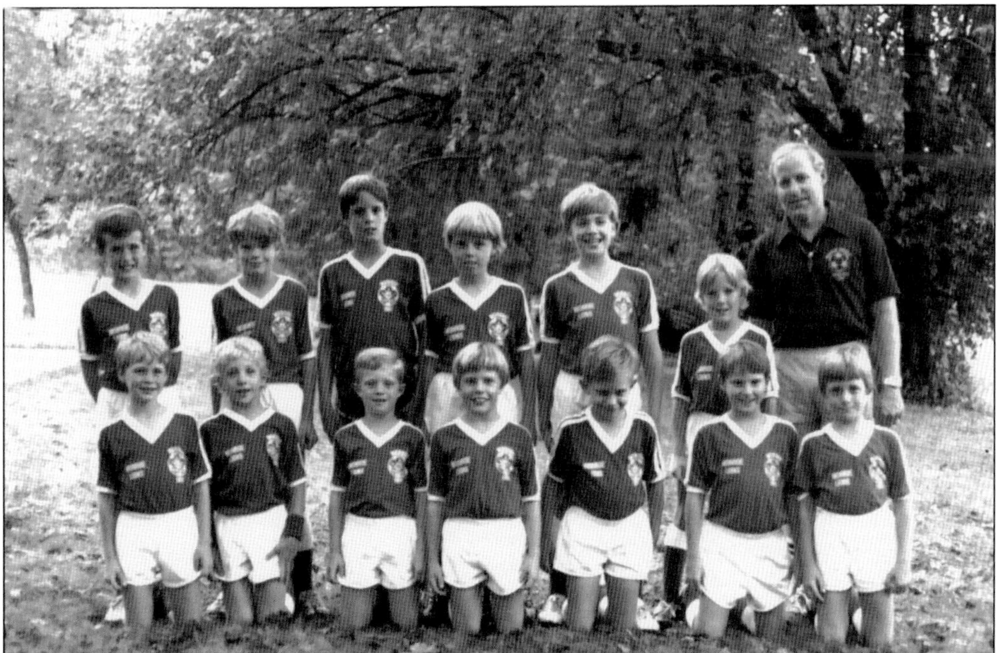

The Monroe Sports Association began its soccer program in 1978. In 1981, the Monroe Soccer Program had 23 teams with 301 boys and girls. This photograph is of the 1981 Lions sponsored team. (Courtesy of the Monroe Lions Club. Reprinted with permission from Lloyd Little.)

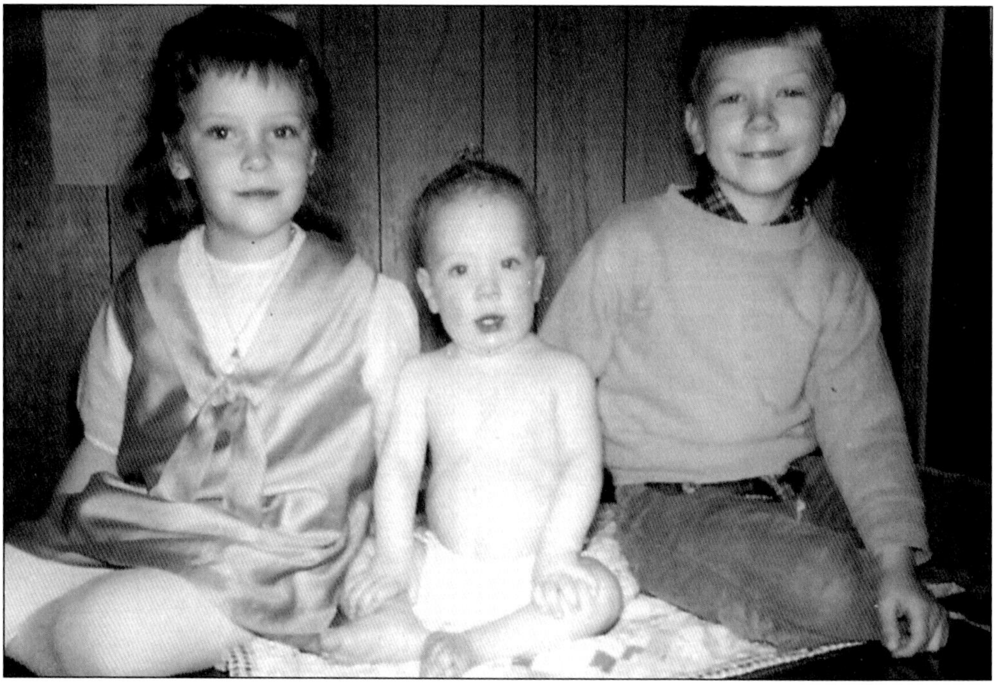

From left to right, Carmon, Scott, and Joe Patrick pose for this 1965 photograph. The Patrick family lived on Ohio Avenue during the early 1960s. Carmon and Joe attended Monroe Elementary School. The family relocated to Trenton in 1966. (Courtesy of Joe and Joyce Patrick.)

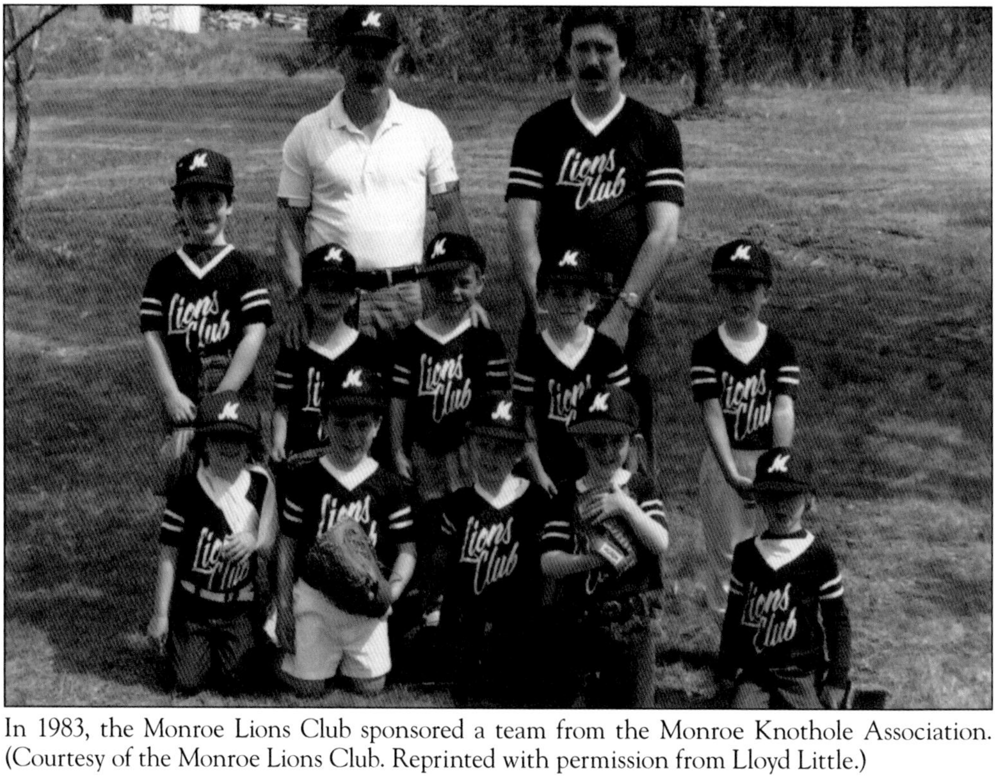

In 1983, the Monroe Lions Club sponsored a team from the Monroe Knothole Association. (Courtesy of the Monroe Lions Club. Reprinted with permission from Lloyd Little.)

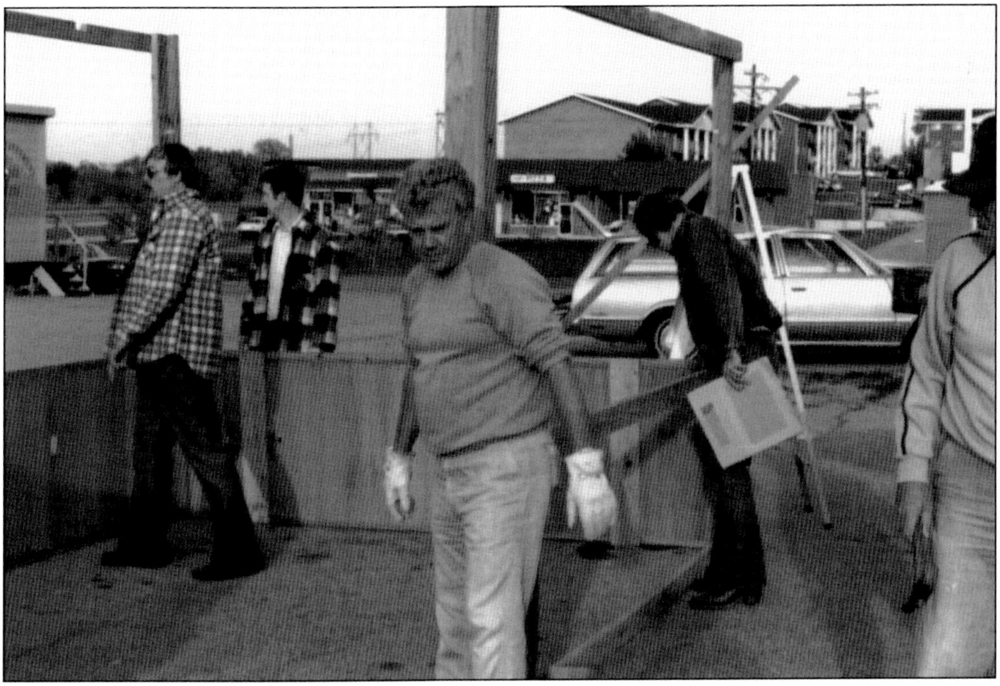

From left to right, Monroe Lions Doug Ward, unidentified, Joe Ponder, Joe Beatty, and Ed MacDonald assemble the Pepsi Pitch booth for the 1982 Log Cabin Days festival. (Courtesy of the Monroe Lions Club.)

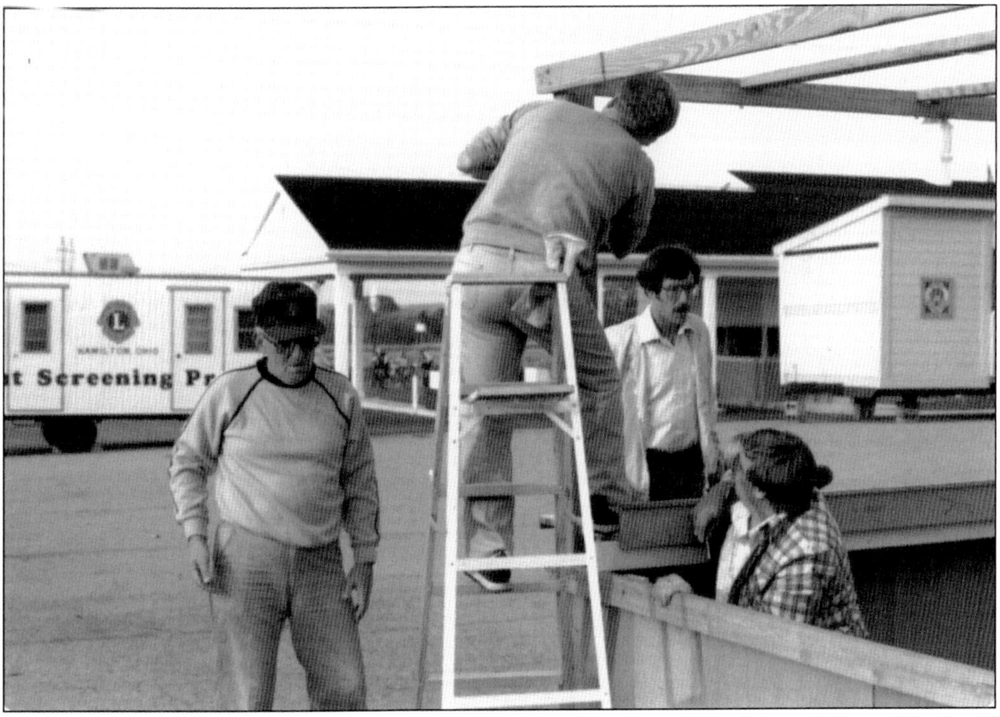

From left to right, Lions Ed MacDonald, Joe Ponder, Dr. Gary Schudel, and Doug Ward add finishing touches to the Pepsi Pitch booth. (Courtesy of the Monroe Lions Club.)

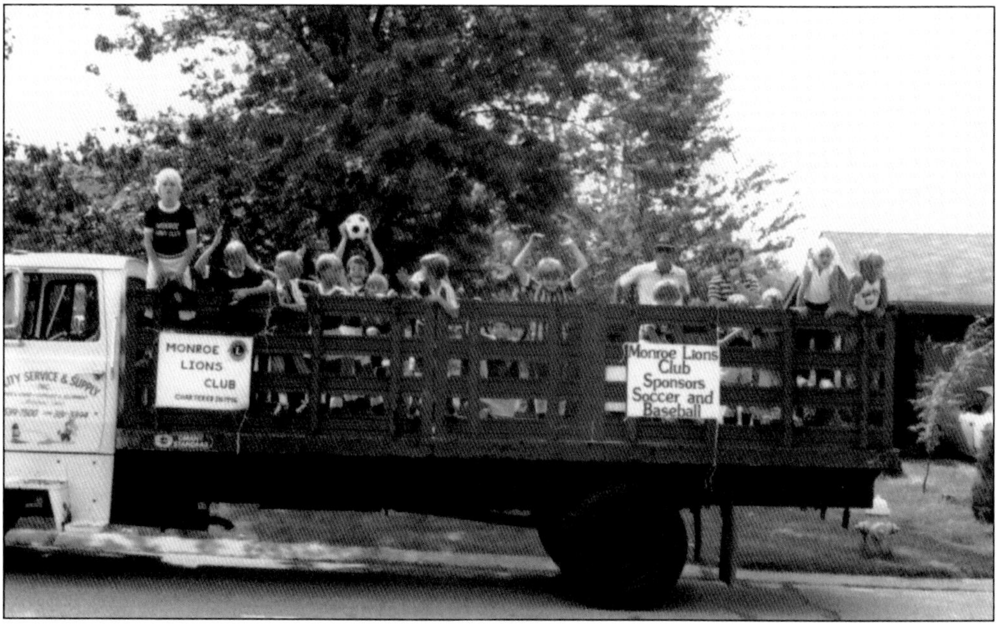

The Lions Club had created a float for the Log Cabin Days parade. Lions Gale and Joe Beatty provided their company truck to use in the parade. Utility Service and Supply was founded in October 1952 by C. E. Beatty. The family business was located on Winton Street in Middletown. In 1959, it moved to 233 South Main Street in Monroe, and in 1989, it relocated to its current office on Lawton Avenue. (Courtesy of the Monroe Lions Club.)

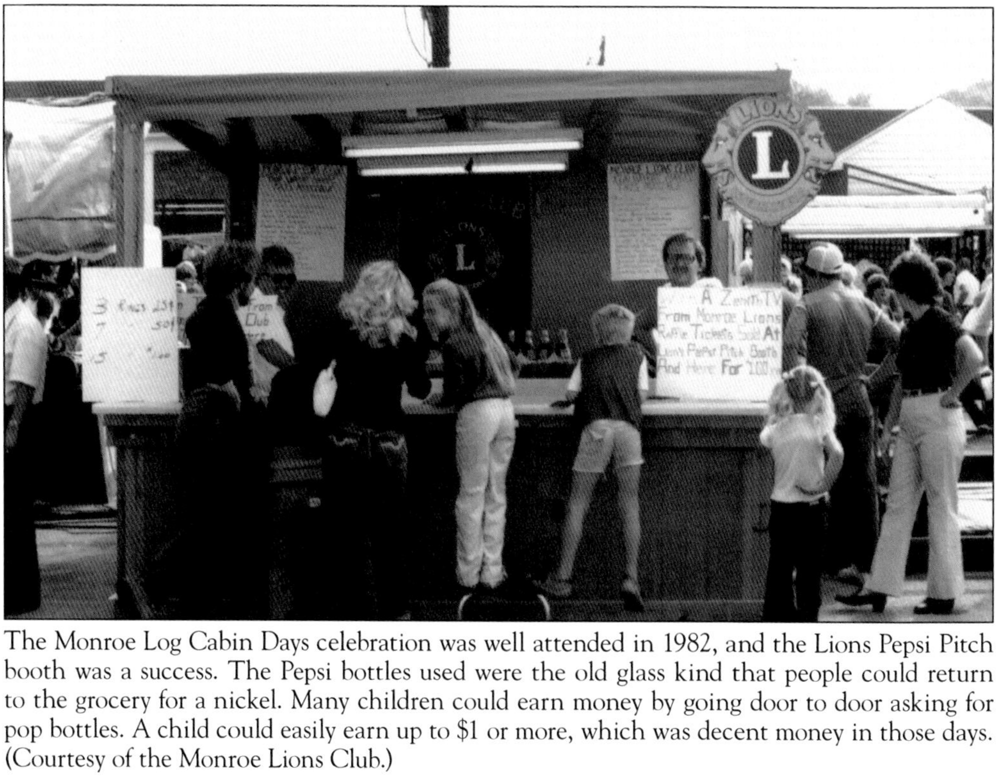

The Monroe Log Cabin Days celebration was well attended in 1982, and the Lions Pepsi Pitch booth was a success. The Pepsi bottles used were the old glass kind that people could return to the grocery for a nickel. Many children could earn money by going door to door asking for pop bottles. A child could easily earn up to $1 or more, which was decent money in those days. (Courtesy of the Monroe Lions Club.)

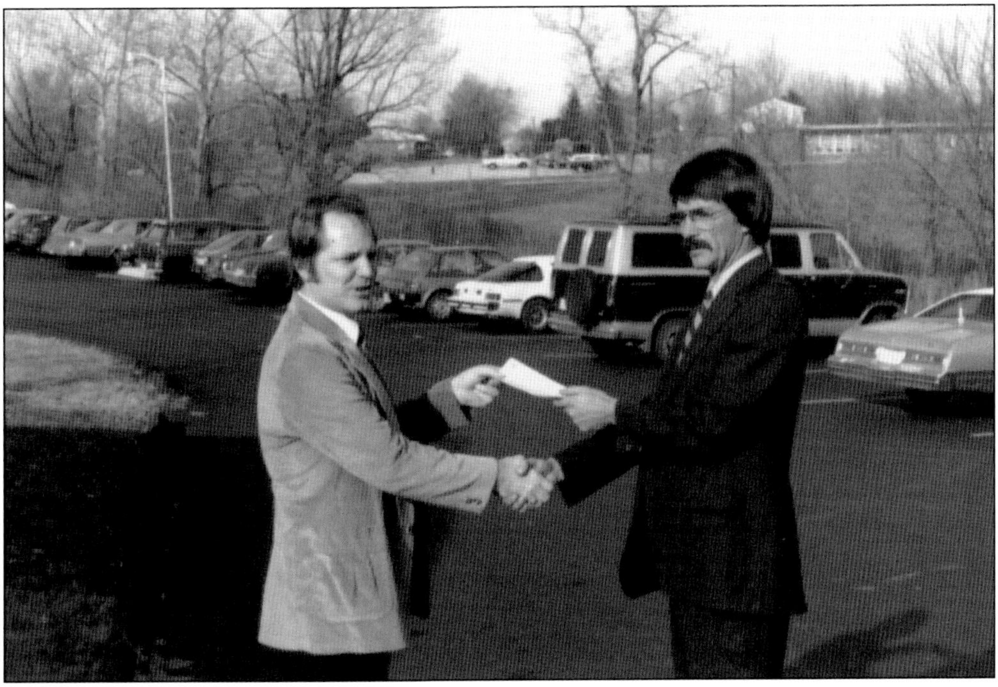

In December 1982, Lions vice president Joe Beatty (left) gave a $150 check to Doty House administrator Tom Neal (right) for the Doty House Christmas Fund. The fund was used to purchase a present for each child who attended Doty House and give them a Christmas party. Doty House provided educational and therapy services for special-needs children that were not available at that time in the public schools. It is now called Abilities First. (Courtesy of the Monroe Lions Club.)

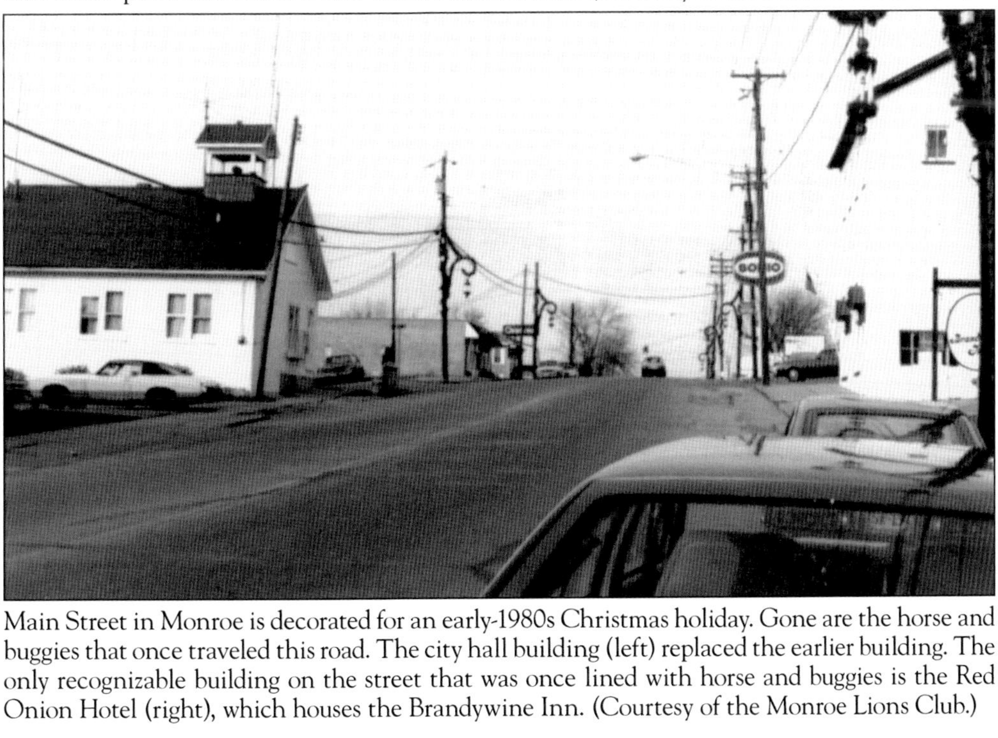

Main Street in Monroe is decorated for an early-1980s Christmas holiday. Gone are the horse and buggies that once traveled this road. The city hall building (left) replaced the earlier building. The only recognizable building on the street that was once lined with horse and buggies is the Red Onion Hotel (right), which houses the Brandywine Inn. (Courtesy of the Monroe Lions Club.)

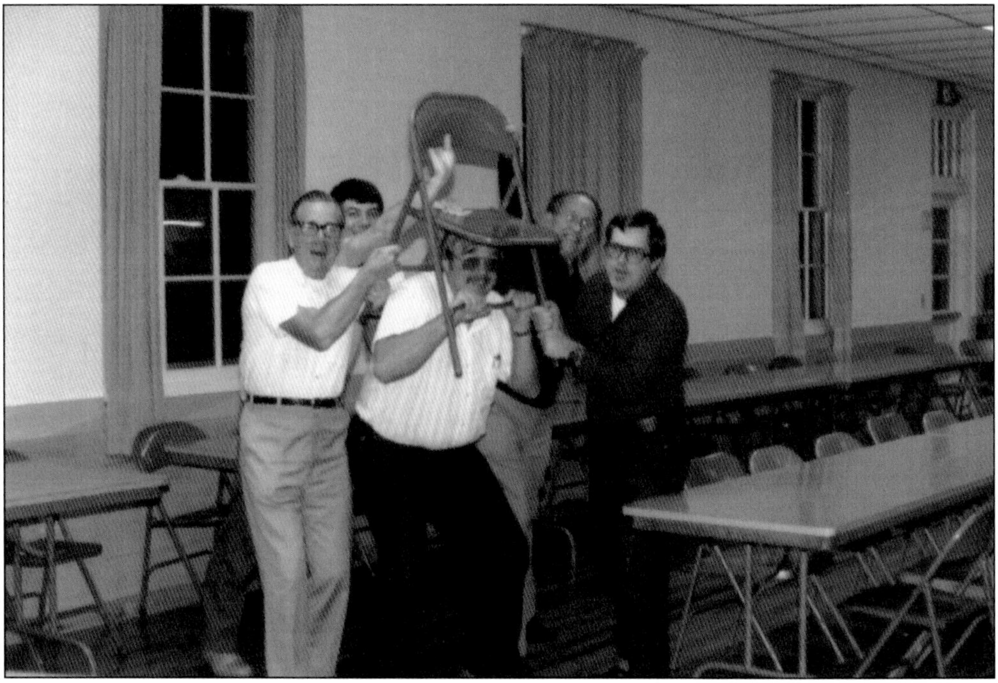

Monroe Lions Club members ham it up before their Christmas party, which was held at the Seven Dolors Catholic Church. The club members would cook and serve the holiday dinner to their wives. It was always a fun and festive occasion. (Courtesy of the Monroe Lions Club.)

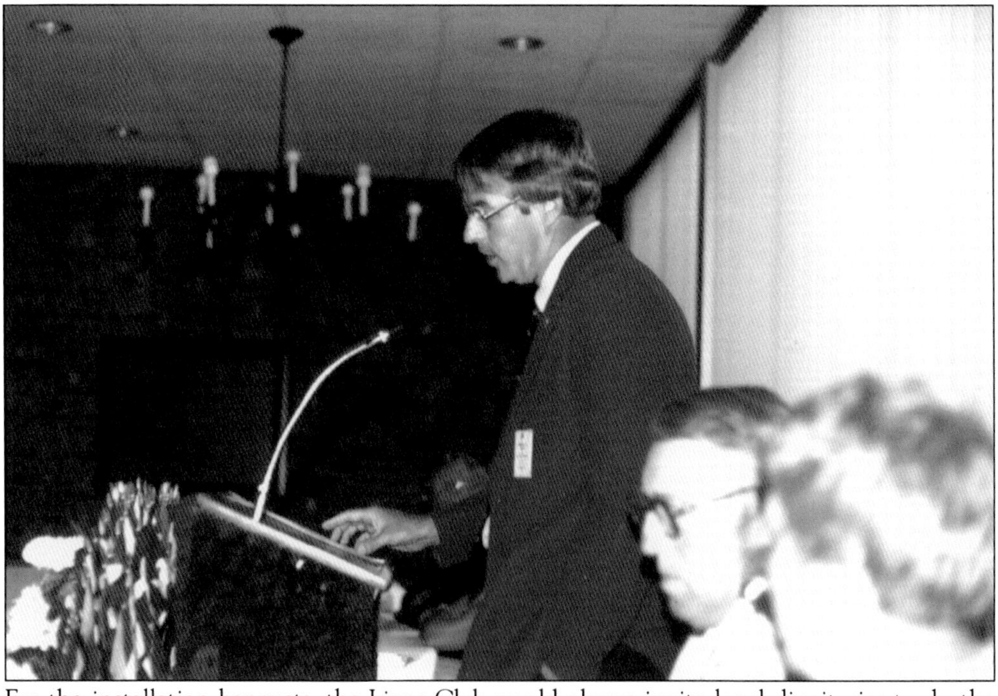

For the installation banquets, the Lions Club would always invite local dignitaries to do the honors. Mike Long of Insurance Associates and past Lions district governor presided over this meeting. (Courtesy of the Monroe Lions Club.)

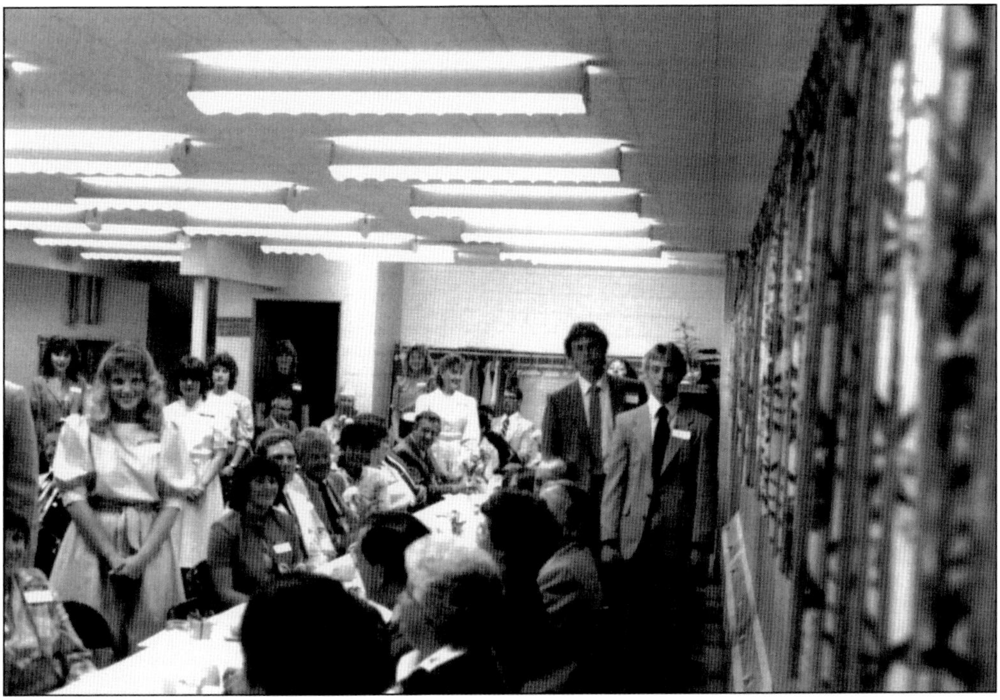

The 1983 Scholarship Recognition Banquet was held on May 9 of that year. The students were honored with a certificate and medallion for their achievement. The guest speaker was Allen Cooper, who was the former director of the corporate responsibility with Armco. He also served on the staff of Wright State University. (Courtesy of the Monroe Lions Club.)

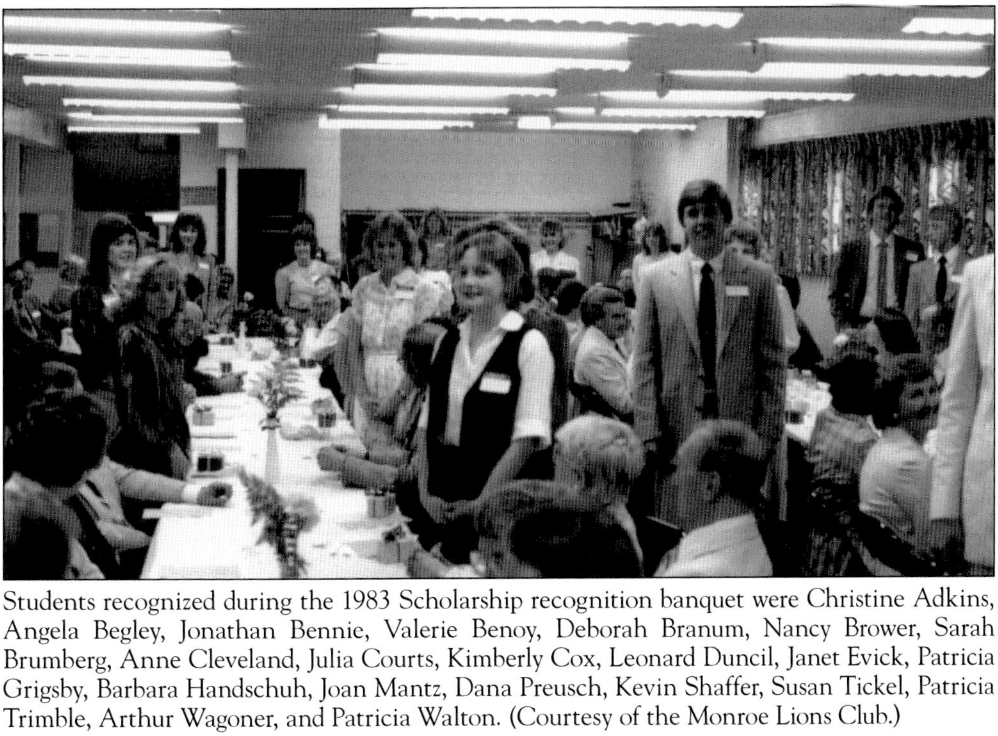

Students recognized during the 1983 Scholarship recognition banquet were Christine Adkins, Angela Begley, Jonathan Bennie, Valerie Benoy, Deborah Branum, Nancy Brower, Sarah Brumberg, Anne Cleveland, Julia Courts, Kimberly Cox, Leonard Duncil, Janet Evick, Patricia Grigsby, Barbara Handschuh, Joan Mantz, Dana Preusch, Kevin Shaffer, Susan Tickel, Patricia Trimble, Arthur Wagoner, and Patricia Walton. (Courtesy of the Monroe Lions Club.)

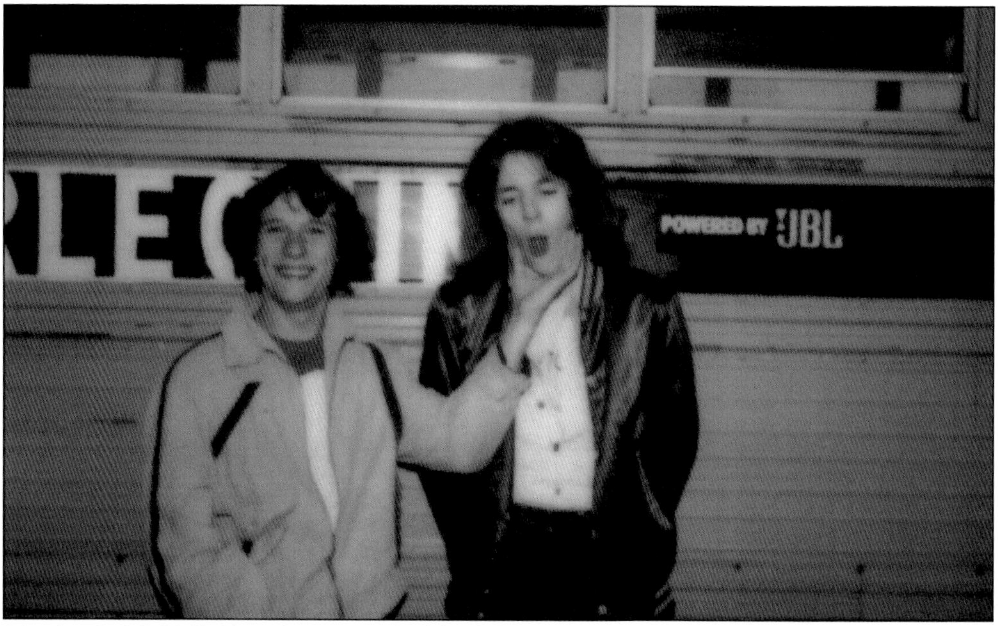

Charlie Crihfield (left) and Matt Basford (right) ham it up before boarding the bus during the early 1980s. Basford joined the band Harlequin at the tender age of 17. Members of Harlequin in 1980 were Coy Jackson, John Hutton, Matt Basford, Mike Basford, Terry Wingett, and Scott Whitt. Harlequin disbanded during the early 1980s and Basford became a founder of Yankee Grey, which disbanded in 2002. He is currently lead guitarist for country star Lee Greenwood. (Courtesy of Liz Hutton-Taylor.)

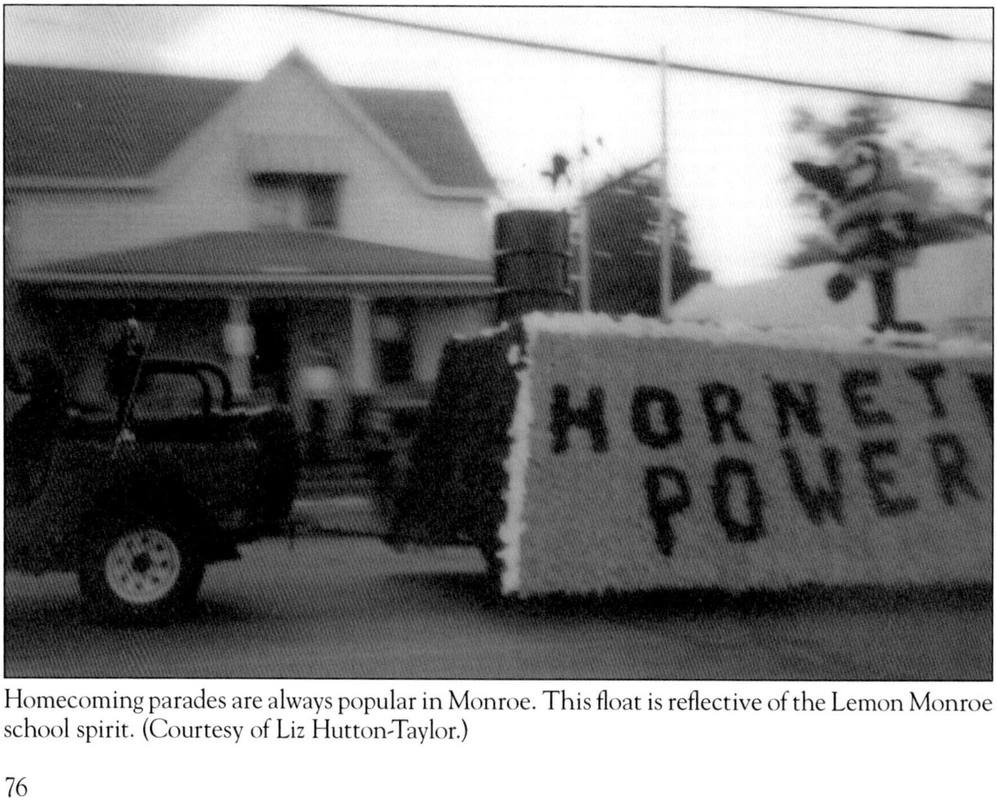

Homecoming parades are always popular in Monroe. This float is reflective of the Lemon Monroe school spirit. (Courtesy of Liz Hutton-Taylor.)

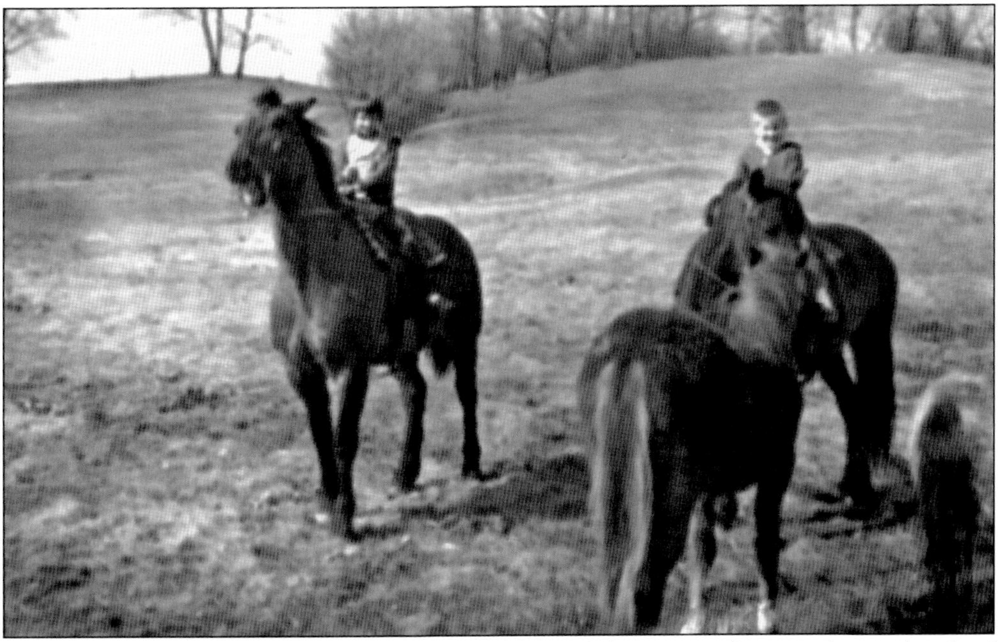

This photograph was taken in 1967 in a pasture east of the Matson farm on the north side of Route 63 at the Macready Avenue intersection. Ruthie Pierce (left) was seven and her brother Jamie (right) was six. The horses were in the sesquicentennial parade in 1967 and pulled a buggy and surrey. In 2000, Jamie was elected president of the newly formed Monroe Local School Board. (Courtesy of Richard Pierce.)

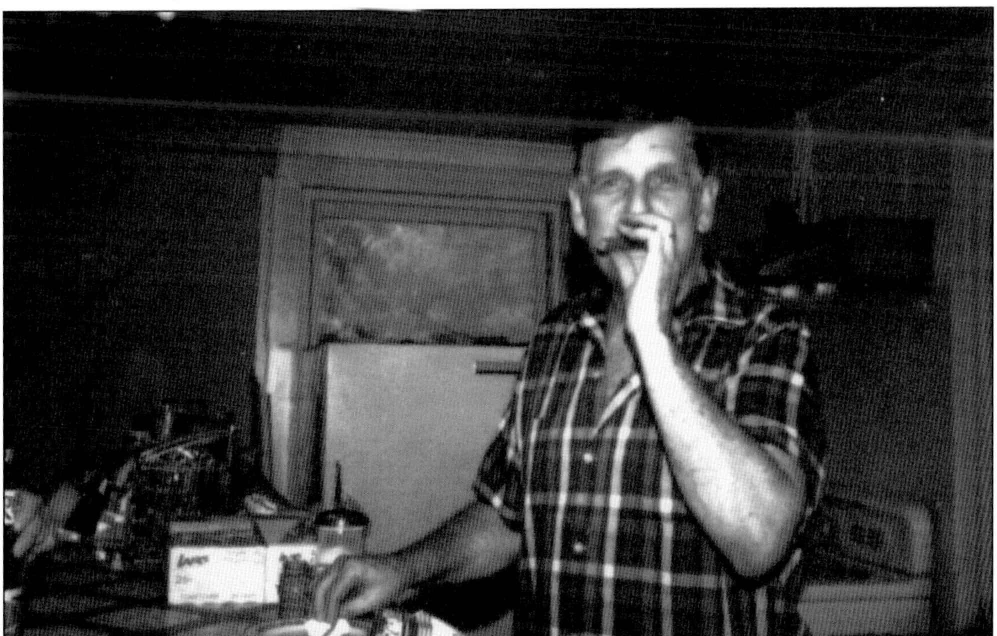

Dick Miller's pool hall was located on Church Street and boasted a simple but tasty lunch menu. Dick's homemade chili was a big hit with his patrons. The pool hall was a popular hang out in Monroe during the 1960s through the 1980s. (Courtesy of Liz Hutton-Taylor.)

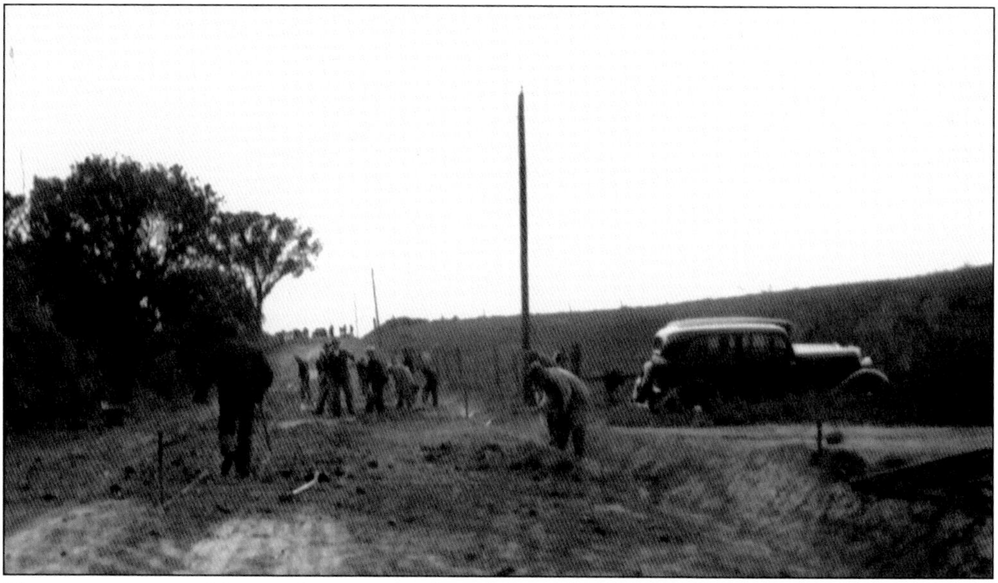

The construction of Britton Lane opened up the north end of Monroe for future development of the Brittany Heights subdivision and the Mount Pleasant Retirement Community during the late 1950s and early 1960s. (Courtesy of Boyd and Virginia Smith.)

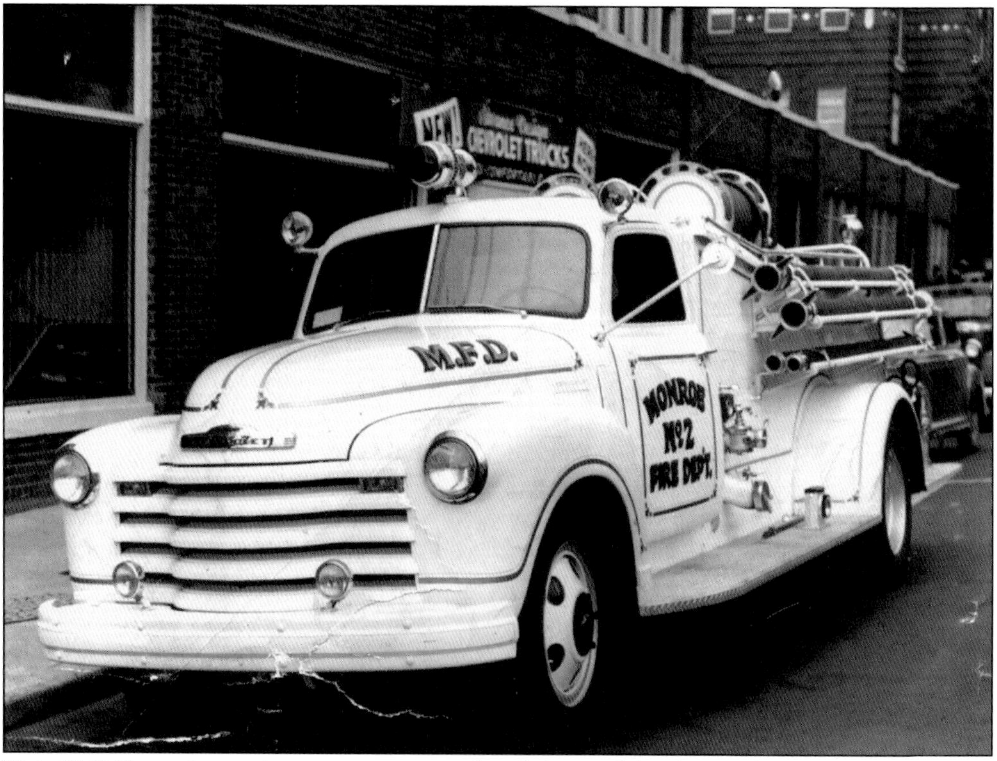

This 1947 Chevrolet combination pumper replaced the Model T during the late 1940s. The new engine faithfully served the Lemon Township and Monroe area for over 20 years. It is now in the private collection of Chip Lytle in nearby Blueball. (Courtesy of the Monroe Fire Department. Reprinted with permission from the Middletown Journal.)

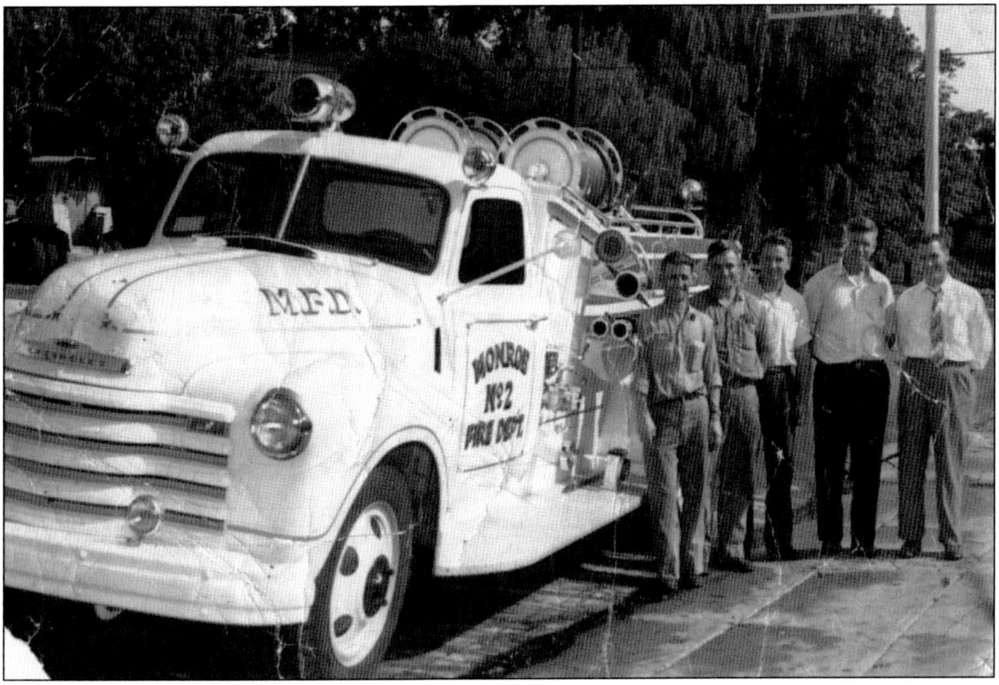

Standing in front of the new fire truck are, from left to right, Earl "Squirrly" Hiteshue, Russell "Stumpy" Hiteshue, and three unidentified men. Earl was fire chief and Russell was assistant chief. Earl is the father of Juanita Hiteshue Doty of Monroe. (Courtesy of the Monroe Fire Department. Reprinted with permission from the Middletown Journal.)

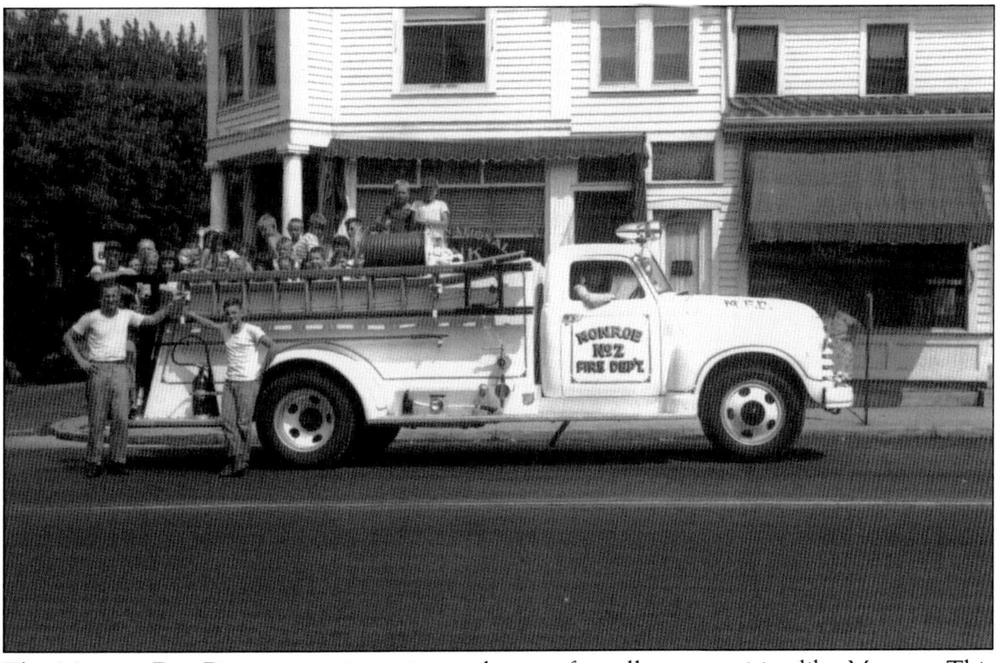

The Monroe Fire Department is an integral part of small communities like Monroe. This photograph was taken in front of Monroe National Bank and the Gorman Insurance Company. (Courtesy of the Monroe Fire Department.)

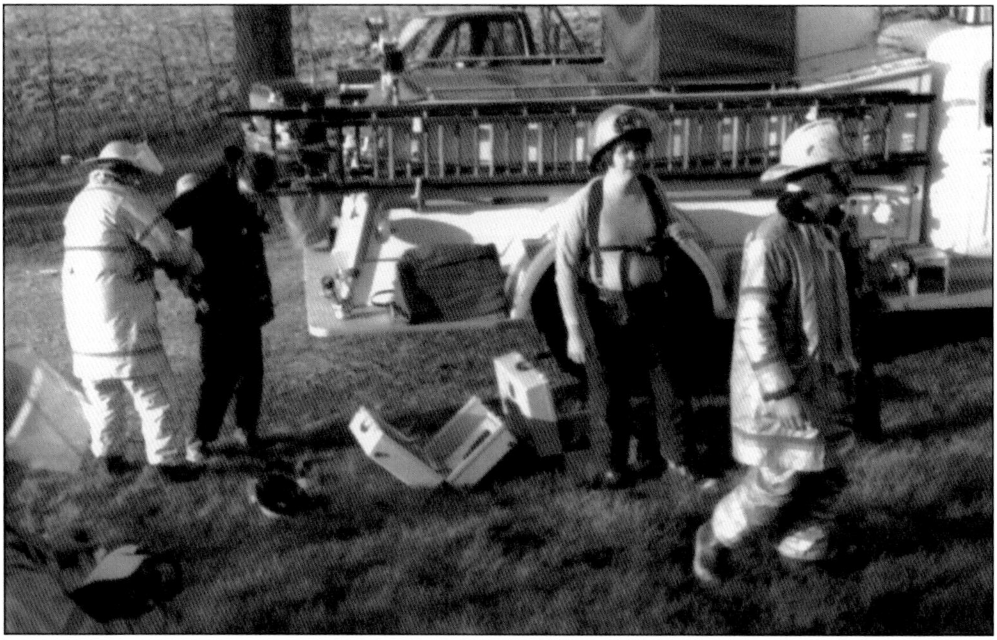

The Monroe Fire Department works hard within the community. (Courtesy of the Monroe Fire Department.)

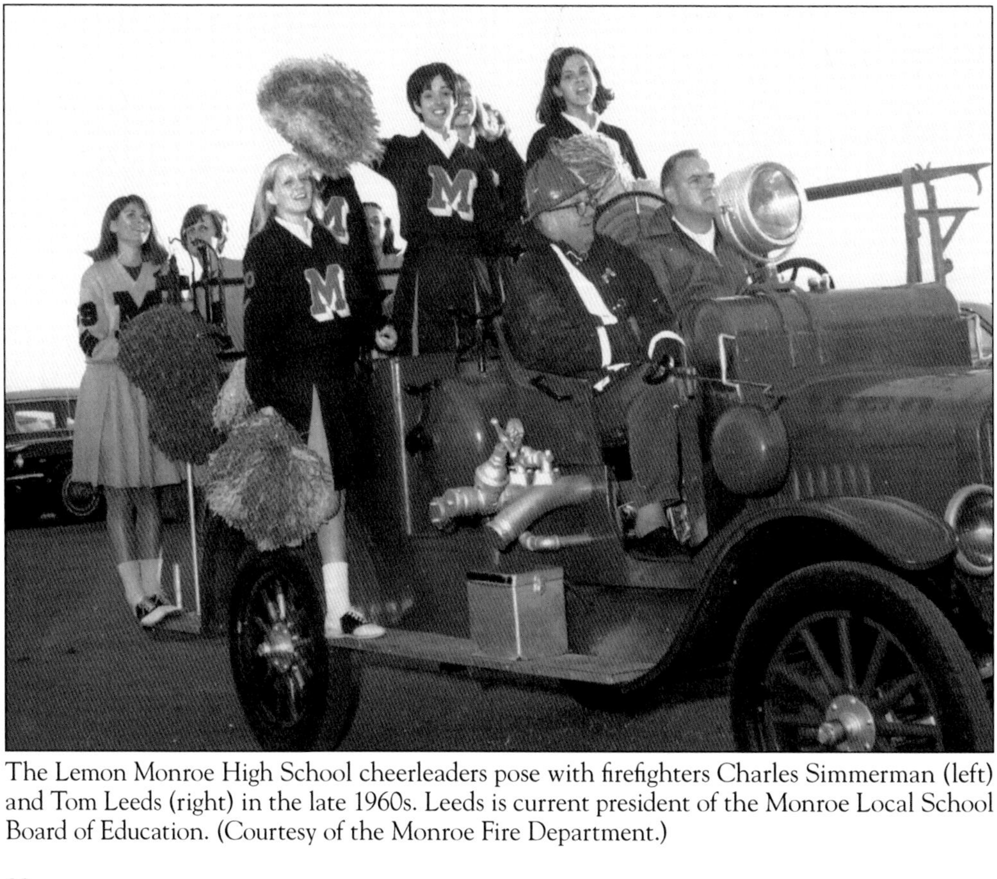

The Lemon Monroe High School cheerleaders pose with firefighters Charles Simmerman (left) and Tom Leeds (right) in the late 1960s. Leeds is current president of the Monroe Local School Board of Education. (Courtesy of the Monroe Fire Department.)

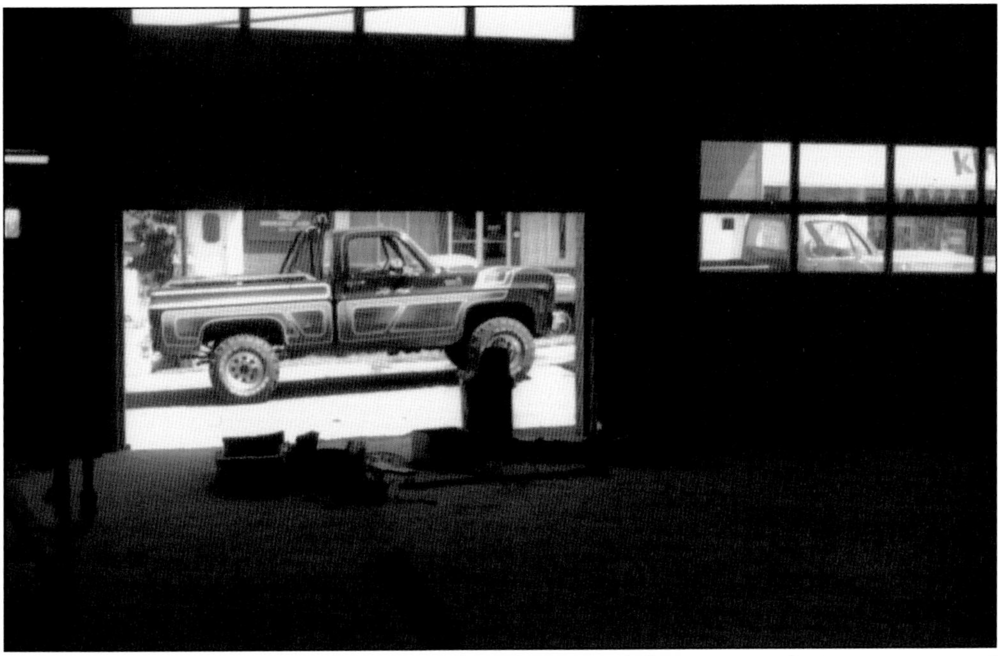

As the fire department grew, it became evident that it needed more space for its apparatus and other equipment. This photograph was taken during the remodeling of the firehouse in the mid-1980s. The old King Quik convenient store on Main Street was directly across from the firehouse. (Courtesy of the Monroe Fire Department.)

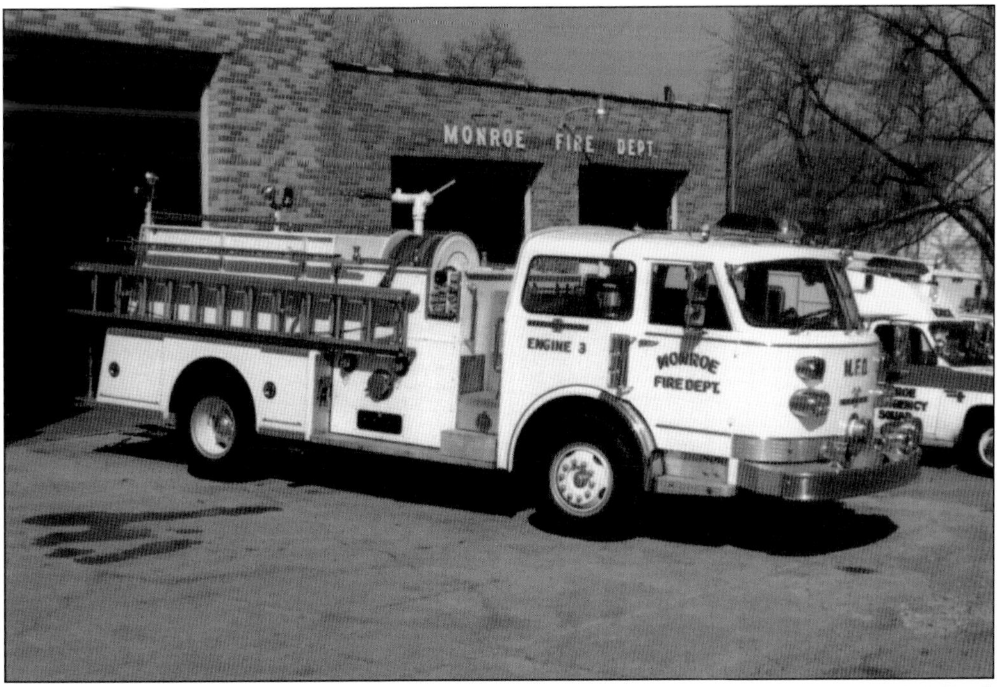

Engine No. 3 stands in front of the newly remodeled firehouse in 1988. No. 3 was a 1967 Ford. The fire station was eventually torn down to build the current one, which was dedicated in 2002. (Courtesy of the Monroe Fire Department.)

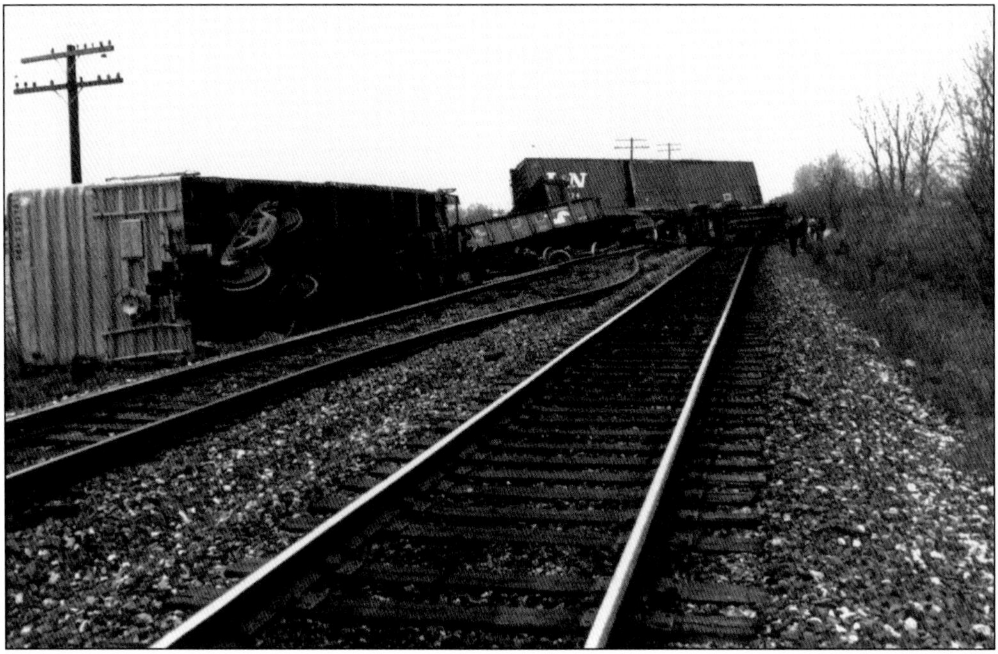

Firemen handle all sorts of emergencies, like this train wreck. (Courtesy of the Monroe Fire Department. Reprinted with permission from the Middletown Journal.)

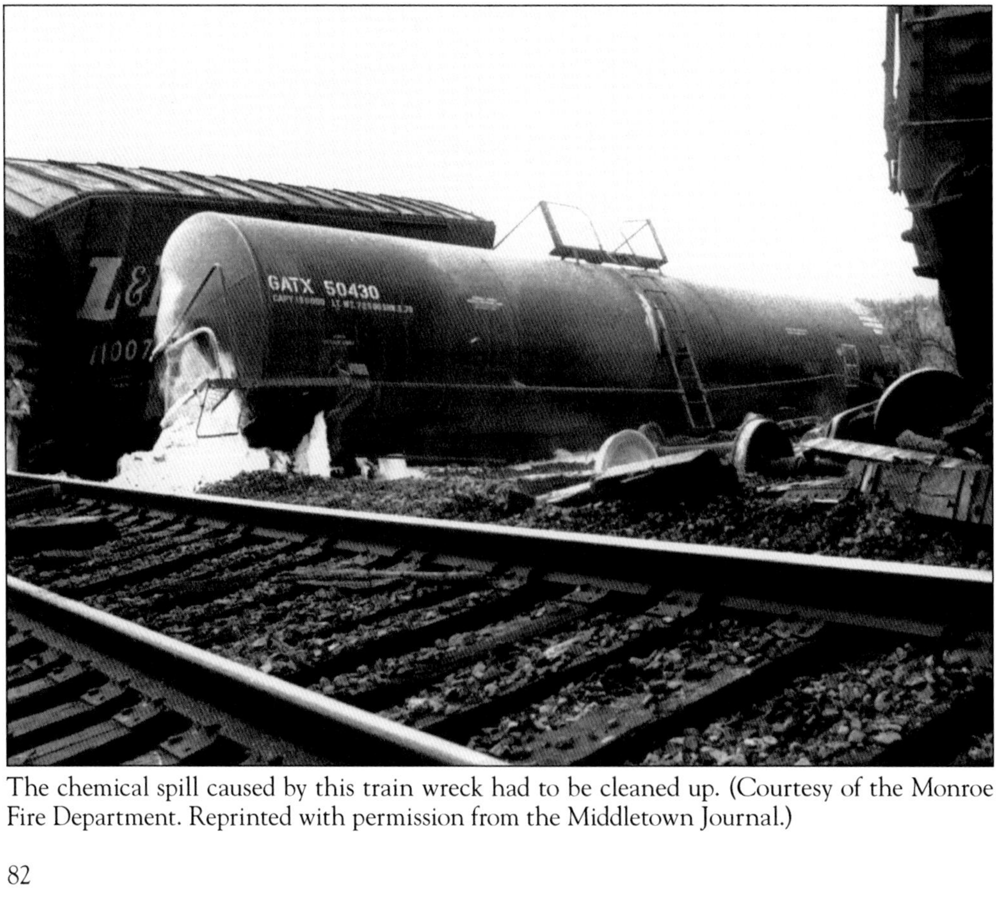

The chemical spill caused by this train wreck had to be cleaned up. (Courtesy of the Monroe Fire Department. Reprinted with permission from the Middletown Journal.)

Monroe men fight a house fire. In the early years, Monroe was a volunteer fire department. (Courtesy of the Monroe fire Department. Reprinted with permission from the Middletown Journal.)

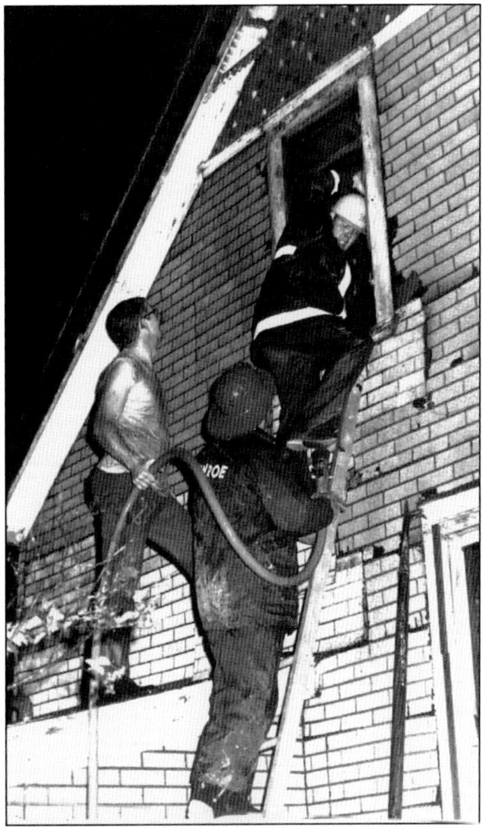

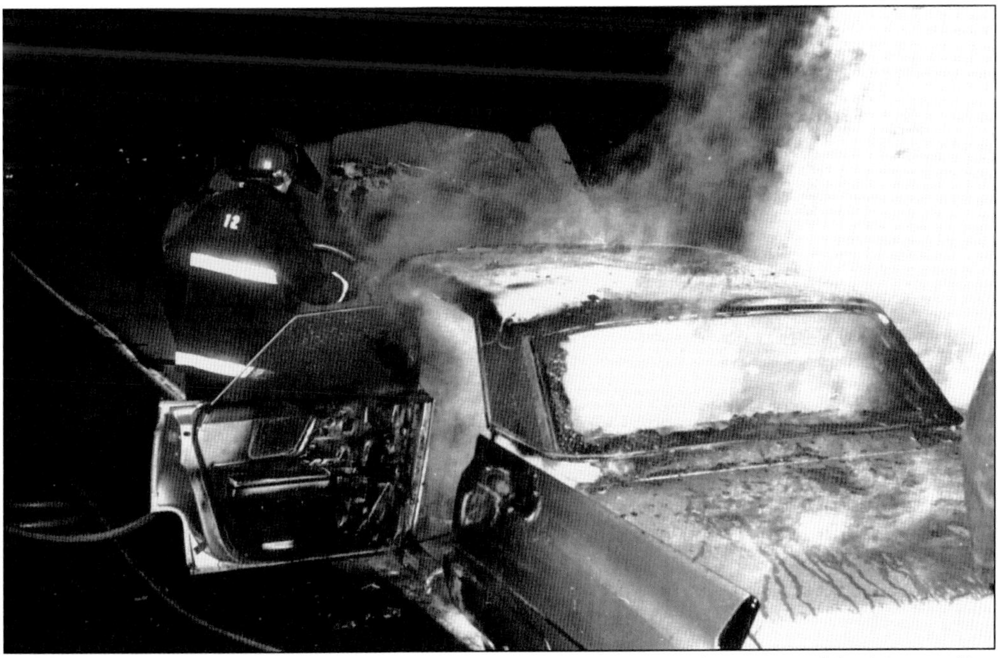

The brave Monroe firefighters put out this car fire in January 1974. (Courtesy of the Monroe Fire Department. Reprinted with permission from the Middletown Journal.)

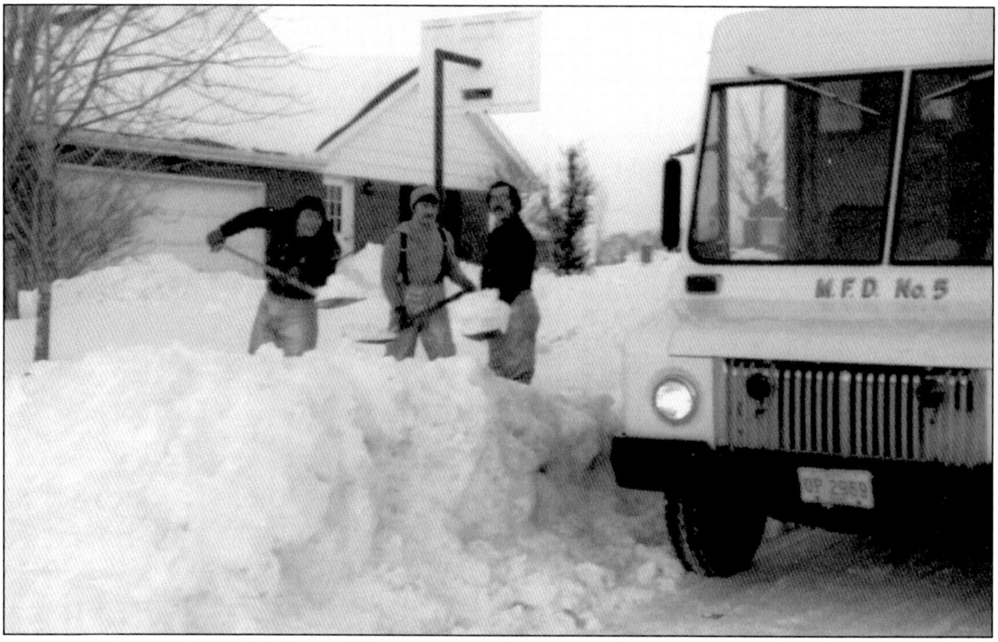

After the blizzard of 1978, it became necessary for firefighters to dig out the fire plugs. The storm hit early Thursday morning on January 26 and continued through Friday January 27. The high, 50-to-70-mile-per-hour winds, followed by the Arctic cold front, shut down the entire area, and the normal pace of society did not resume until about five days later. Radio stations had abandoned their regular programming to broadcast storm information and served as communication links when telephones and electricity failed. Volunteers with four-wheel-drive vehicles would distribute food and other supplies to those isolated people who were in need. (Courtesy of the Monroe Fire Department.)

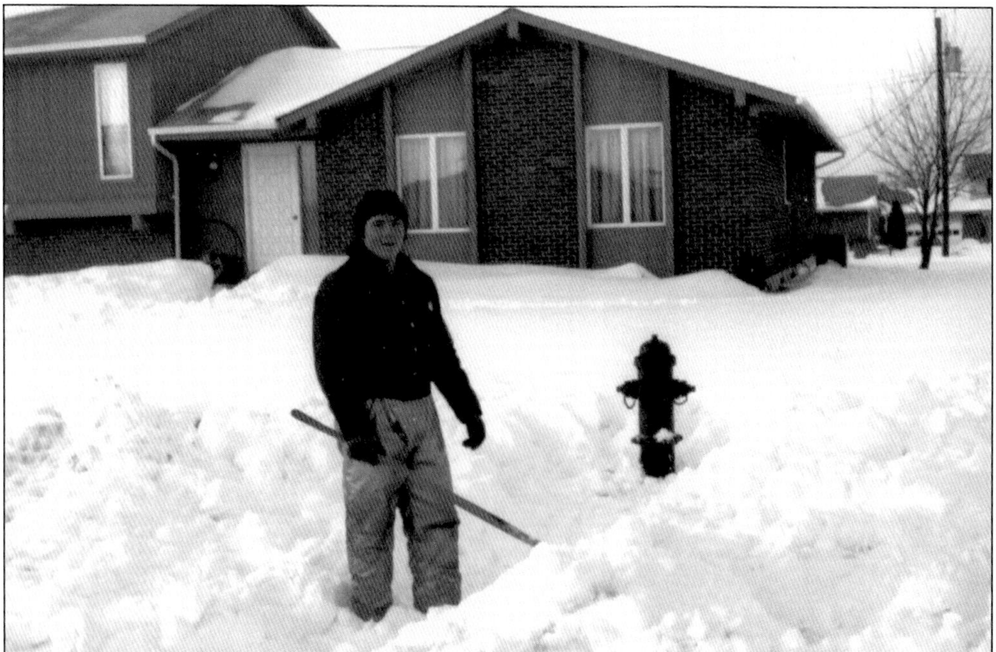

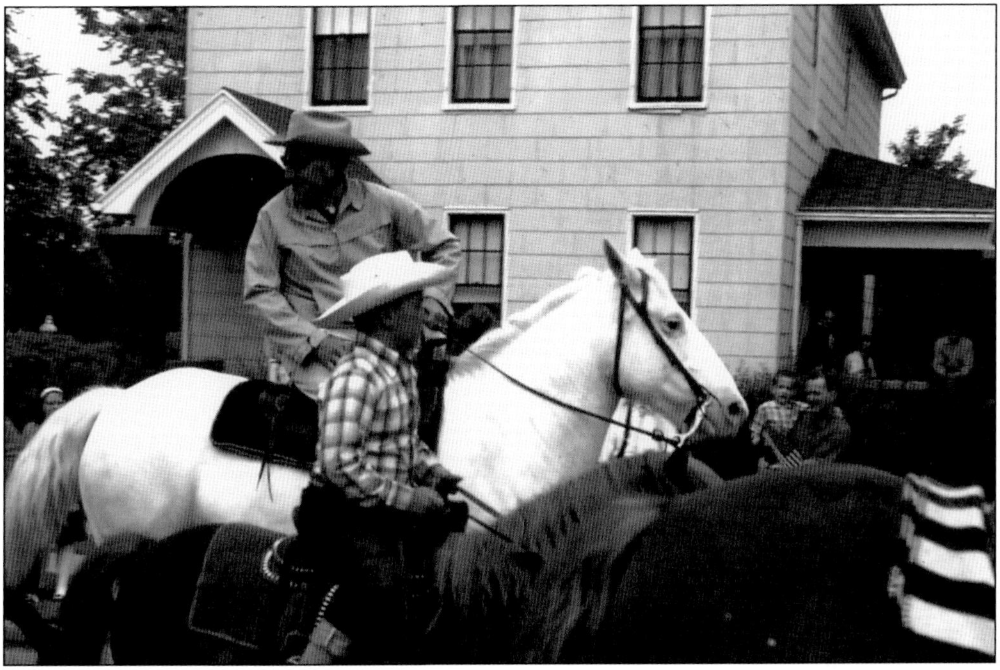

Monroe has always held many parades. Ed MacDonald (back) and John MacDonald (front) ride their horses in a parade during the mid-1960s. (Courtesy of Ed and Marge MacDonald.)

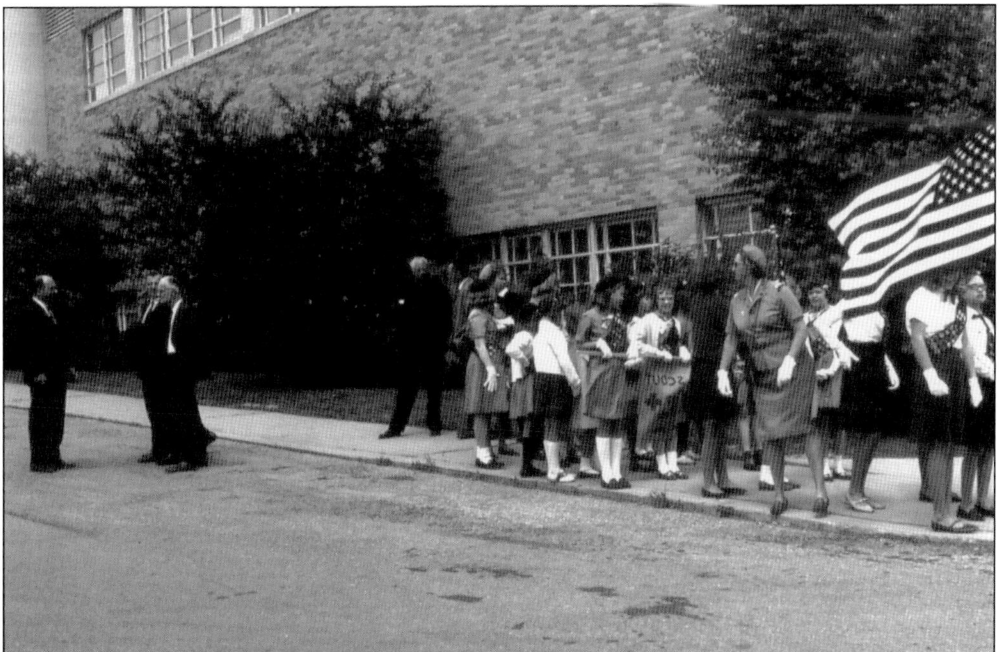

Girl Scouts are preparing for a parade in this 1960s photograph. Both Boy and Girl Scouting were popular activities in Monroe during that time period. (Courtesy of Ed and Marge MacDonald.)

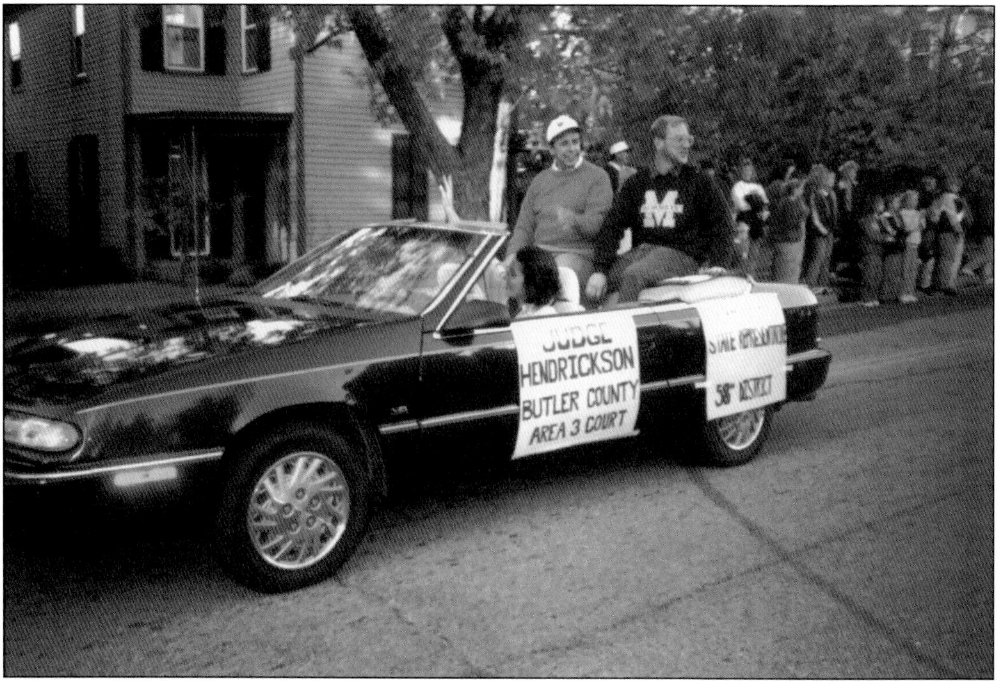

Judge Robert Hendrickson and state representative Gary Cates share an automobile in this parade. (Courtesy of Ed and Marge MacDonald.)

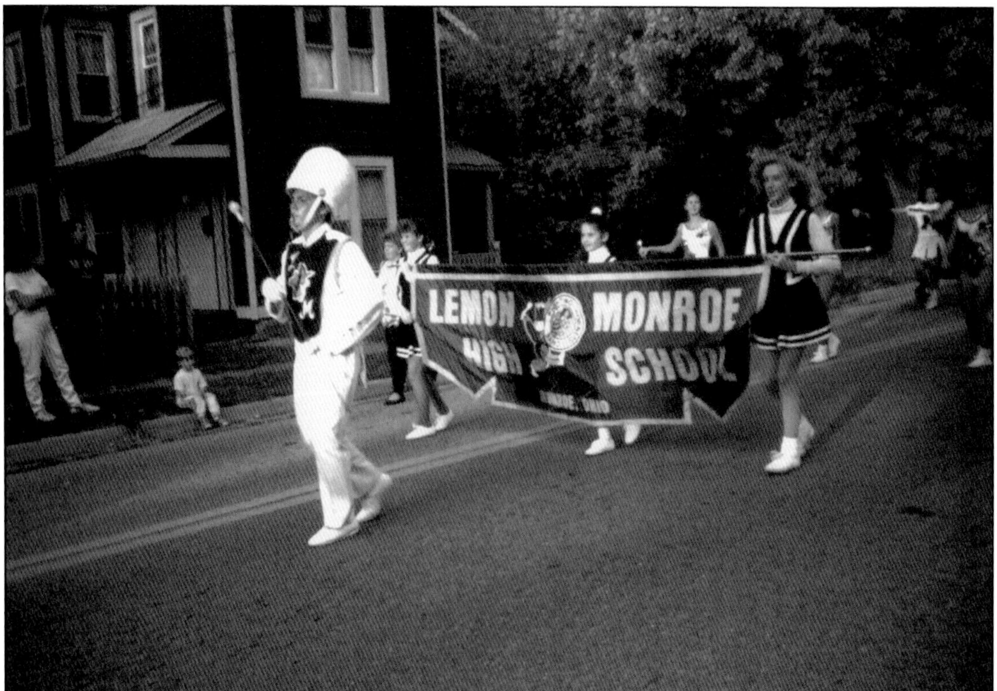

The Fighting Hornets Marching Band from Lemon Monroe High School participated in the local parades. (Courtesy of Ed and Marge MacDonald.)

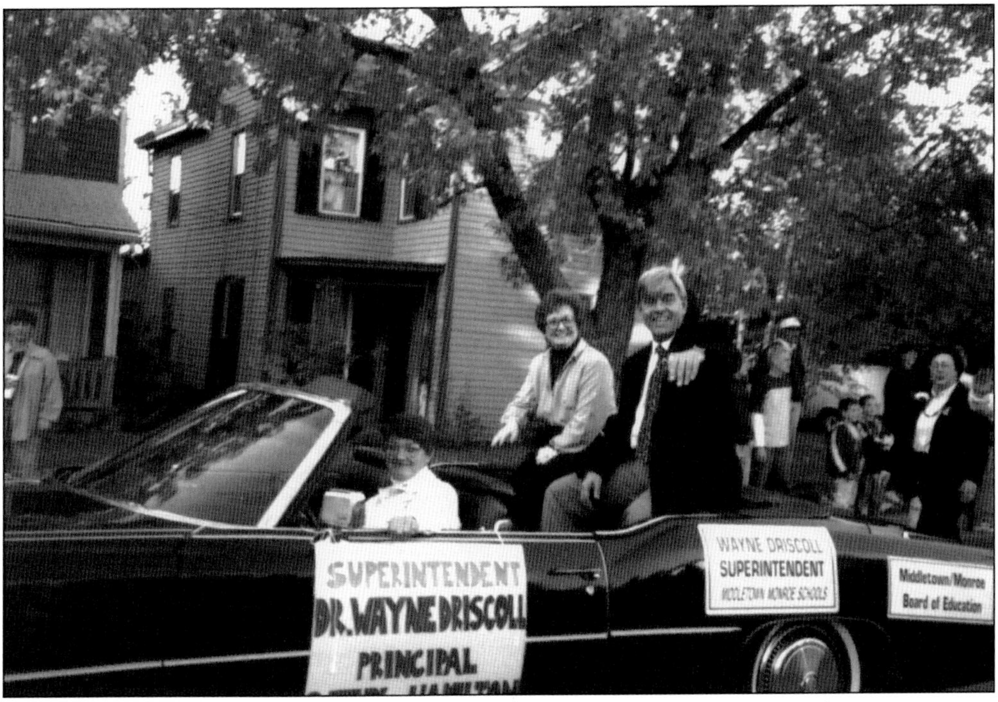

Superintendent of the Middletown City Schools Dr. Wayne Driscoll (right) and Lemon Monroe High School principal Cathy Hamilton (center) ride in the parade. Monroe schools joined Middletown City Schools in 1952 and became independent from the Middletown district in 2000. The newly formed district is called Monroe Local Schools. (Courtesy of Ed and Marge MacDonald.)

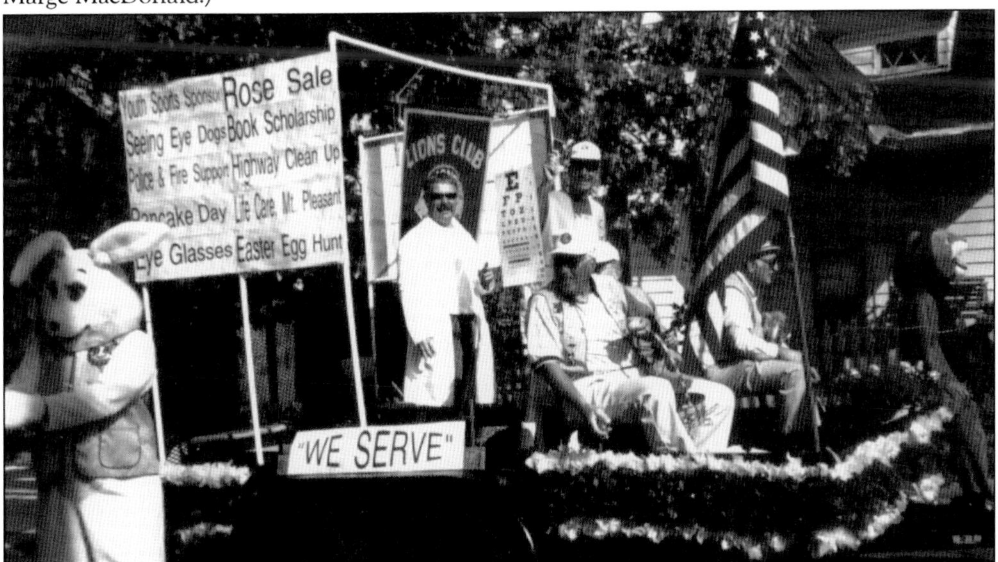

The Lions Club is a regular participant in the parades and continues to serve the community through its support of the fire and police departments, Life Care at Mount Pleasant, scholarships, providing eye glasses and seeing eye dogs, the highway clean up, the Easter egg hunt, and the rose sale and pancake breakfast. (Courtesy of Ed and Marge MacDonald.)

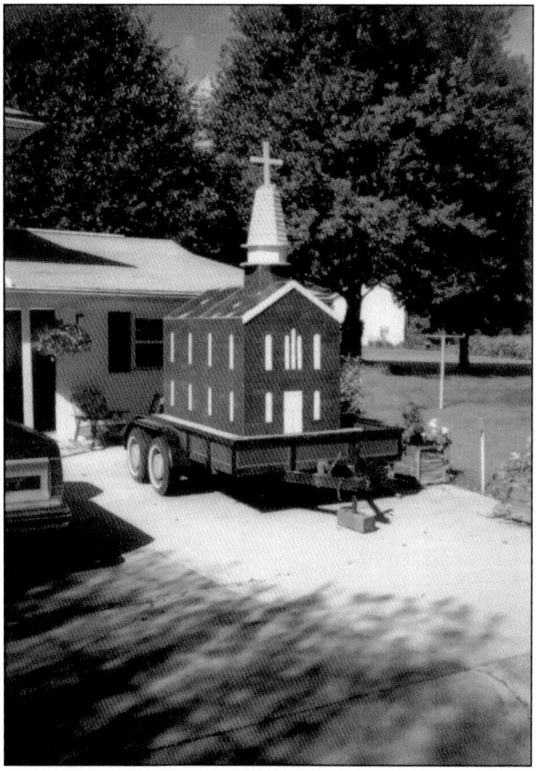

This float appeared in a 1998 parade and was constructed by Ed MacDonald. The replica of the old Methodist church commemorated the beginning of the congregation's 175th year in Monroe, from 1823 to 1998. (Courtesy of Ed and Marge MacDonald.)

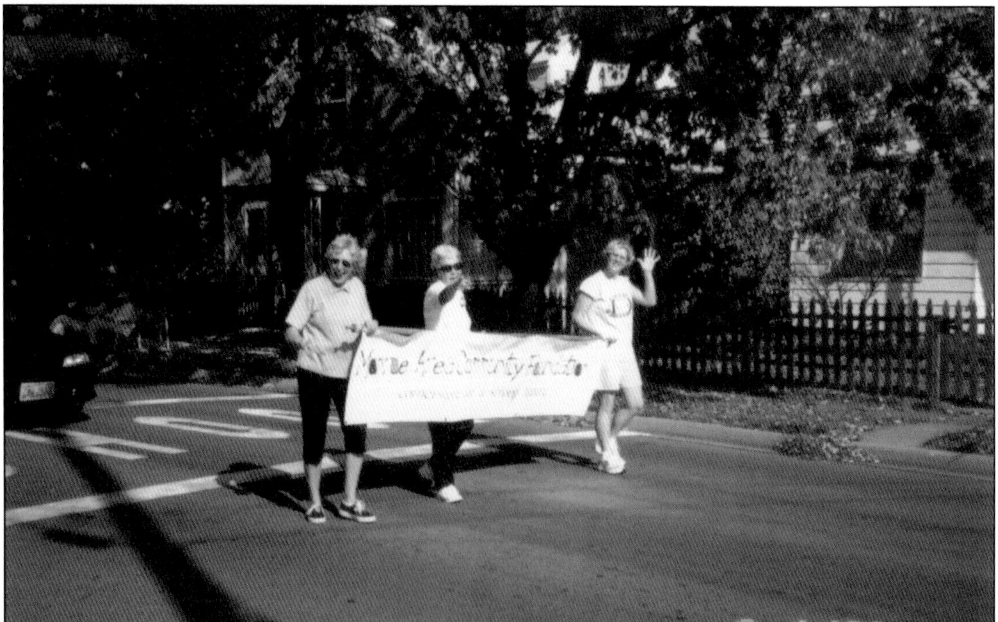

The Monroe Community Foundation participates in a parade. It was founded during the late 1990s by Gloria Miltenberger in honor of her late husband and former city council member Richard Miltenberger. Gloria served as executive director for the first 10 years. Ron Tubbs is currently serving as executive director. (Courtesy of Ed and Marge MacDonald.)

Kim Neu shows her Monroe Hornets spirit by carrying a banner in a parade. (Courtesy of Ed and Marge MacDonald.)

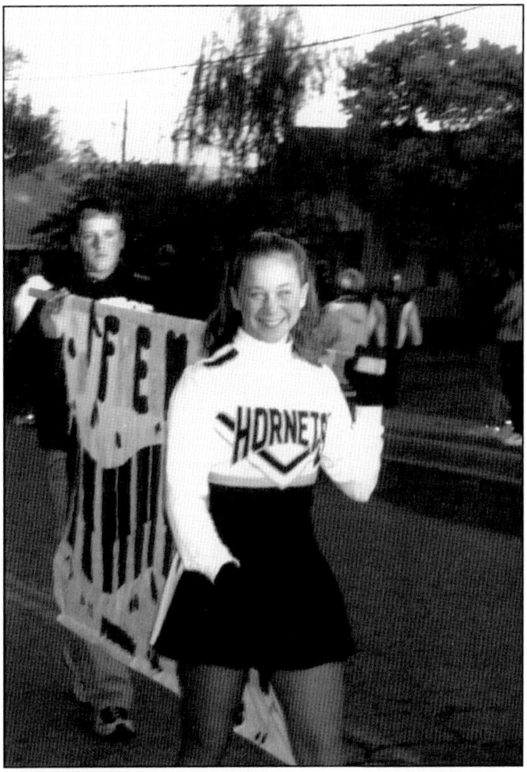

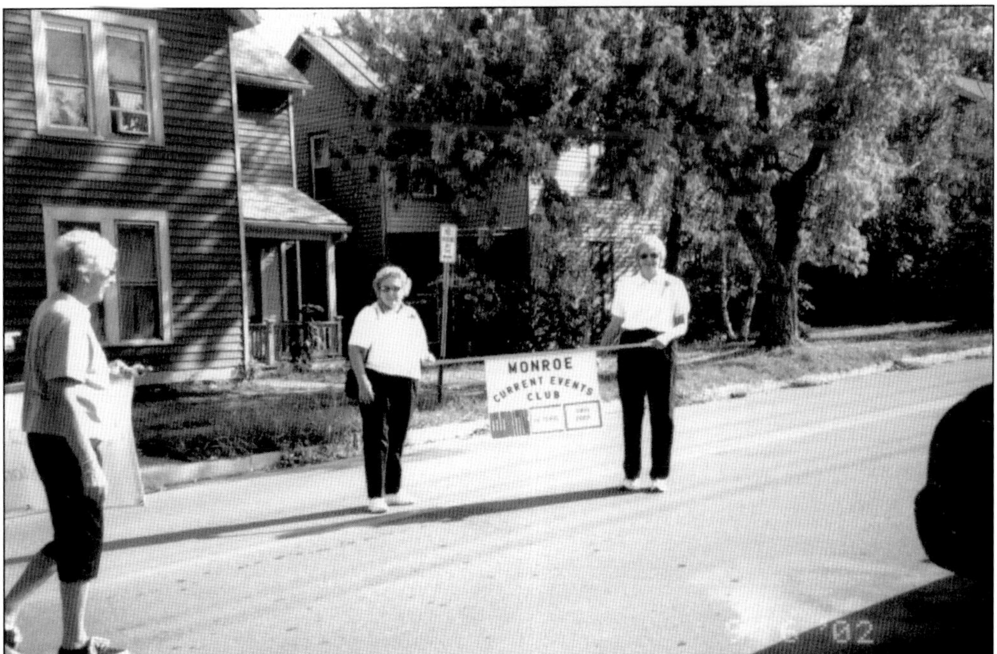

The Monroe Current Events Club always participates in the parades. Organized in 1903, its objective is to study current events of the day and promote intellectual and social culture of its members. It is the oldest civic organization in Monroe. (Courtesy of Ed and Marge MacDonald.)

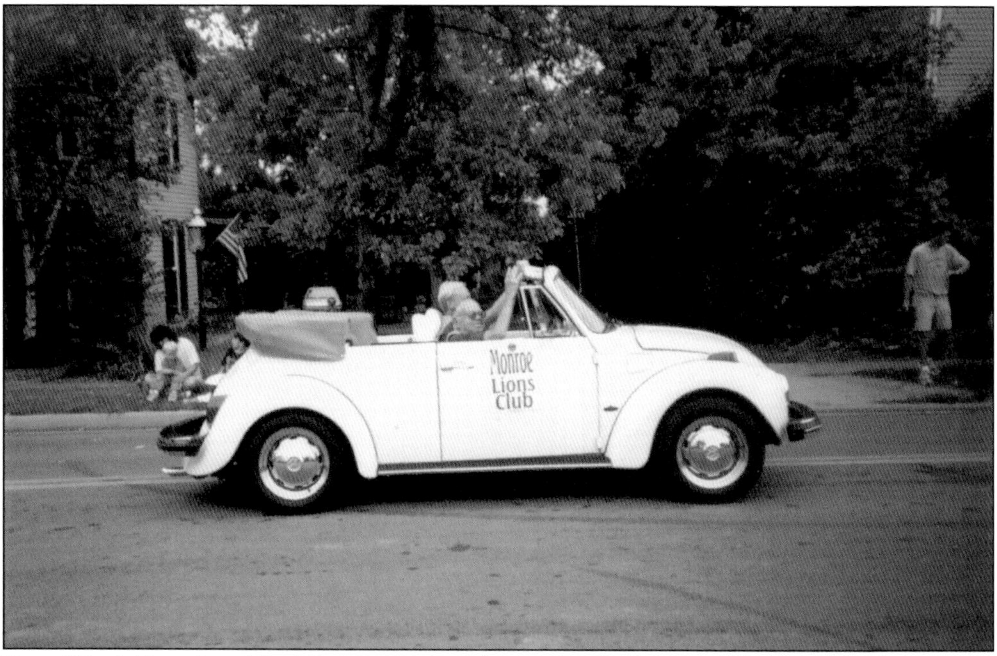

Doug Ward (driver) and Paul Buker promote the Lions Club in a Monroe parade. Buker joined the club during the 1950s and is its oldest member. He married Elizabeth Macready, daughter of Dr. Charles Macready, and Ward married Paul's daughter Alice Buker. (Courtesy of Ed and Marge MacDonald.)

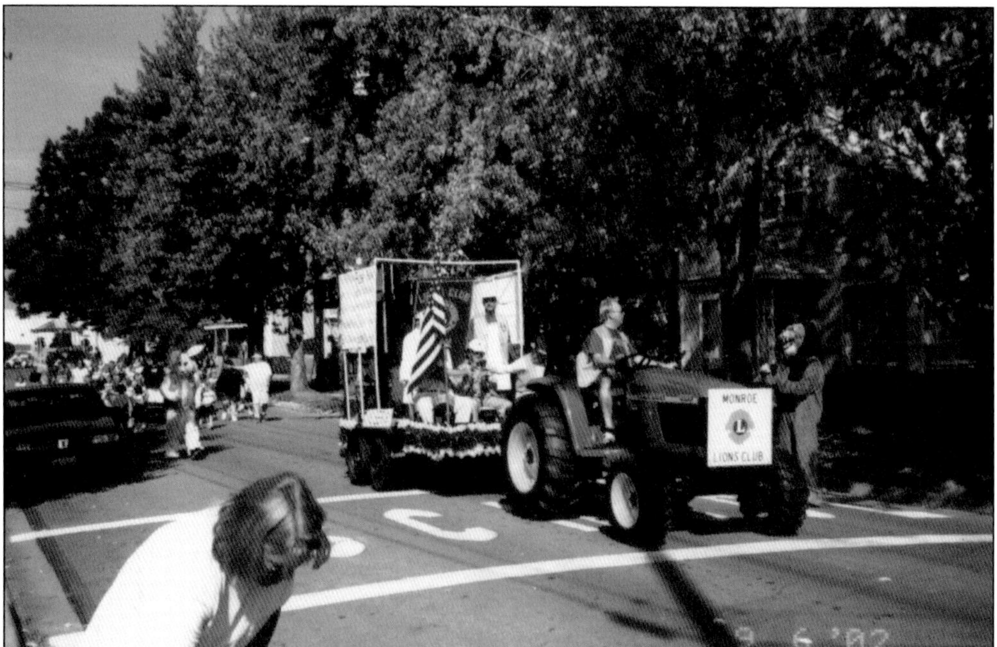

Doug Ward pulls the Lions float with his John Deere tractor and converses with Larry MacCartt, who is in a lion costume. Joe Beatty walks behind the float as the Easter Bunny. The Lions participate annually in the Fourth of July parade. (Courtesy of Ed and Marge MacDonald.)

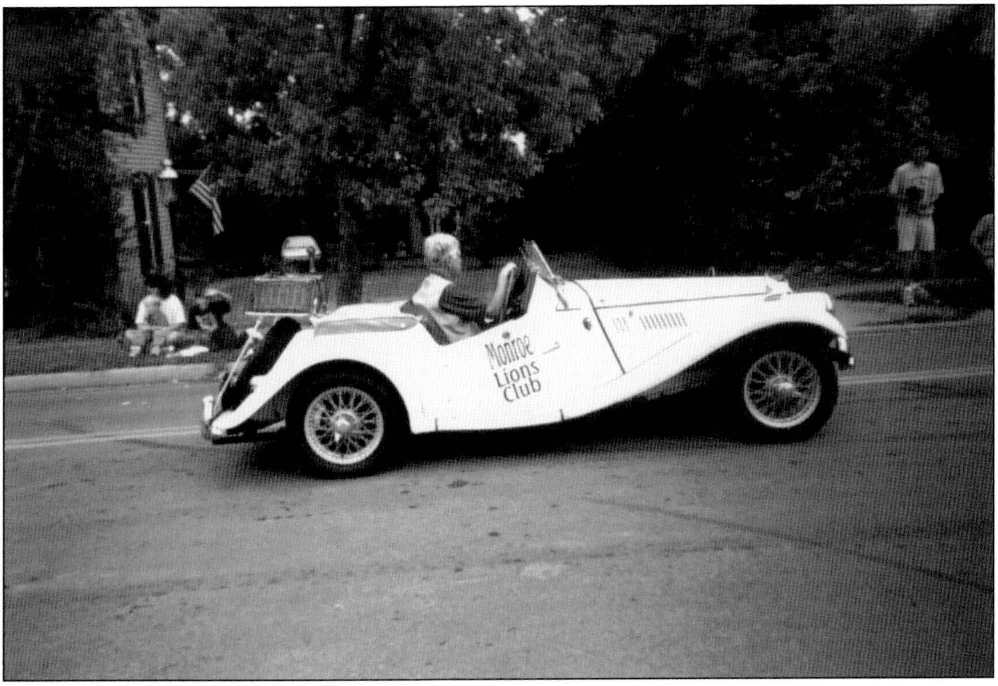

Larry McCartt is driving his MGTF in a Monroe parade for the Lions Club. (Courtesy of Ed and Marge MacDonald.)

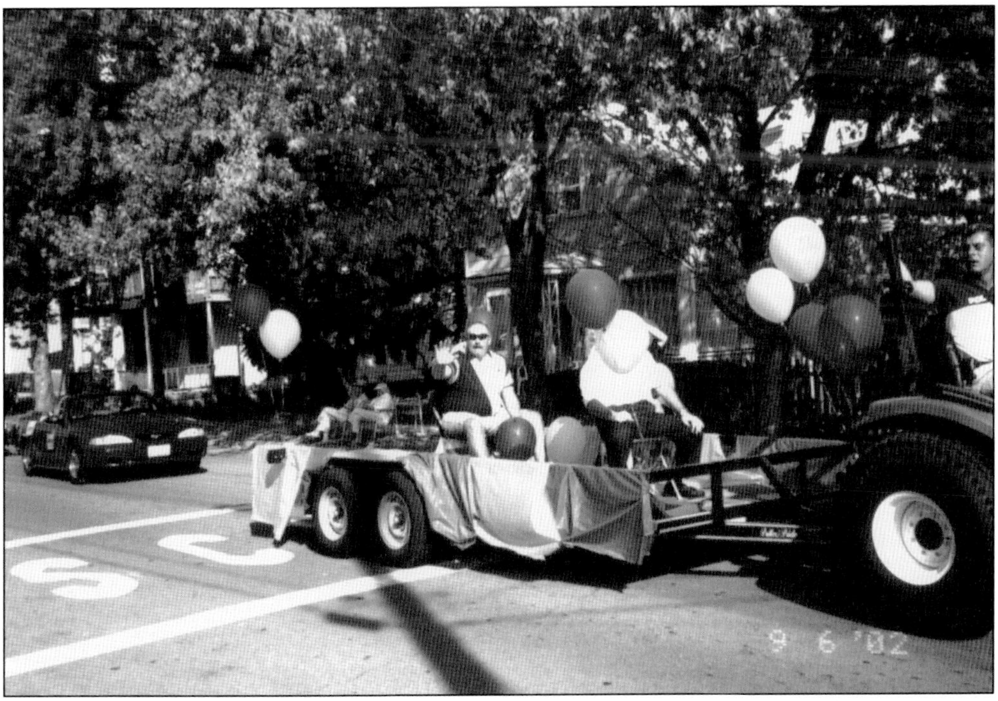

Decorating floats and riding in the parade has always been a fun way to greet the community. This float is decorated in the Monroe school colors of blue and gold. (Courtesy of Ed and Marge MacDonald.)

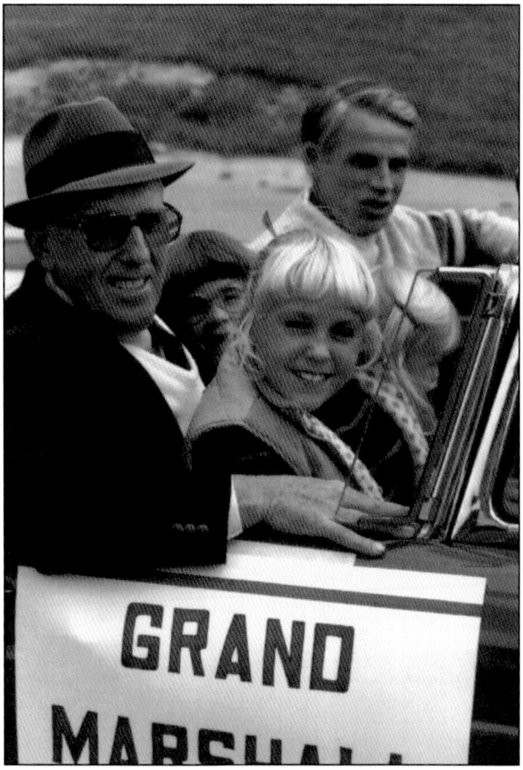

Every parade needs a grand marshal, and Monroe always has one. In 1985, Ed MacDonald (left) was grand marshal. He is seated with his two granddaughters, Kelly Williams-Gomia (right) and Judy Williams (center). (Courtesy of Ed and Marge MacDonald.)

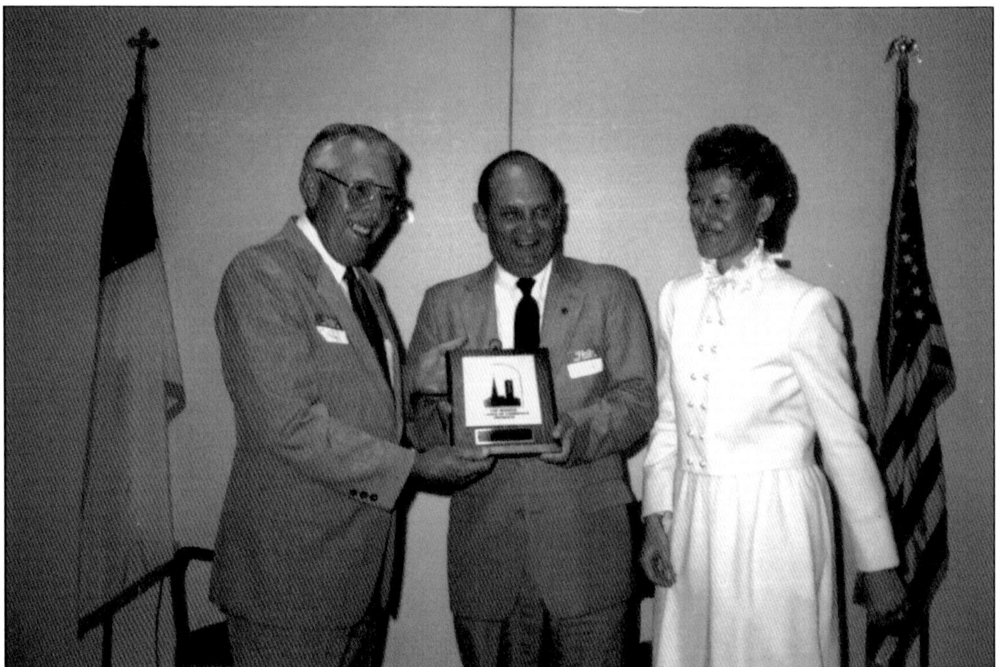

Gale Beatty (center) and Dr. Katherine Bednarczuk Youtsler (right) are presenting the 1983–1984 Business Man of the Year Award to Ed MacDonald (left). (Courtesy of Ed and Marge MacDonald.)

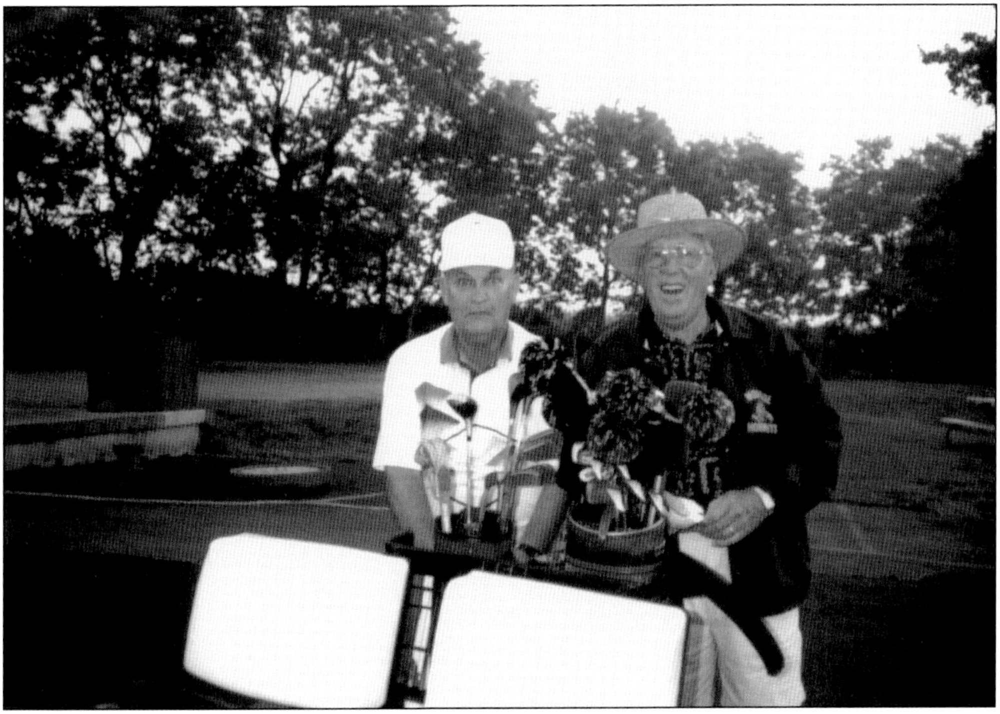

These two businessmen, Gale Beatty (left) and Ed MacDonald (right), shared many rounds of golf together. (Courtesy of Ed and Marge MacDonald.)

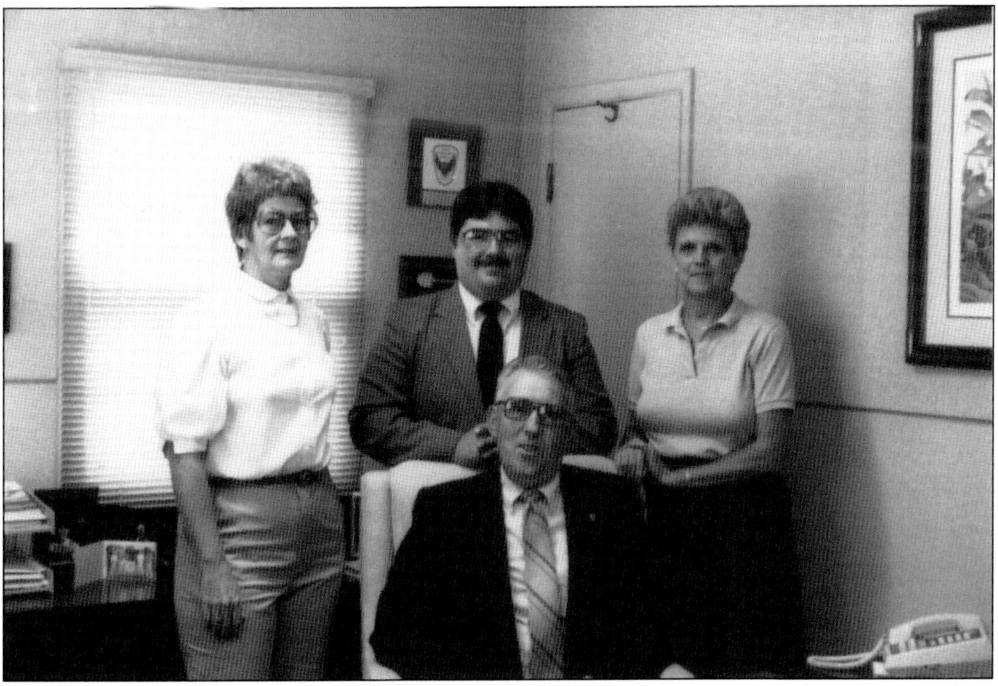

Ed MacDonald (front) and John MacDonald (center) posed with their employees Sharon Collier (left) and Joyce Tannreuther (right) for this photograph that was taken at MacDonald Insurance during the 1980s. (Courtesy of Ed and Marge MacDonald.)

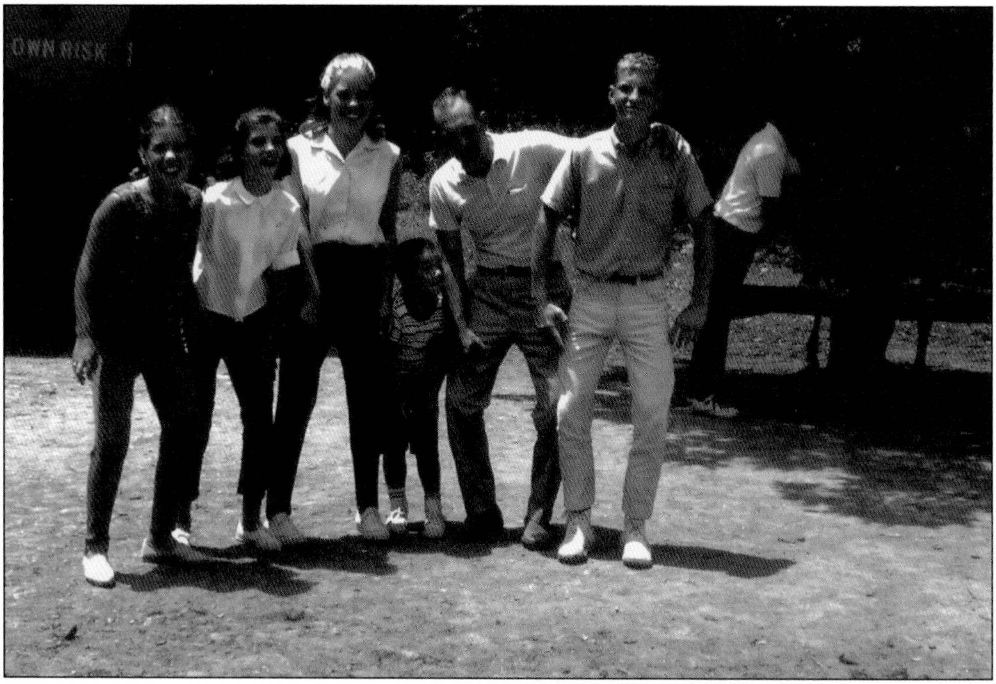

Many Monroe families enjoyed spending leisure time together in the early 1960s. The Beatty and MacDonald families had great fun on this camping trip. From left to right are Cheryl MacDonald, Pam Beatty, Karen MacDonald, John MacDonald, Gale Beatty, and Joe Beatty. (Courtesy of Ed and Marge MacDonald.)

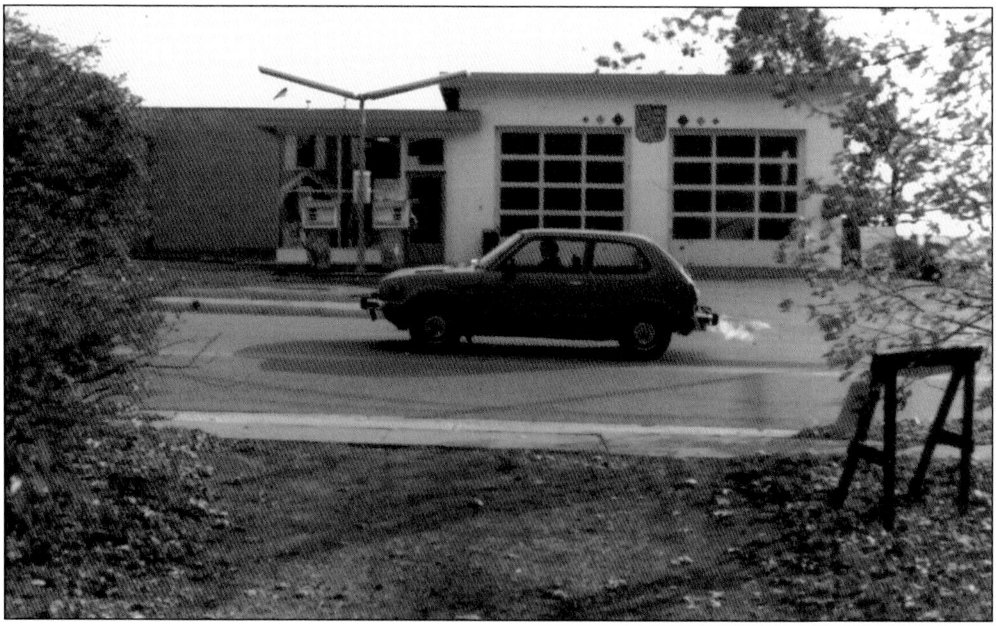

Many of the Monroe baby boomers left for college and found a life outside of the small village of Monroe. Sabrina McCartt, pictured here in her automobile, remained in St. Louis after graduation and later relocated to New York City. Behind her is the old Sinclair Station, which later became Auto Techniques and is currently Monroe Auto Repair. (Courtesy of Larry McCartt.)

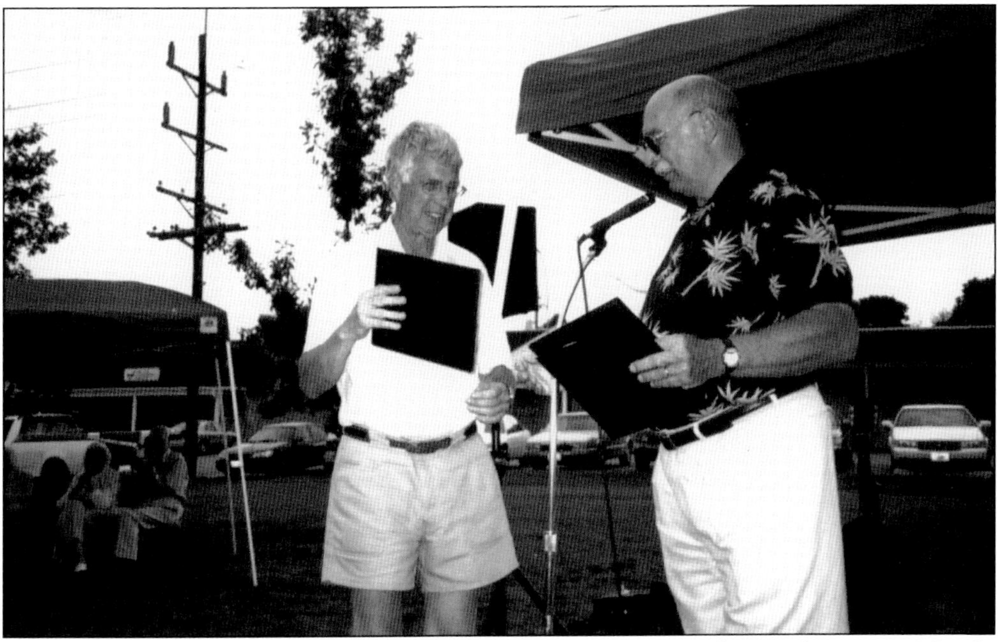

Monroe mayor Elbert Tannreuther (right) presents Larry McCartt with a proclamation of thanks for his design, which was adopted as the Monroe city seal in 2001. (Courtesy of Larry McCartt.)

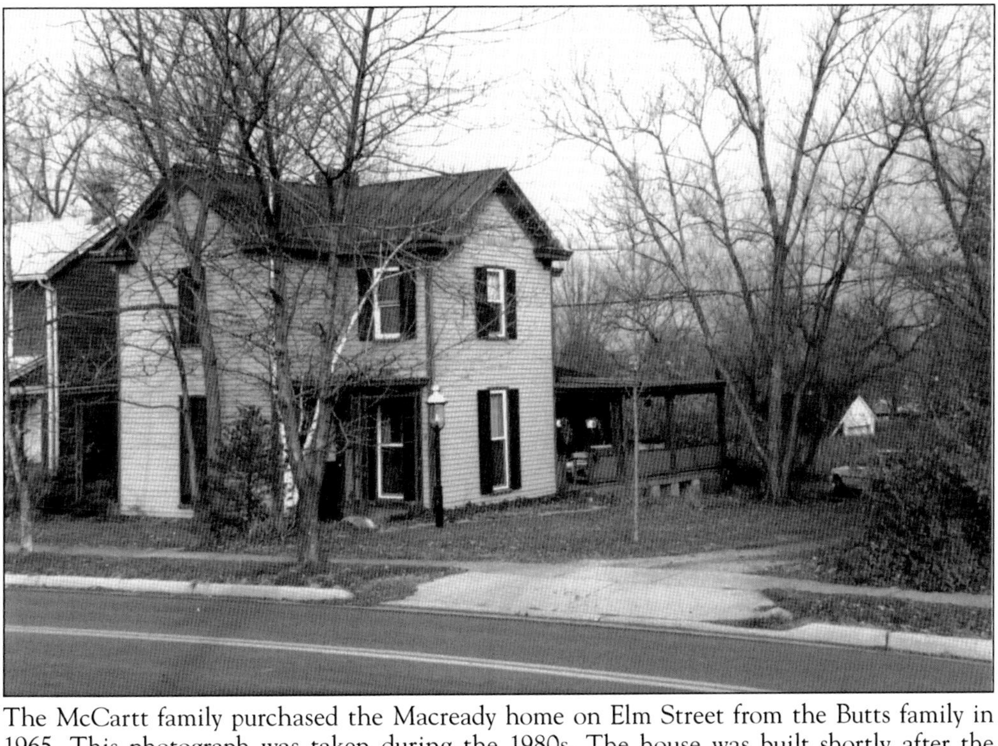

The McCartt family purchased the Macready home on Elm Street from the Butts family in 1965. This photograph was taken during the 1980s. The house was built shortly after the Civil War and served as both the office and home for Dr. James and Dr. Charles Macready. The Macready family lived in the house until the 1950s when the Butts family purchased it. (Courtesy of Larry McCartt.)

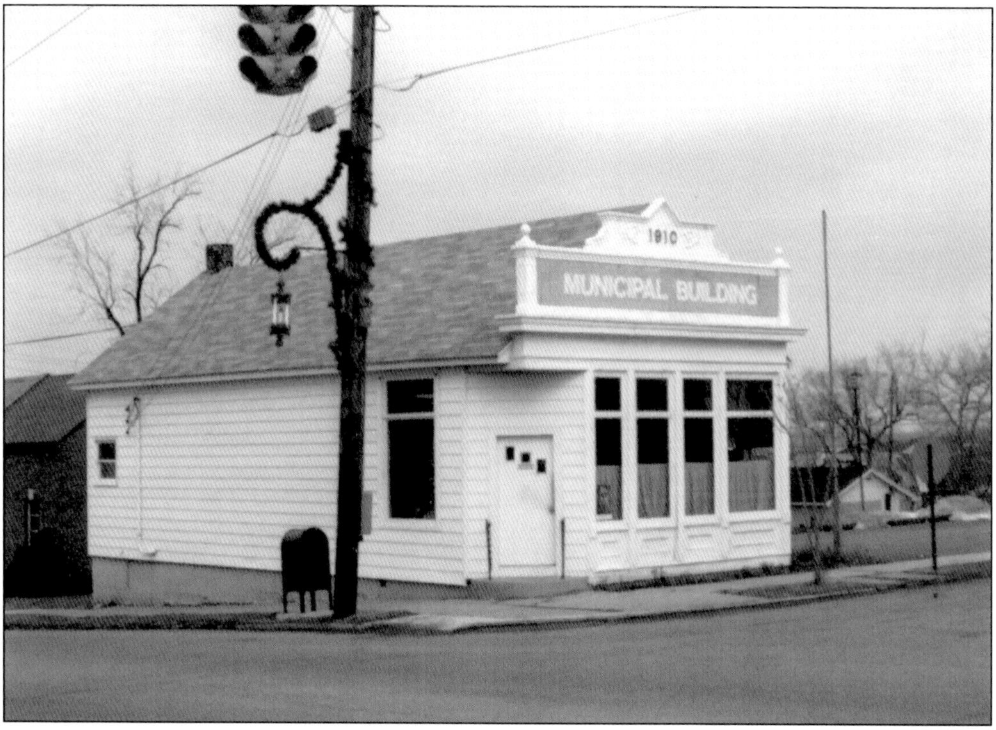

The 1910 Warner corner store eventually became the municipal building for the Village of Monroe. (Courtesy of Larry McCartt.)

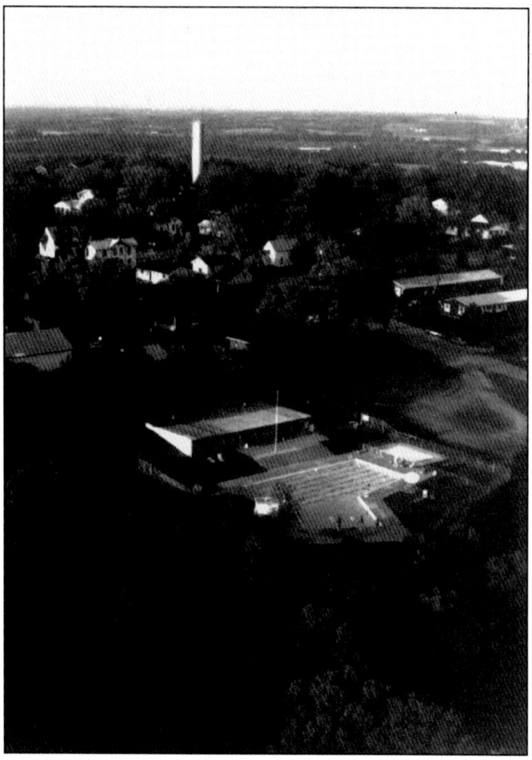

This aerial view of the water tower and swim club was taken during an evening balloon ride over the village of Monroe in the 1980s. (Courtesy of Larry McCartt.)

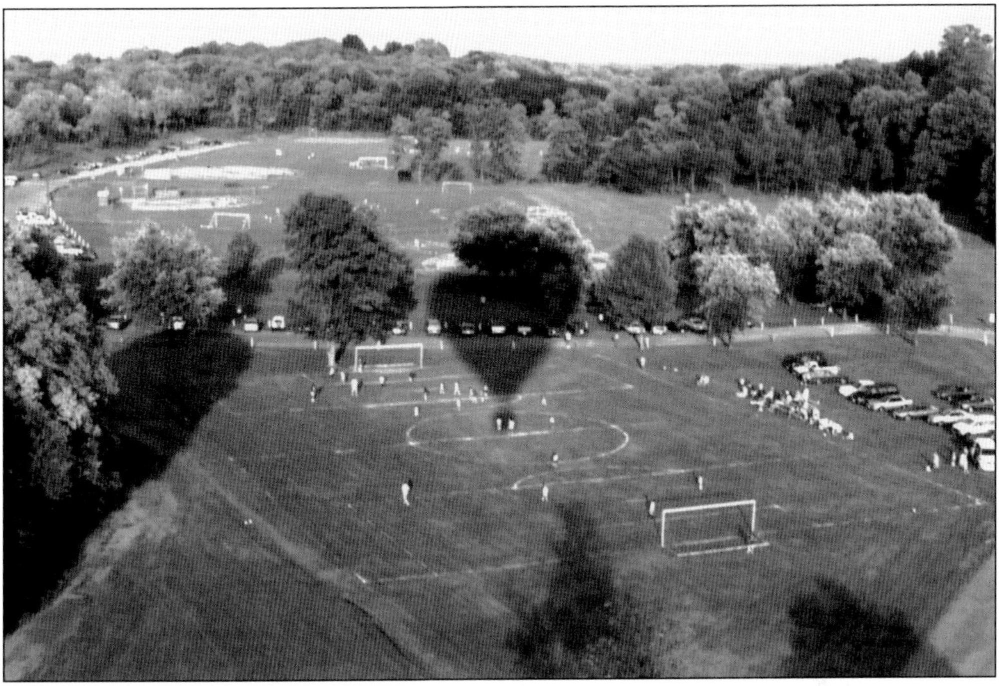

This is an aerial view of the Monroe Community Park, which was founded in 1958 and was operated by the Lions Club for many years. (Courtesy of Larry McCartt.)

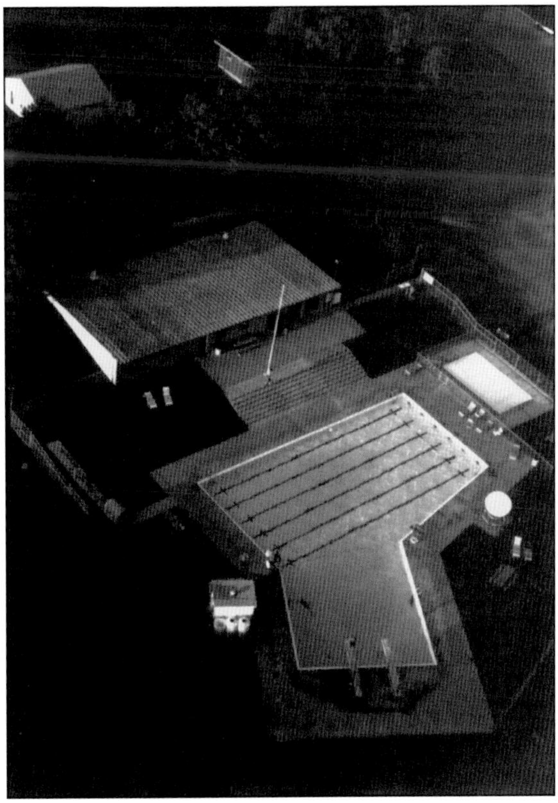

This is an aerial view of the Monroe Swim Club, which was started in 1962 to provide swimming facilities for the many families who were living in Monroe at that time. (Courtesy of Larry McCartt.)

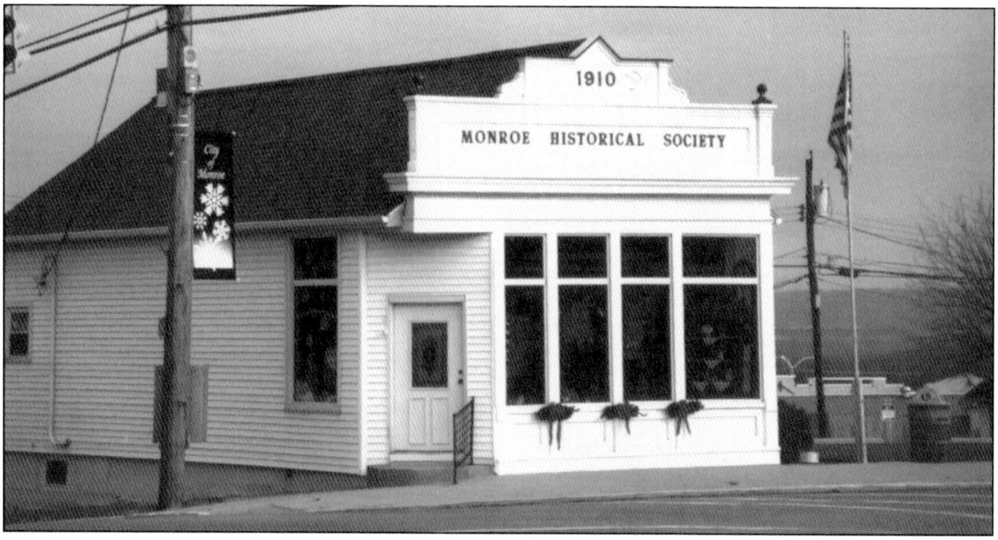

After the 1910 building ceased to be the municipal building, Jim Price provided it to the Monroe Historical Society. The historical society later built a larger building in the lot next to the corner museum. (Courtesy of Larry McCartt.)

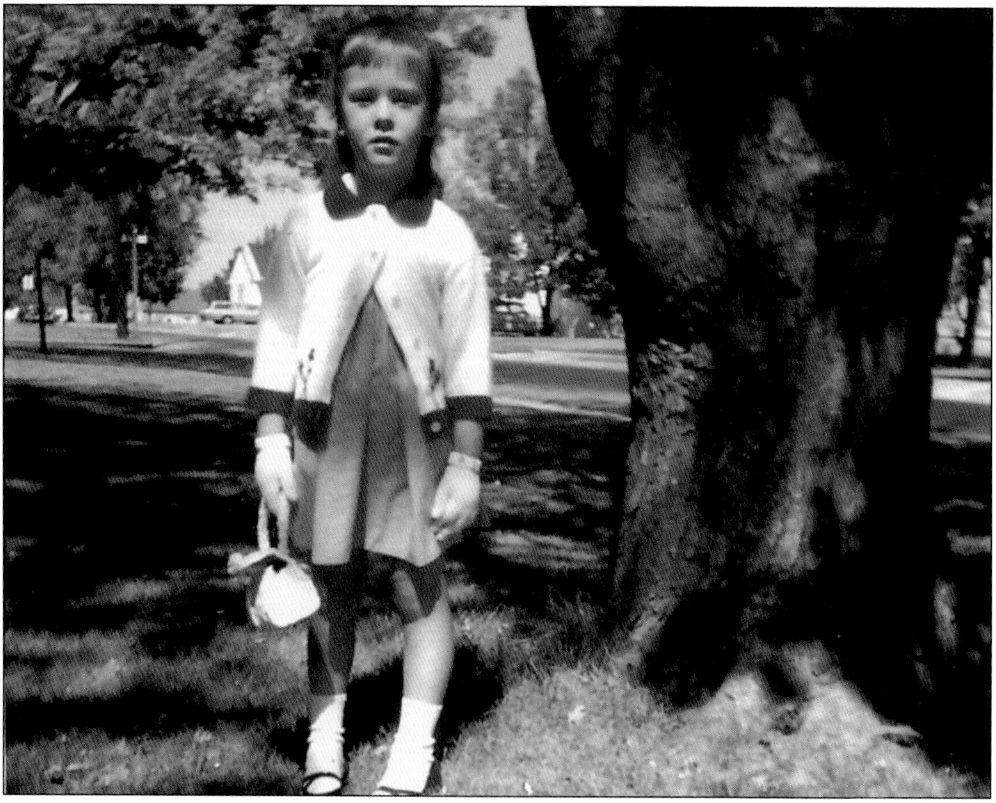

Carmon Patrick is returning from Sunday school at Monroe Presbyterian Church in 1964. This photograph was taken outside of their home at 55 Ohio Avenue. Patrick eventually became a columnist for the *Middletown Journal* and wrote for the Trenton community page. (Courtesy of Joe and Joyce Patrick.)

Three

THE 1969 TORNADO

It was not a typical Saturday in the village of Monroe. It was the Saturday before Mother's Day. The entire town was bustling with activity. Staff at the old folks home were scurrying about, getting ready to receive Sunday visitors and planning alternate activities for the residents and shut-ins. The florist was filling last minute orders for procrastinating husbands, and long checkout lines were found at the local IGA. The Dutch Pantry and Congress Inn were attending to food inventories and making last-minute schedules in anticipation of the busy Sunday lunch. Mount Pleasant Presbyterian Church was conducting a prayer meeting.

Arthur "Grandpa" Apple had picked up his grandson, Mike, and took him out for the day. Kitty Apple ran a beauty parlor in town. The force of the wind blew down the stadium light pole across the street shattering Kitty's windows before blowing through the Macready barn, and leaping through the IGA parking lot on Main Street to devastate the Holly Hill Manor Apartments by Route 63.

Marcia Helton was nine years old when the tornado damaged her family's home. The following is her story:

> I thought we were going to die. As the tornado plowed through our house and tore off the roof, it was almost like an explosion. Dirt rained through the floorboards as the cement block wall between the garage and family room came crashing down. We were in the southwest corner of the basement nearest the garage. My father grabbed us and pulled us back. I thought the entire house was being devoured by this monster.
>
> It was over in a matter of minutes. We ascended the stairs and my parents raced ahead and opened the door. All we could see was sky. My mother started searching and found a coat for me to drape around my chilled body. I wasn't cold. Just scared and numb from the shock. The danger was past, but there was no way we could stay in this house. Carolyn Hall raced to make sure her neighbors were okay. Several devastated families gathered at her house on Mason Avenue and the corner house at Sands to comfort one another and figure out what to do next.

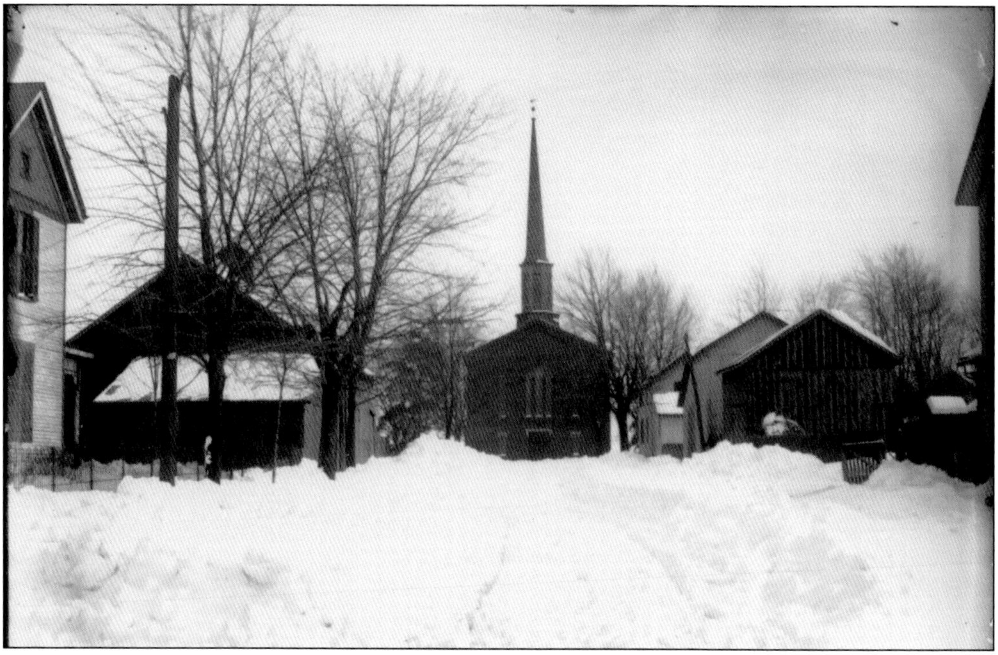

This c. 1918 photograph shows the Methodist church proudly holding its steeple and weathering the storm. The church would lose the steeple 50 years later during the tornado. (Courtesy of the Monroe Historical Society.)

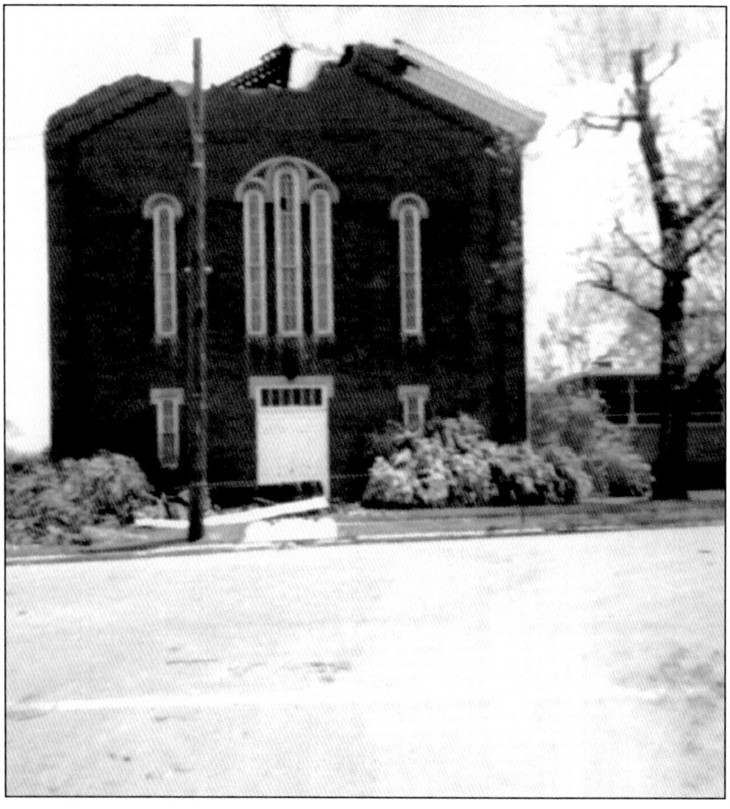

The Methodist church stands, after the tornado, with no steeple. Anna Hale remembers it vividly. From her Britton Lane home she watched the steeple spinning as it shot through the air. The old sanctuary was later razed. (Courtesy of Anna Hale.)

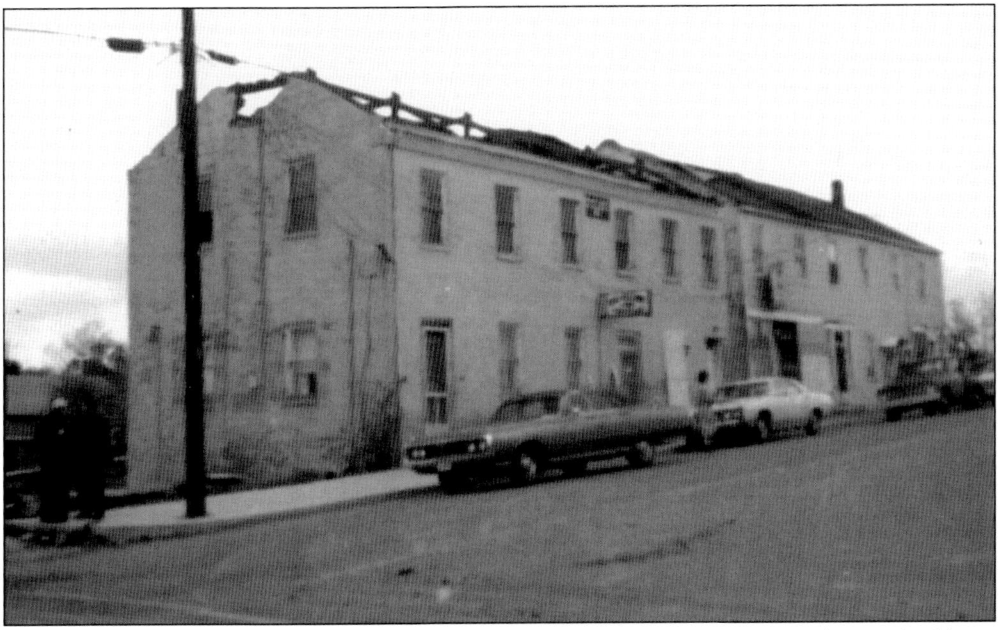

The IOOF hall on Main Street lost its roof and suffered substantial damage. The two buildings pictured here were later razed. The IOOF rebuilt its lodge on the current Britton Lane site. (Courtesy of Anna Hale.)

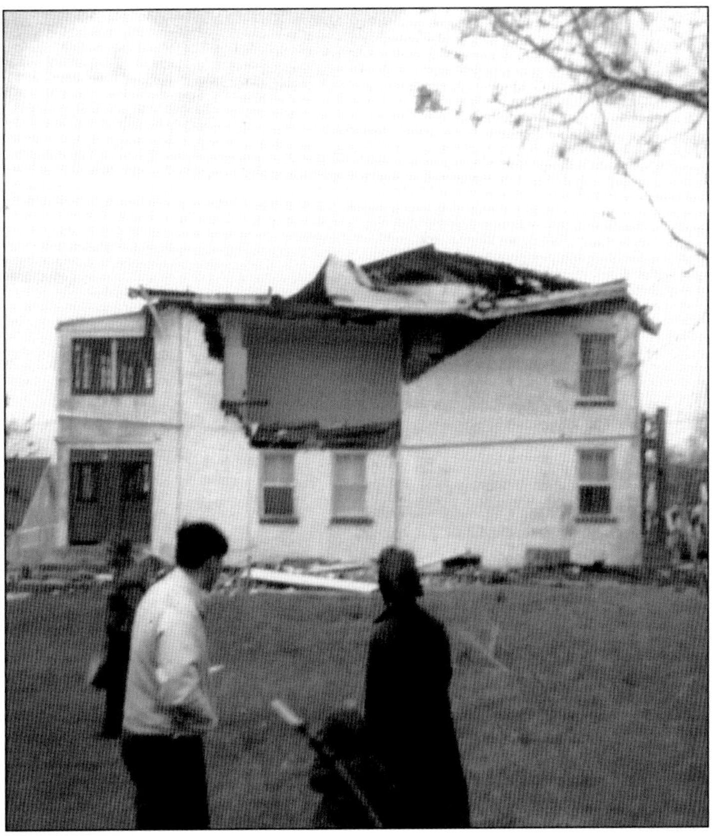

From left to right, Kelly, Autumn, and Anna Hale view the heavily damaged Red Onion building. (Courtesy of Anna Hale.)

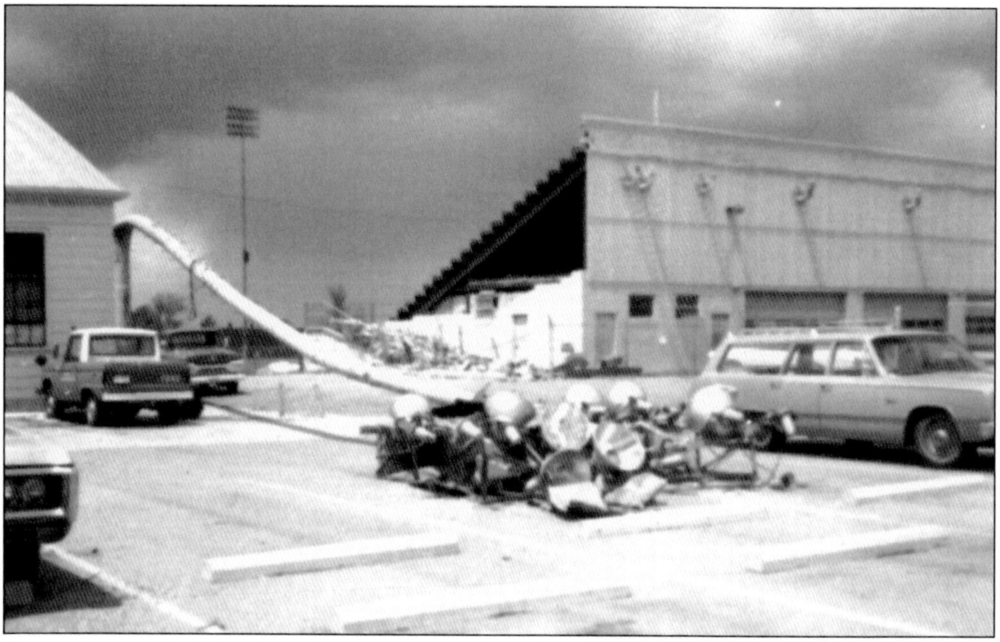

This photograph of the downed stadium light shows how powerful and dangerous the storm was. (Courtesy of Anna Hale.)

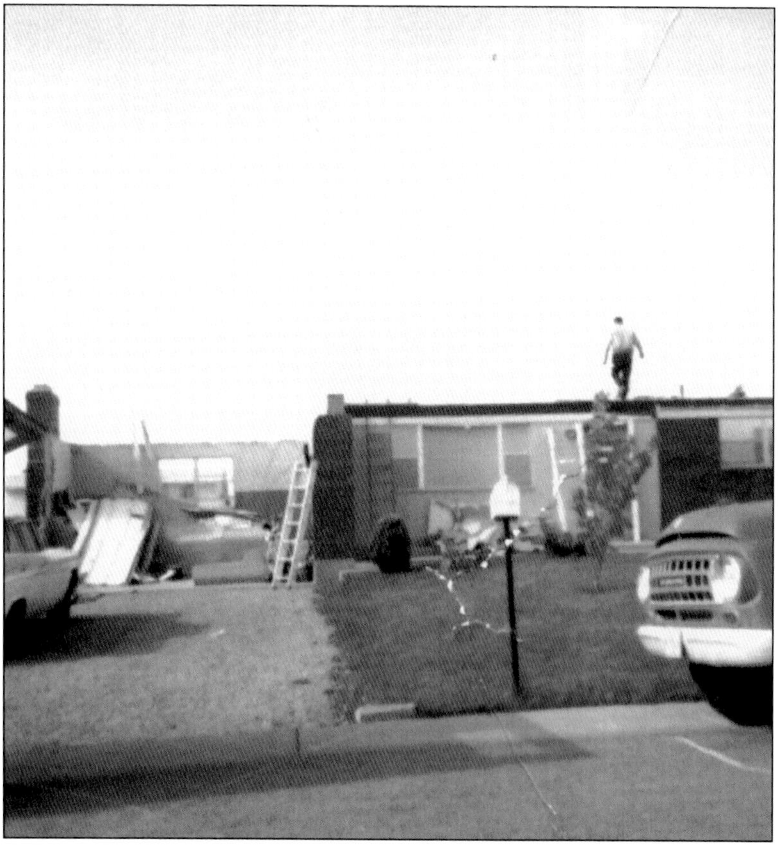

The Helton house at 320 Mason Avenue suffered heavy damage. The tornado roared through the house like a freight train, ripping off the roof in the process. Insulation from the attic covered everything. Even though repairs began immediately, as shown in this photograph, it was not until the end of summer that the family was able to move back in. (Courtesy of Anna Hale.)

The Estill King home, next to the Helton house on Mason Avenue, was also damaged. The King family was not home at the time of the tornado. (Courtesy of Anna Hale.)

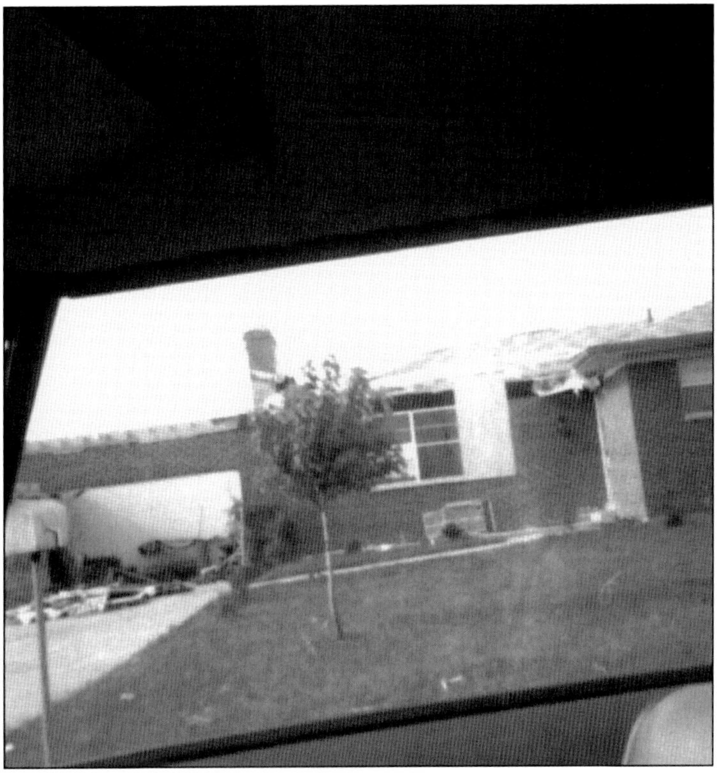

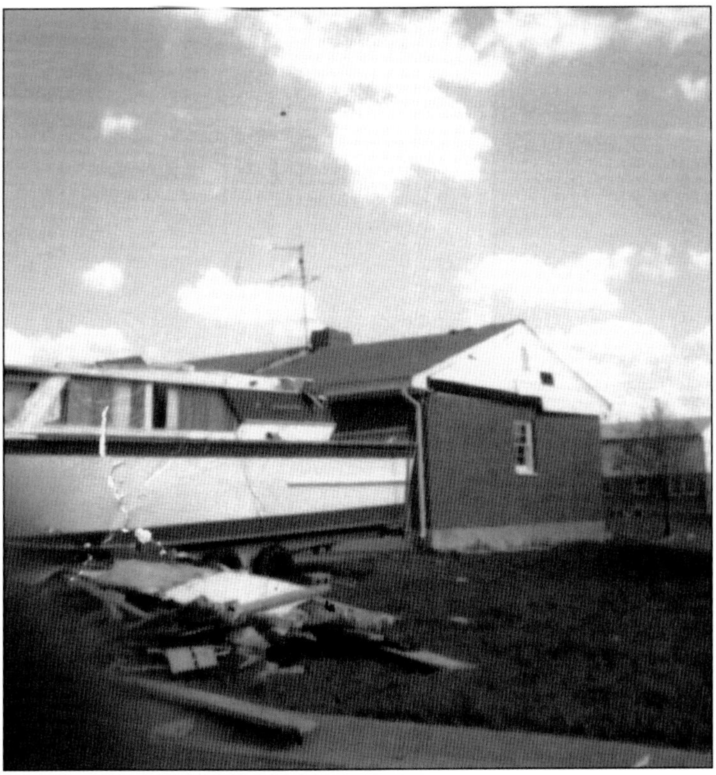

The Wehr house was located on Sunset Court and sat behind the Helton house. It suffered significant damage. (Courtesy of Anna Hale.)

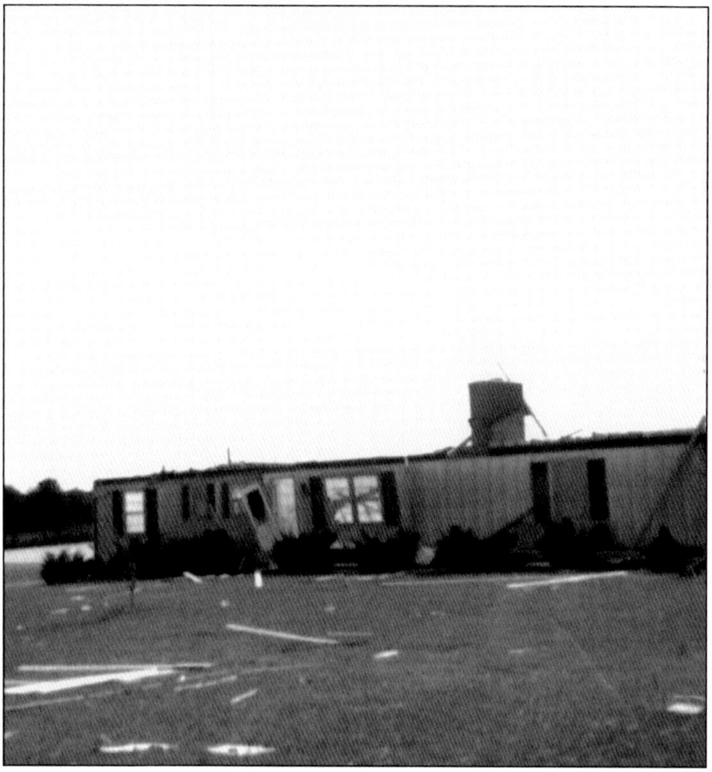

Many homes in the Highview Subdivision, which was located behind the Monroe Elementary School, suffered damage. (Courtesy of Anna Hale.)

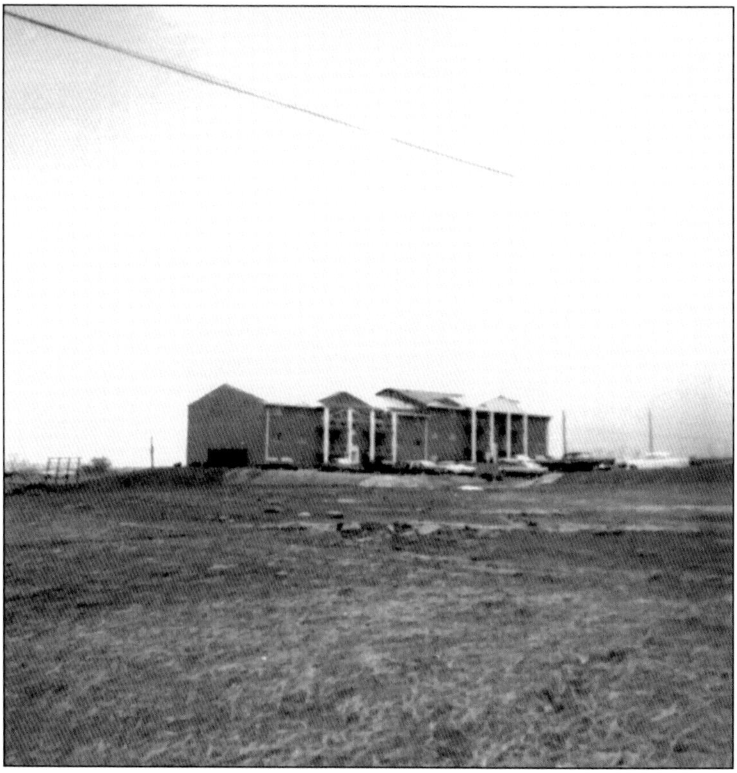

The Holly Hill Manor Apartments near Route 63 lost part of the roof. (Courtesy of Anna Hale.)

This view of the rear of Holly Hill Manor Apartments shows dangling gutters and portions of a roof lie on the ground. (Courtesy of Anna Hale.)

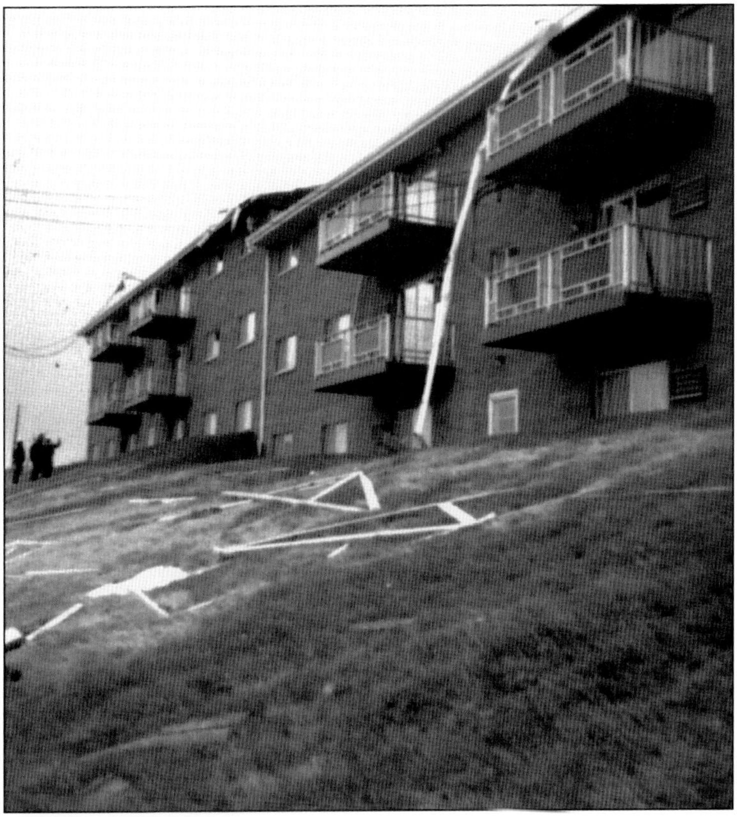

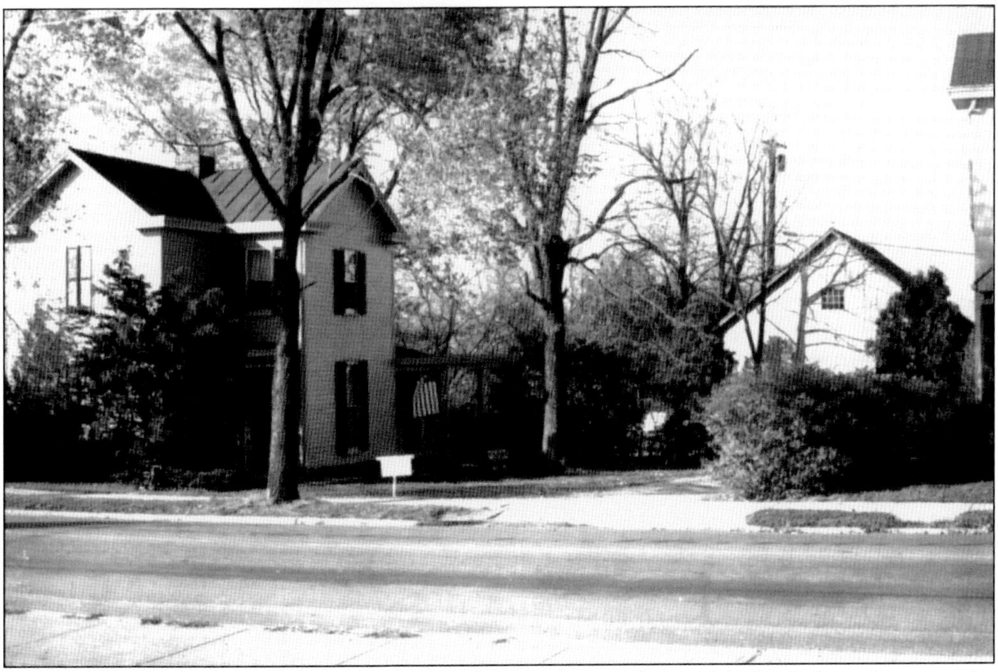

The Macready house and barn are pictured here during the mid-1960s before the tornado. (Courtesy of Larry McCartt.)

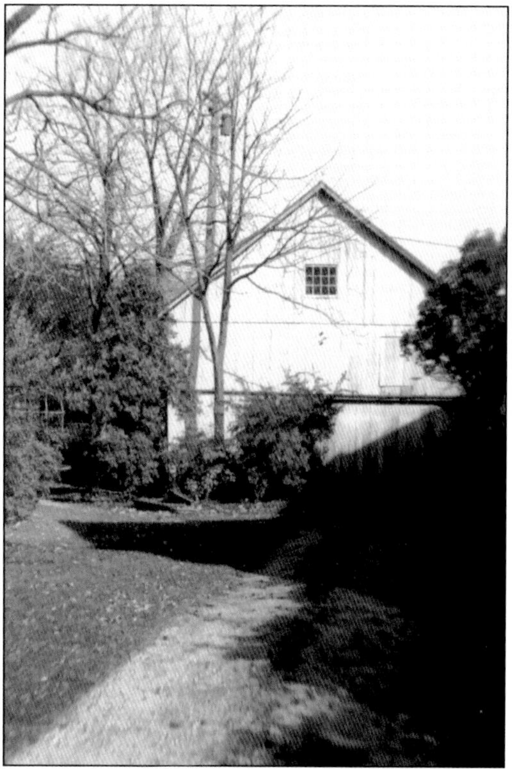

The barn at the Macready house, which was located at 16 West Elm Street, suffered extensive damage from the tornado and had to be razed. This photograph was taken in 1966. (Courtesy of Larry McCartt.)

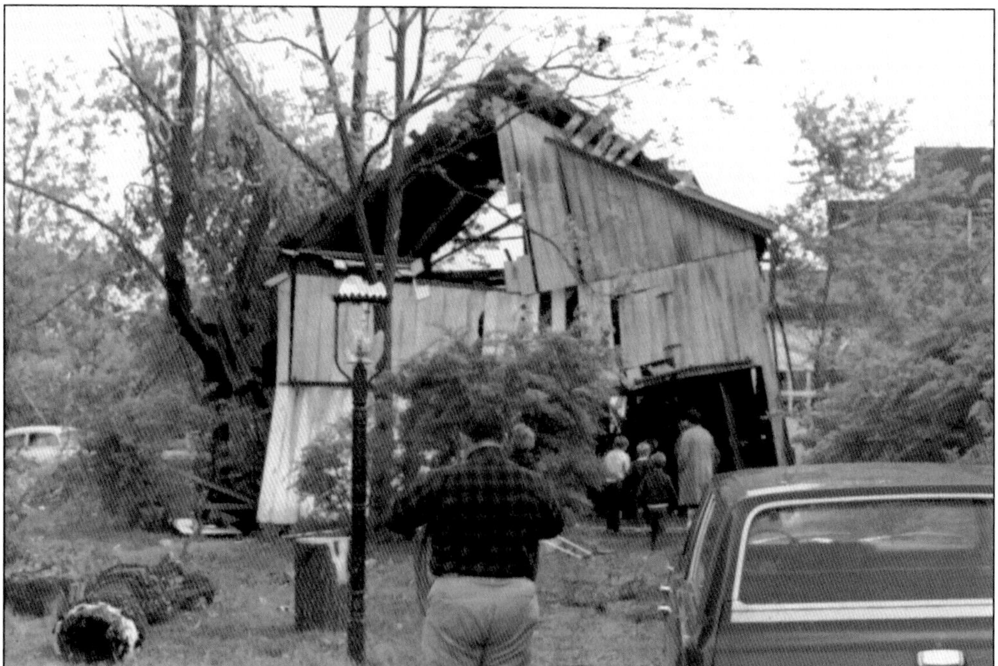

The Monroe community came together after the storm to help their neighbors who were in need. From left to right, Dick Pierce, Sabrina McCartt, Peter McCartt, Andrew McCartt, Jamie Pierce, and Camilla McCartt survey damage to the old Macready barn. (Courtesy of Larry McCartt.)

The Macready barn was in a state of disrepair after the tornado. (Courtesy of Larry McCartt.)

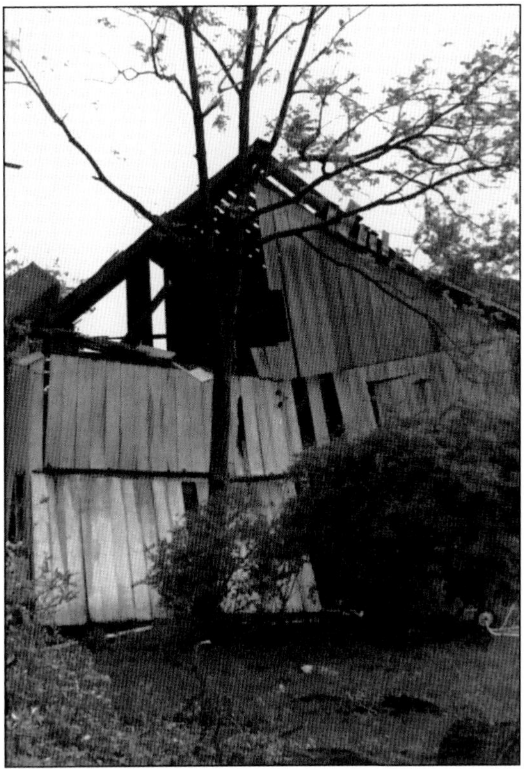

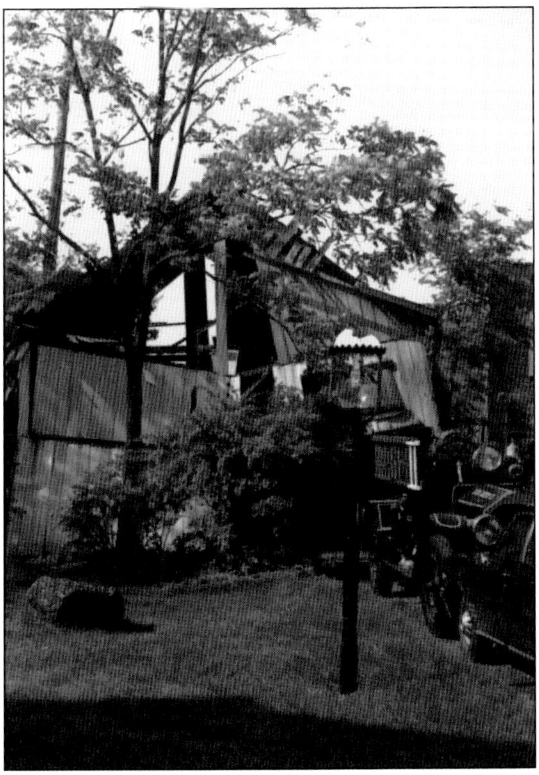

The front of the Macready barn was severely damaged from the high winds. The Apple family house a few doors from the McCartt home on Elm Street also suffered significant damage. (Courtesy of Larry McCartt.)

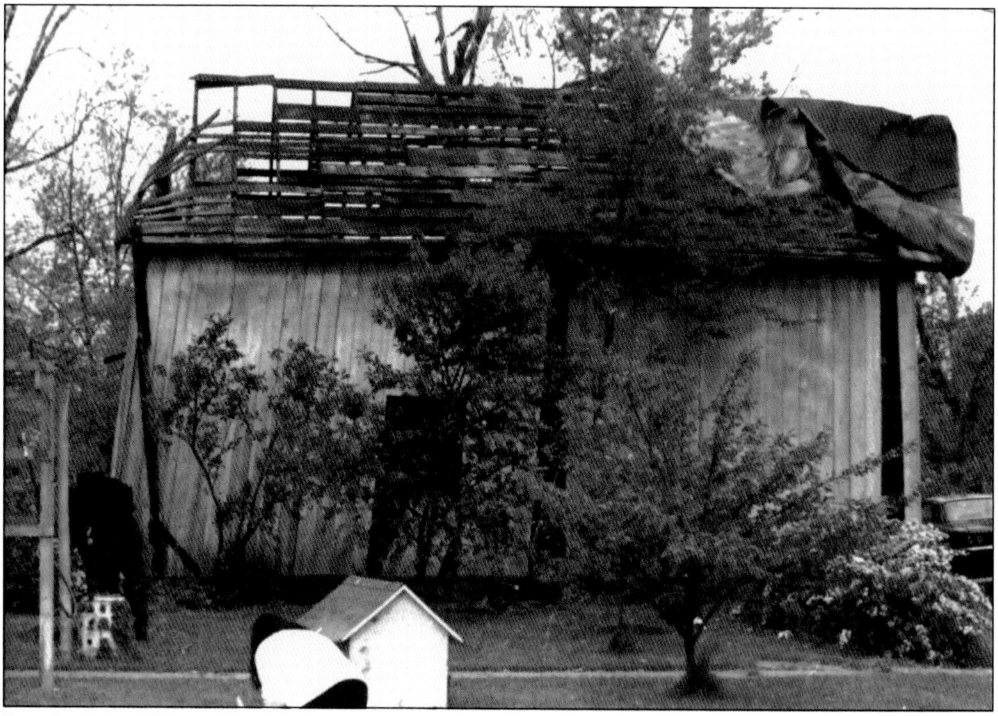

Residents on Elm Street clear debris from the storm. (Courtesy of Larry McCartt.)

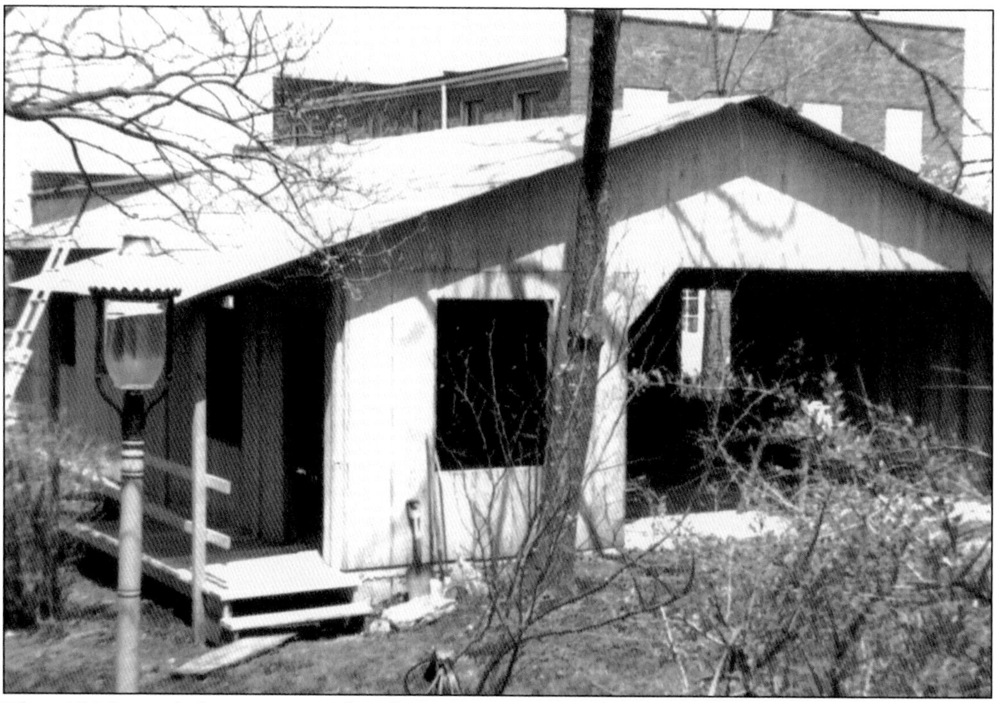

The old Macready barn was razed and new construction for a garage started after the tornado. (Courtesy of Larry McCartt.)

Four

Contemporary History

The village of Monroe became a city in 1995 when the population became at least 5,000. Monroe schools became independent of the Middletown City School District in 2000, and the Monroe Local Schools was formed. According to the 2000 census, there were 7,133 people living in Monroe. The racial makeup was 97.15 percent white; 1.42 percent African American; .10 percent Native American; .34 percent Asian; .77 percent multiracial; and .22 percent other races. Hispanic of any race was .64 percent. Monroe continues to grow and the population is currently around 11,000. In 2008, the mayor of Monroe was Robert Routson and vice mayor was Steve Tannreuther. Council members were Anna Hale, Lora Stillman, Suzi Rubin, Bob Kelley, and Tracy Shell.

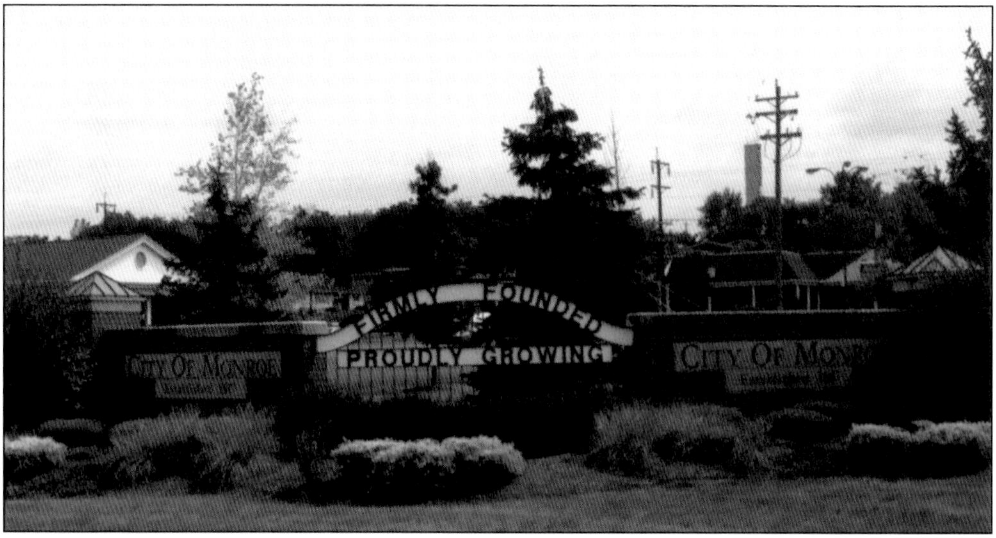

The entrance to the city of Monroe in 2008 at State Route 63 and North Main Street greets newcomers. A committee from the Monroe Historical Society was appointed to come up with a slogan and Pauline Schmidt came up with "Firmly Founded, Proudly Growing," which was approved by the committee and later adopted by the city. (Courtesy of Larry and Marcia McCartt.)

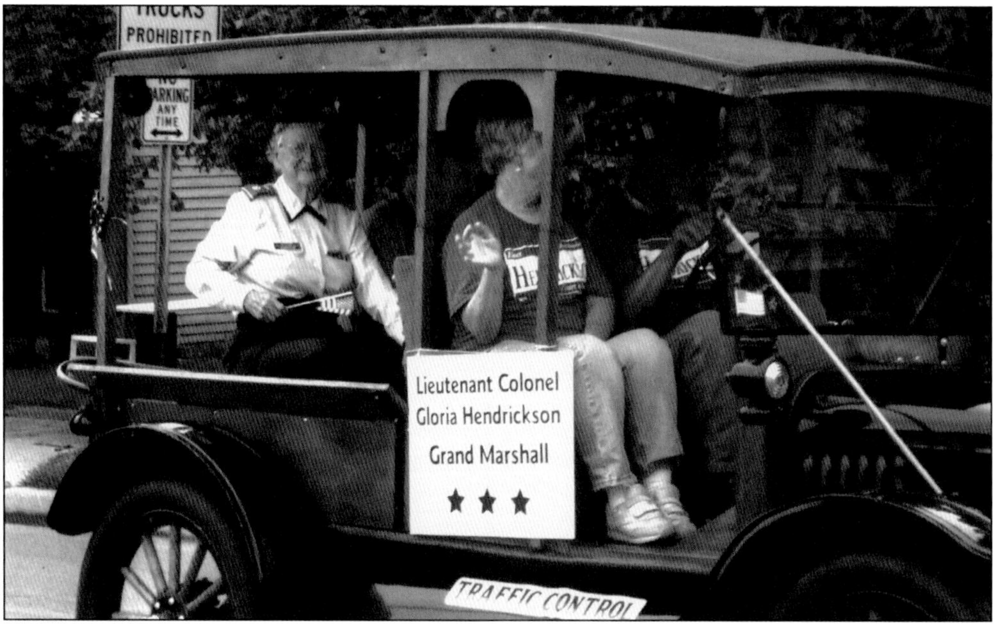

Lt. Col. Gloria Hendrickson was the grand marshal in this July 2008 parade. She joined the Civil Air Patrol (CAP) in 1987. CAP was formed prior to World War II because private pilots feared they would be unable to fly. They patrolled factories and coastlines, sinking a few German submarines. They also delivered mail and medicines from 1938 to 1941. CAP was organized by Gil R. Wilson, backed by Gen. H. Arnold. Pres. Harry S. Truman in 1948 signed a bill to make CAP a civilian auxiliary of the U.S. Air Force. It consists of a cadet program and senior program. Subjects learned aerospace education, search and rescue, and natural disaster and relief operations. (Courtesy of the City of Monroe.)

Bob Hendrickson (left) followed in the footsteps of his father Bill (right) and became a Butler County judge. (Courtesy of Gloria Hendrickson.)

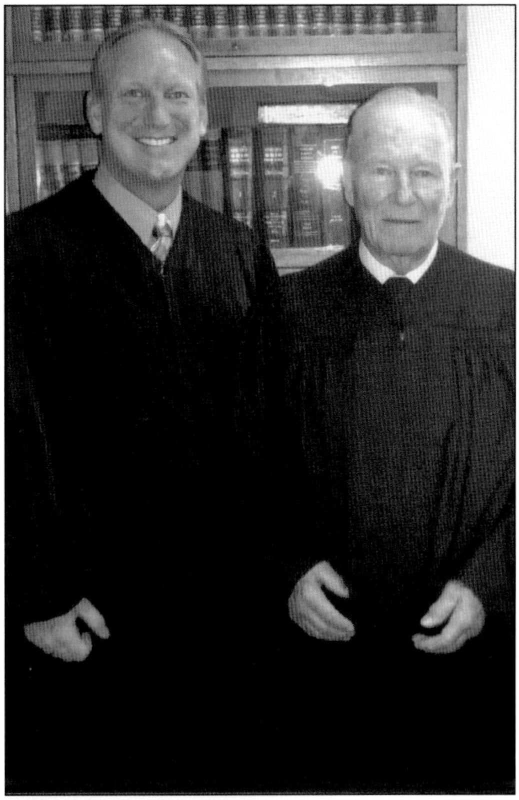

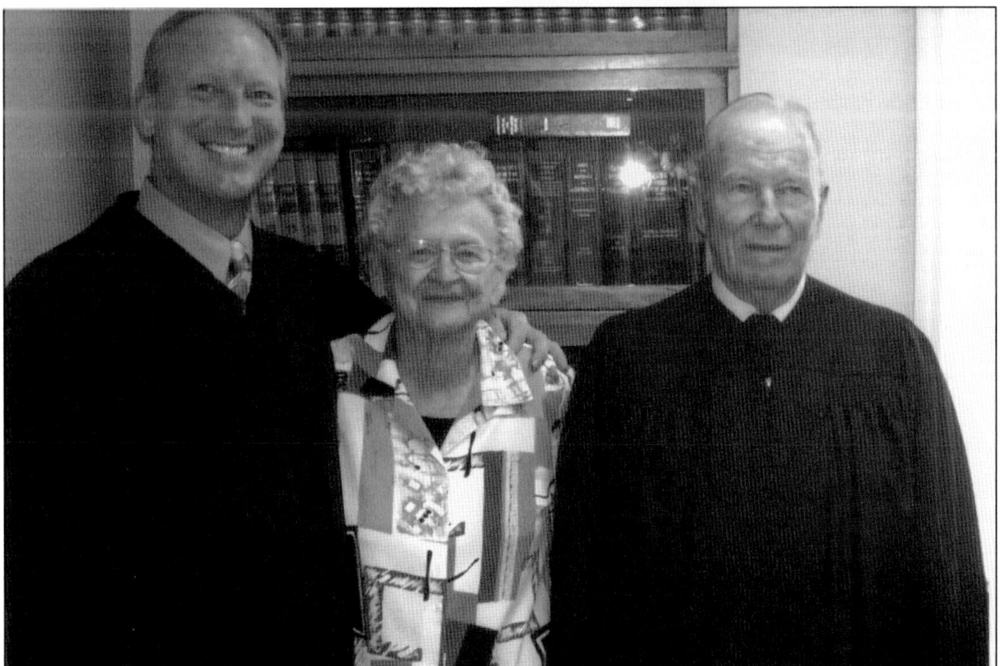

Judge William Hendrickson (right) poses with his wife Gloria (center) and son Judge Robert Hendrickson. (Courtesy of Gloria Hendrickson.)

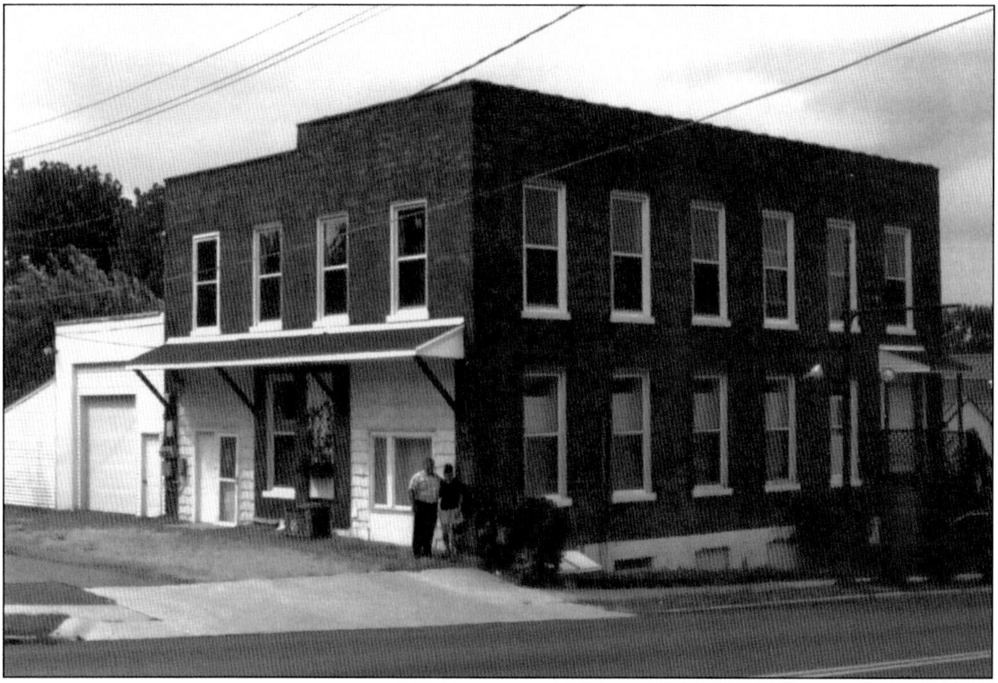

John MacDonald (left) and his wife, Jennifer (right), recently purchased the old Hiteshue building on Main Street. Bussy Hiteshue built the brick building for his buggy and blacksmith shop. Hiteshue later became an automobile mechanic, and the building served as his garage. (Courtesy of Larry and Marcia McCartt.)

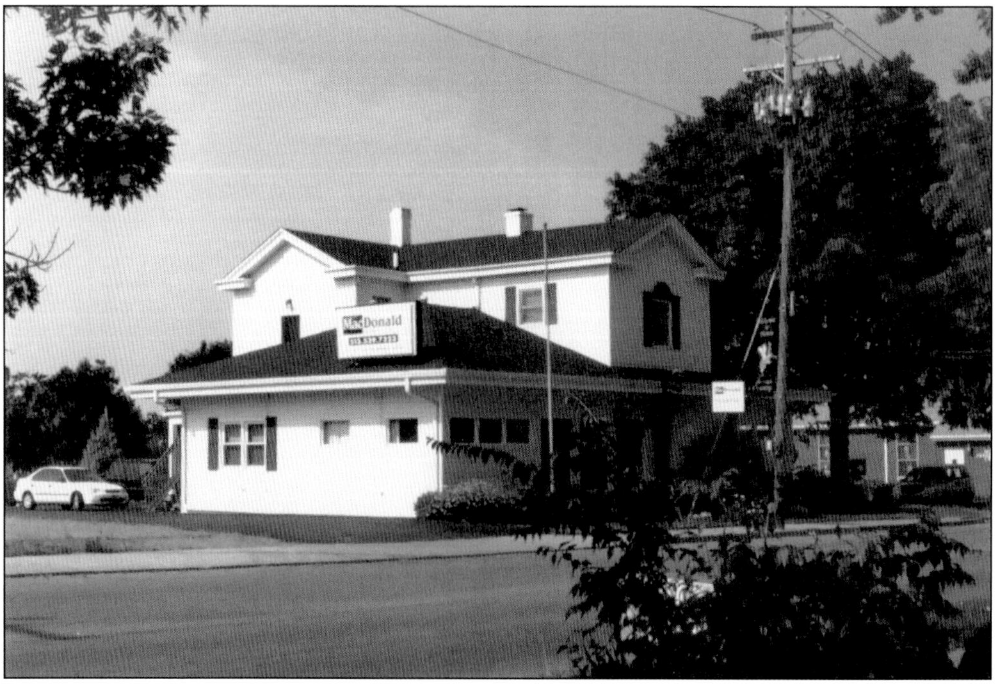

MacDonald Insurance is located on West Elm Street. (Courtesy of Larry and Marcia McCartt.)

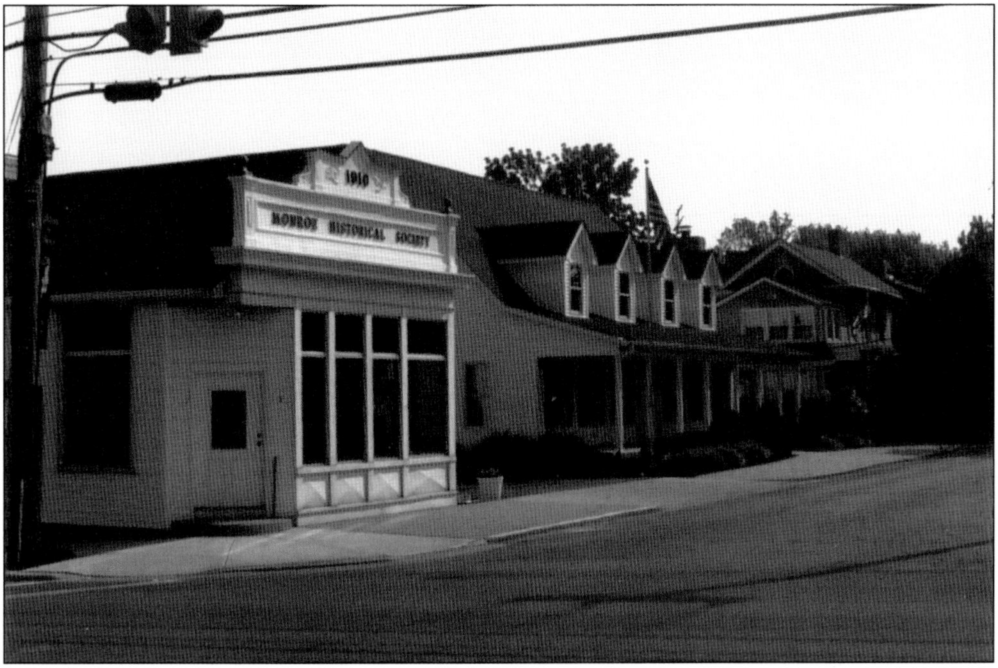

Up the street from MacDonald Insurance, at the corner of Main and Elm Streets, stands the Monroe Historical Society. The 1910 corner building was formerly M. G. Warner's store, the Hornets Nest, and the Monroe Village Hall. The building to the right was built by the historical society in 1999 and the land was provided by Jim Price. (Courtesy of Larry and Marcia McCartt.)

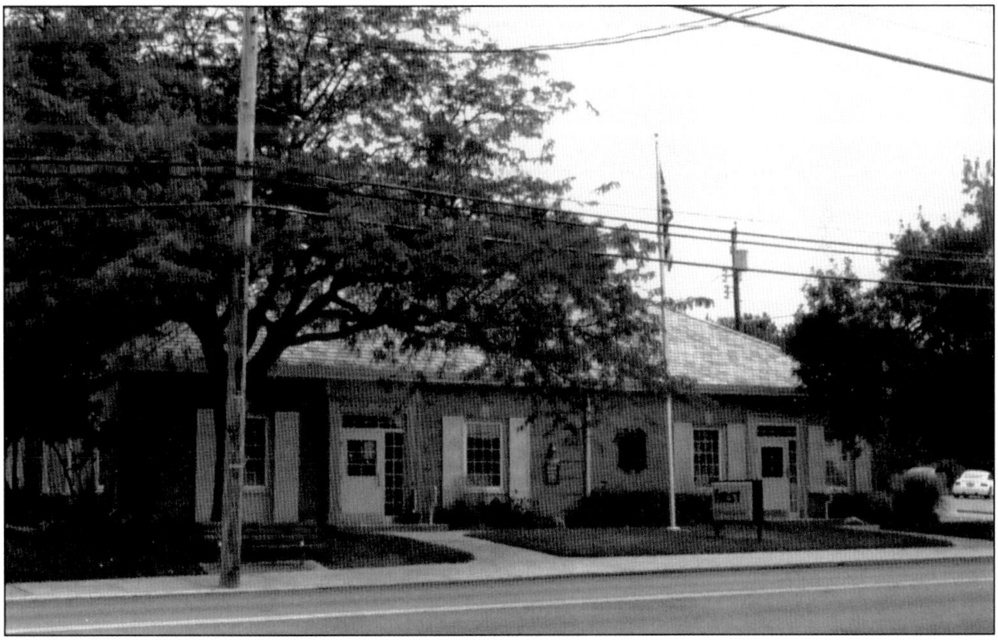

Opposite the Monroe Historical Society stands First Financial Bank. This building was built in 1954 and stands on the site of the first Warner store, which was remodeled as the Monroe National Bank in 1910. The bank has been in operation on this site for nearly 100 years. (Courtesy of Larry and Marcia McCartt.)

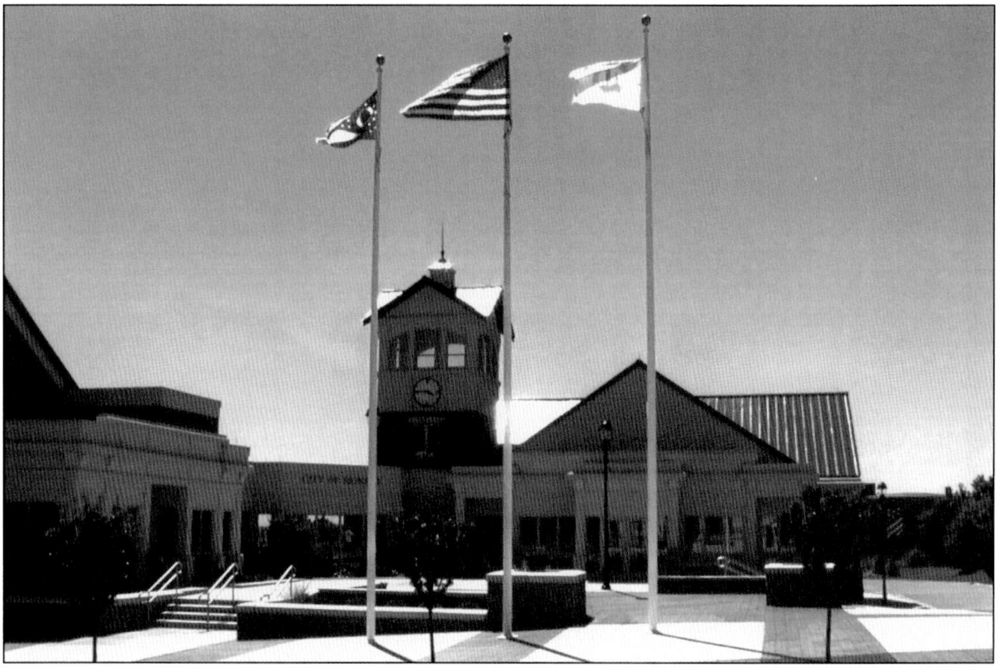

Traveling south on Main Street, one will find the Monroe City Building on the right. This building was constructed in 1999 when Monroe became a city. (Courtesy of the City of Monroe.)

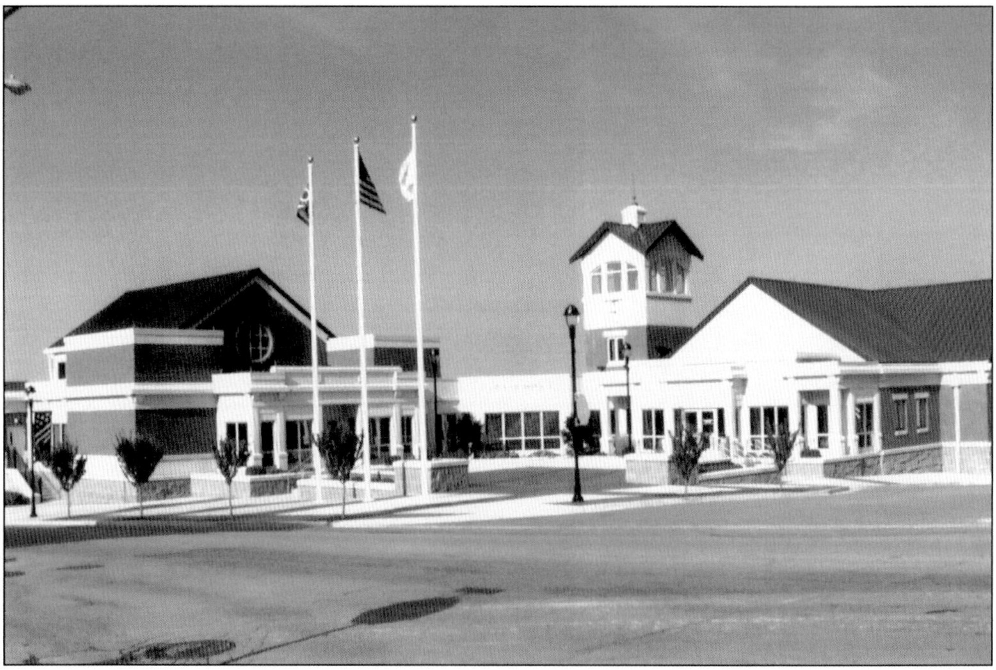

This view shows the Monroe City Building and the mayors court, which stands across from the old Red Onion building on Main Street. (Courtesy of the City of Monroe.)

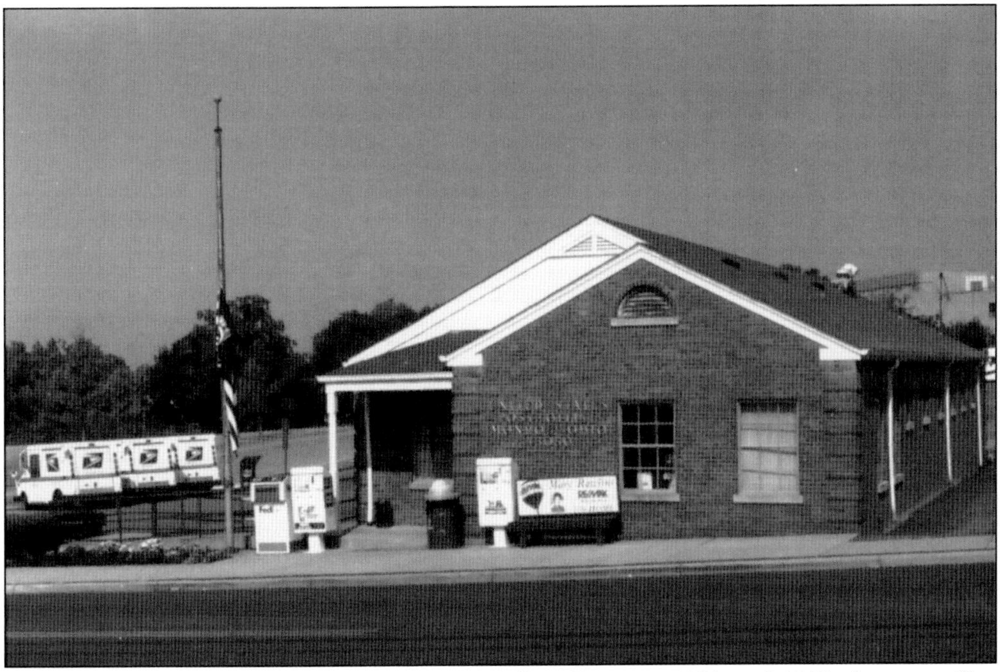

Beside the city building is the Monroe Post Office. Between 1954 and 1967, the post office was located in the bank building at Elm and Main Streets. This building was constructed in 1967 and has served the Monroe community for over 40 years. The current postmaster is Chris Snyder, who also serves as vice president of the Monroe Local School Board. (Courtesy of Larry and Marcia McCartt.)

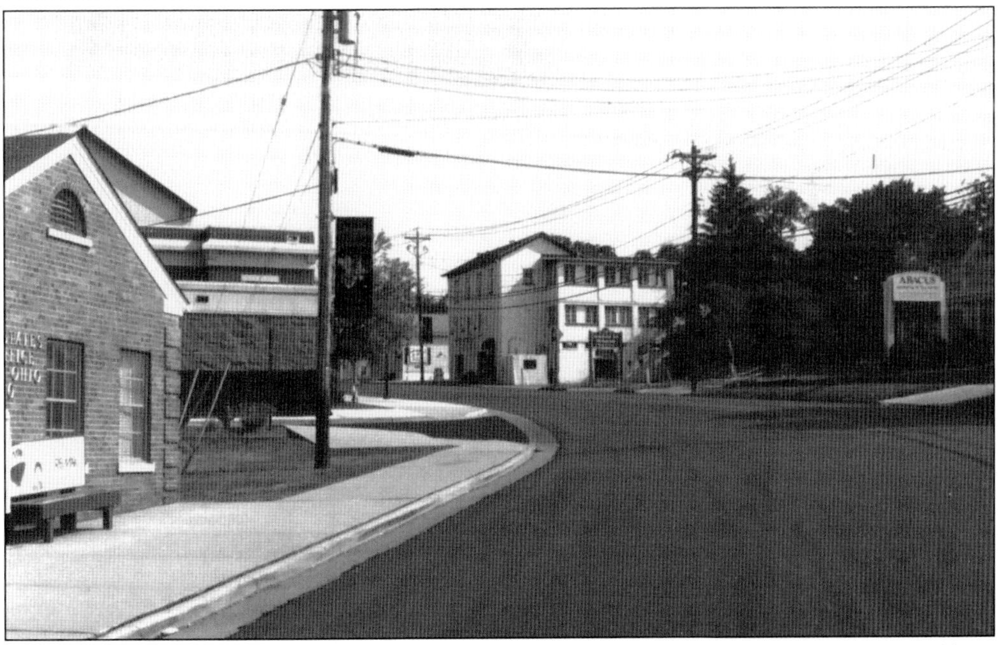

Looking north on Main Street from the Monroe Post Office, one can see the old Red Onion Building, which currently houses both the Red Onion Café and Brandywine Inn. Although Monroe is a growing city, traffic is still light on Sunday mornings. (Courtesy of Larry and Marcia McCartt.)

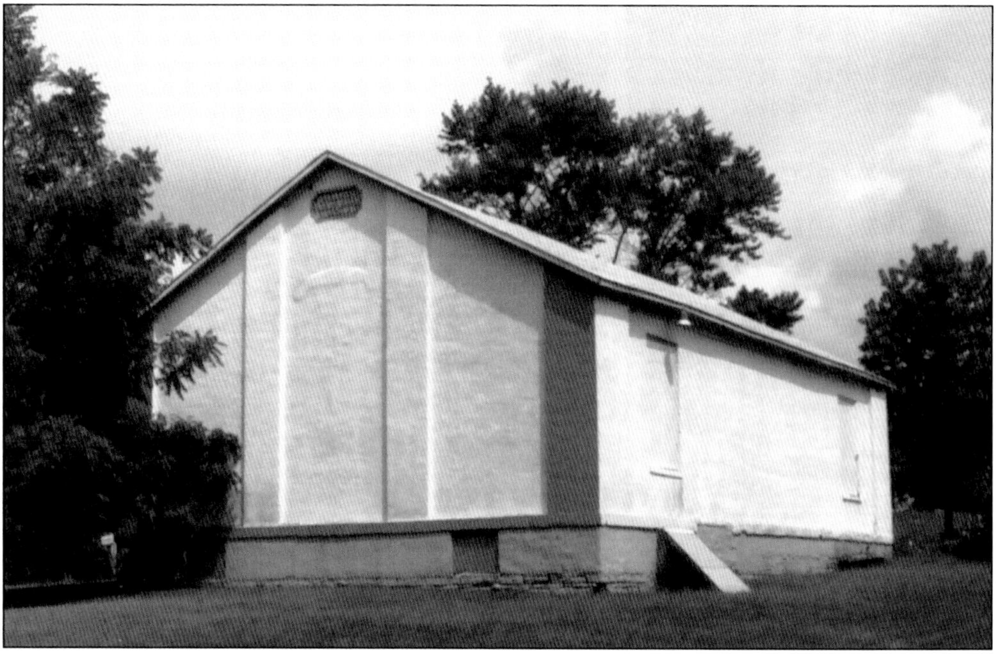

Across from the Monroe Post Office stands the old Presbyterian Academy. The academy was built around 1876 and was part of the First Presbyterian Church, which was founded in 1831. The academy was used as a school before the old consolidated school was built in the early 1880s. The academy is no longer in use. (Courtesy of Larry and Marcia McCartt.)

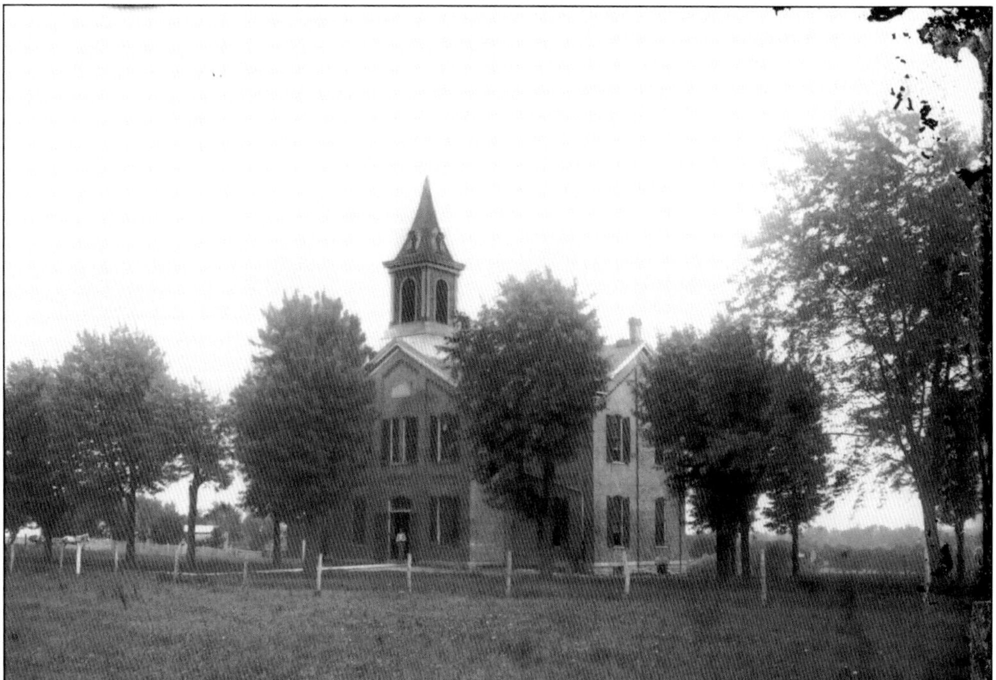

The consolidated school held the first high school class, which was started by James Macready in 1882 and graduated in 1886. (Courtesy of the Monroe Historical Society.)

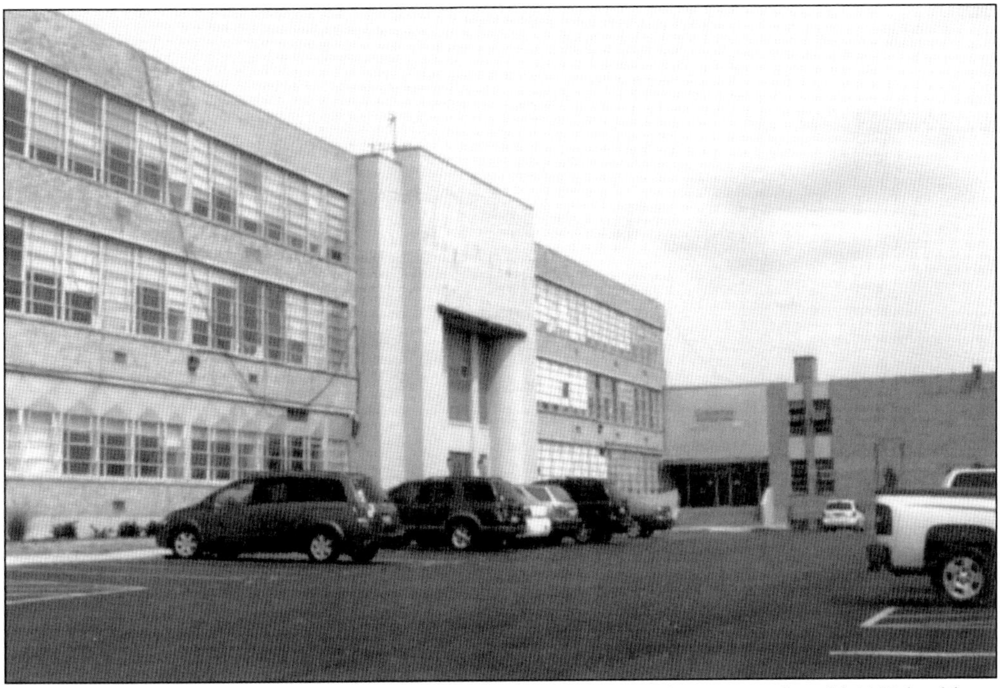

The old Lemon Monroe High School was built in 1948 as a south wing to the old 1912 building. The old high school is currently in use by Butler Tech as Greentree Academy. (Courtesy of Larry and Marcia McCartt.)

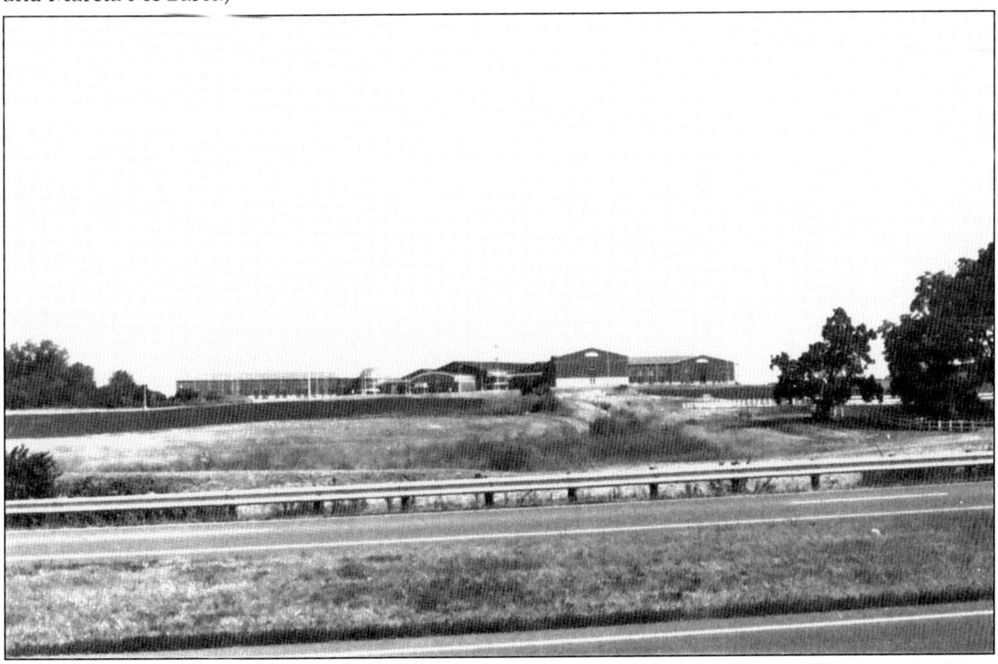

The new Monroe School building houses kindergarten through grade 12. This new building opened in 2004 and stands on land donated by Edith and Margaret Matson. The school district is currently putting the old Monroe Elementary School on Macready Avenue to use, as the district has outgrown the new school building. (Courtesy of Larry and Marcia McCartt.)

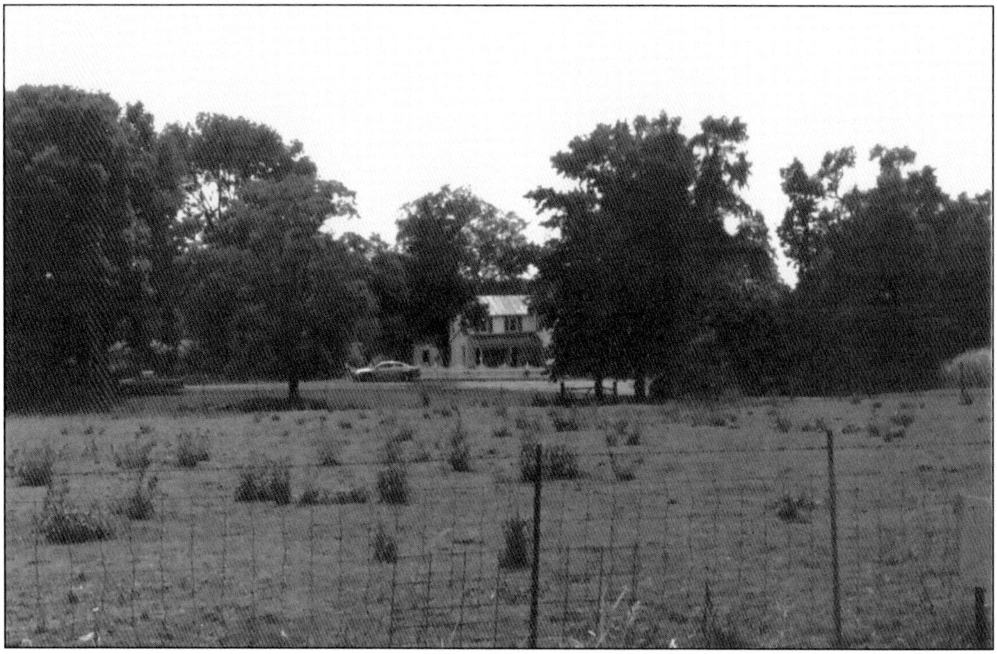

The Coldwater Creek Farm is located on Carson Road and is owned and operated by Tom and Mary Ann Leeds. It is one of the few remaining working farms in Monroe. (Courtesy of Larry and Marcia McCartt.)

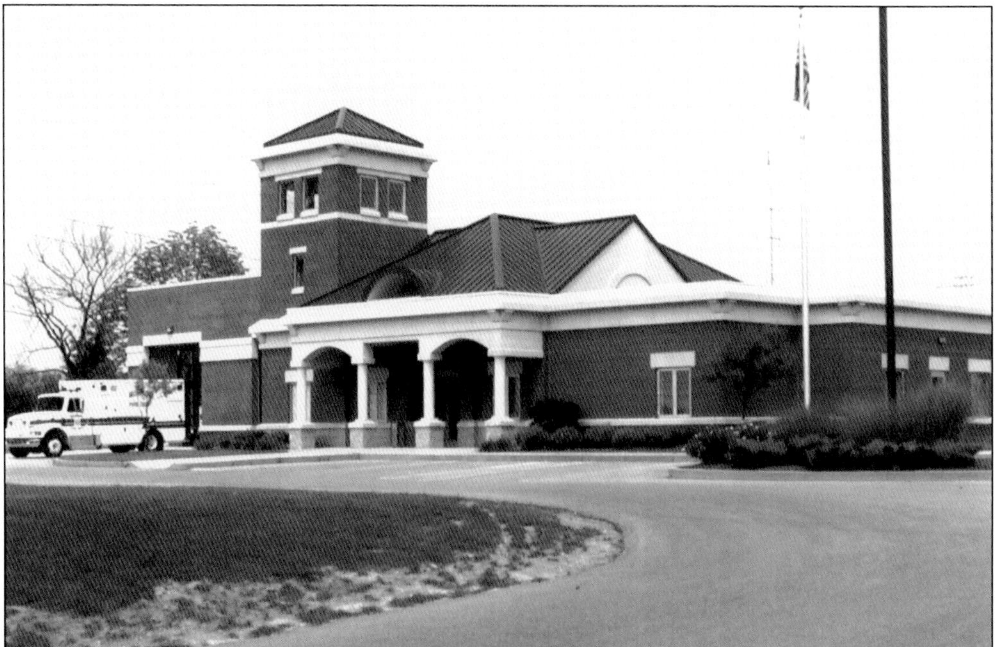

Monroe now has two fire stations. This one is located on State Route 4 between the State Route 63 interchange and Middletown. It houses the office of Fire Chief Mark Neu II. (Courtesy of the City of Monroe.)

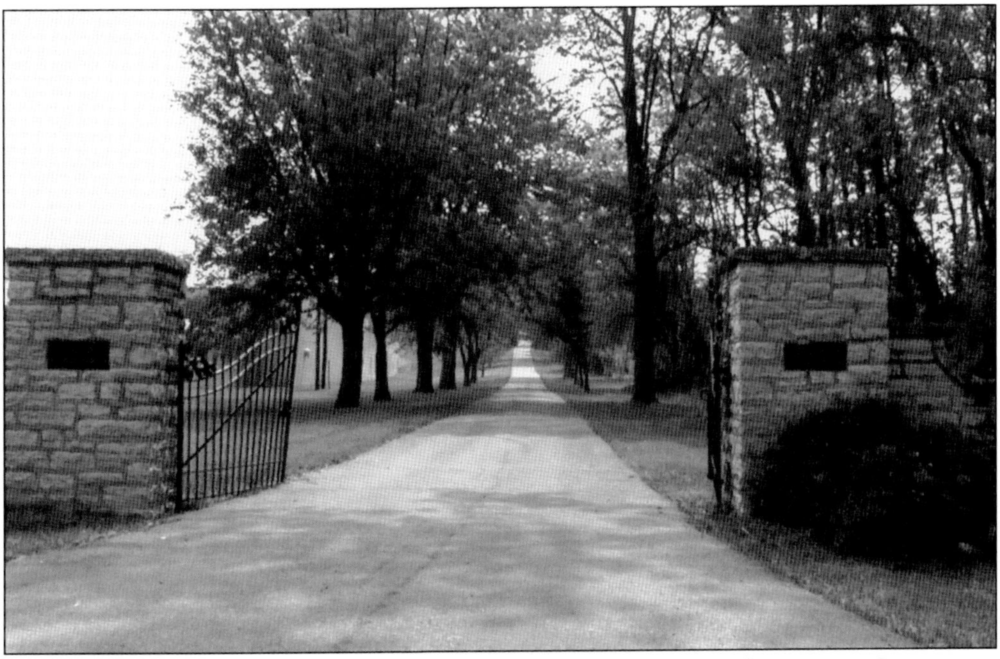

The entrance to Mound Cemetery is located on Main Street below the Monroe Community Park. Mound Cemetery Association was organized in 1859. The Village of Monroe deeded the cemetery to Lemon Township Board of Trustees in 1941 and it reverted back to the City of Monroe during the 1990s. (Courtesy of the City of Monroe.)

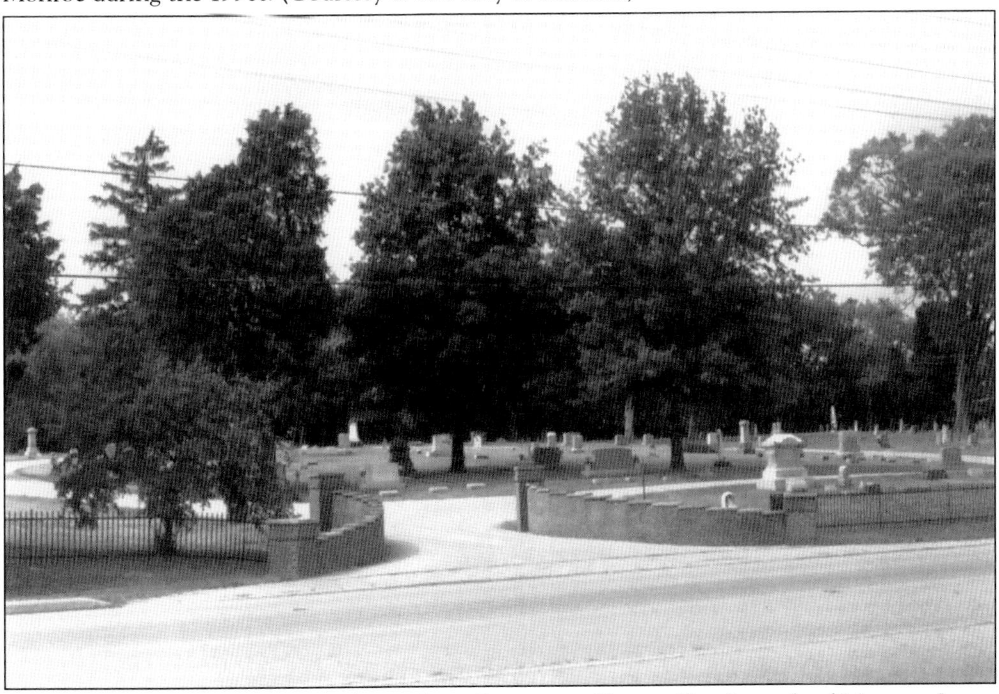

The North Monroe Cemetery is located on Cincinnati Dayton Road, north of Monroe. It was chartered in 1858. The cemetery sits on the former site of the Presbyterian church. (Courtesy of Larry and Marcia McCartt.)

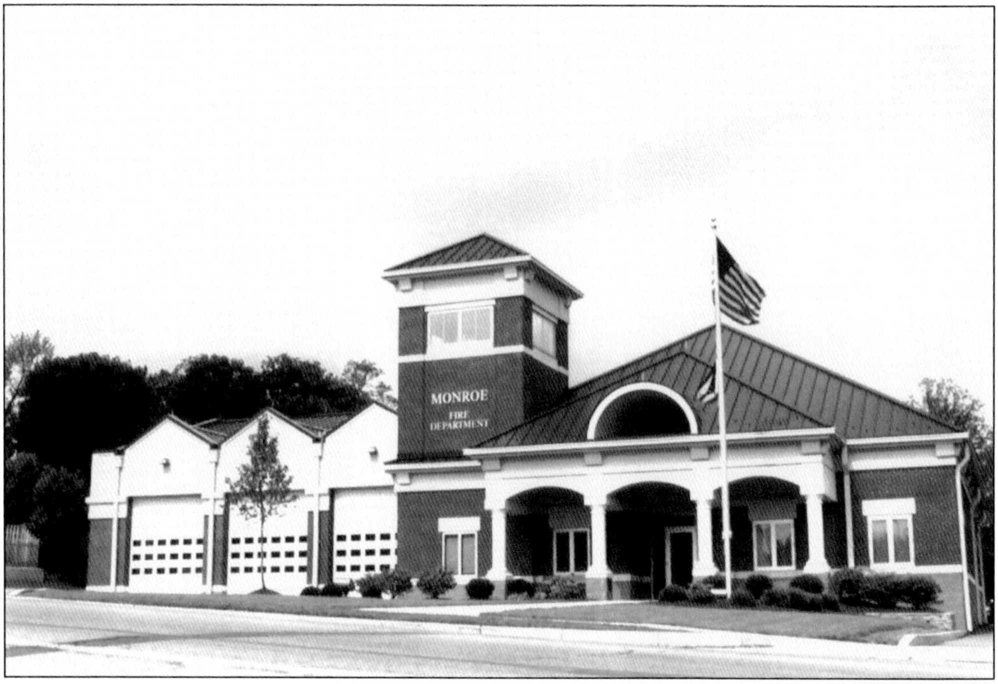

The old firehouse on Main Street was razed and this much larger new building was dedicated in 2002. (Courtesy of the City of Monroe.)

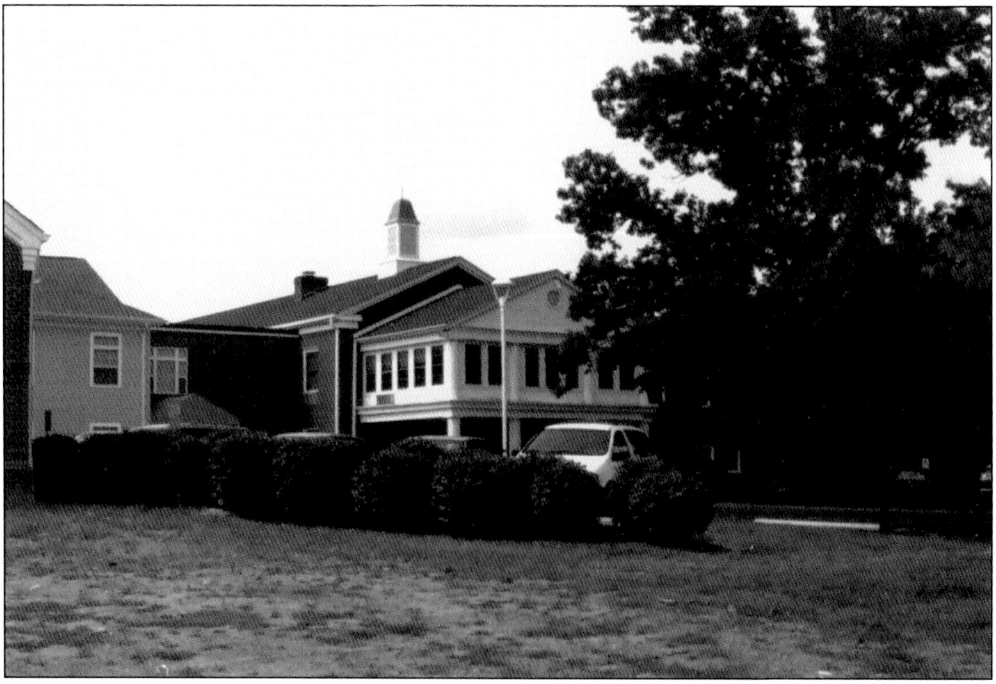
Mount Pleasant Retirement Village, which is located on Britton Lane in Monroe, has been in operation for over 50 years. It is part of the Ohio Presbyterian Retirement Services and is comprised of cottages, ranch homes, new brownstones, apartments, assisted living, and skilled-nursing care. (Courtesy of Larry and Marcia McCartt.)

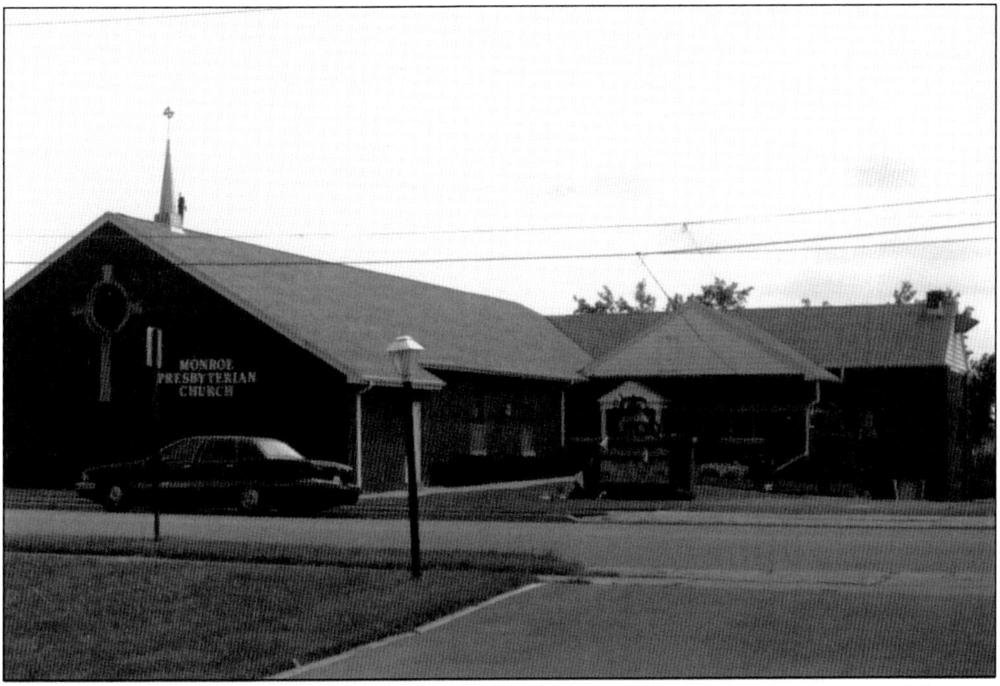

Monroe Presbyterian Church, located on West Elm Street, is the oldest congregation in Monroe. (Courtesy of Larry and Marcia McCartt.)

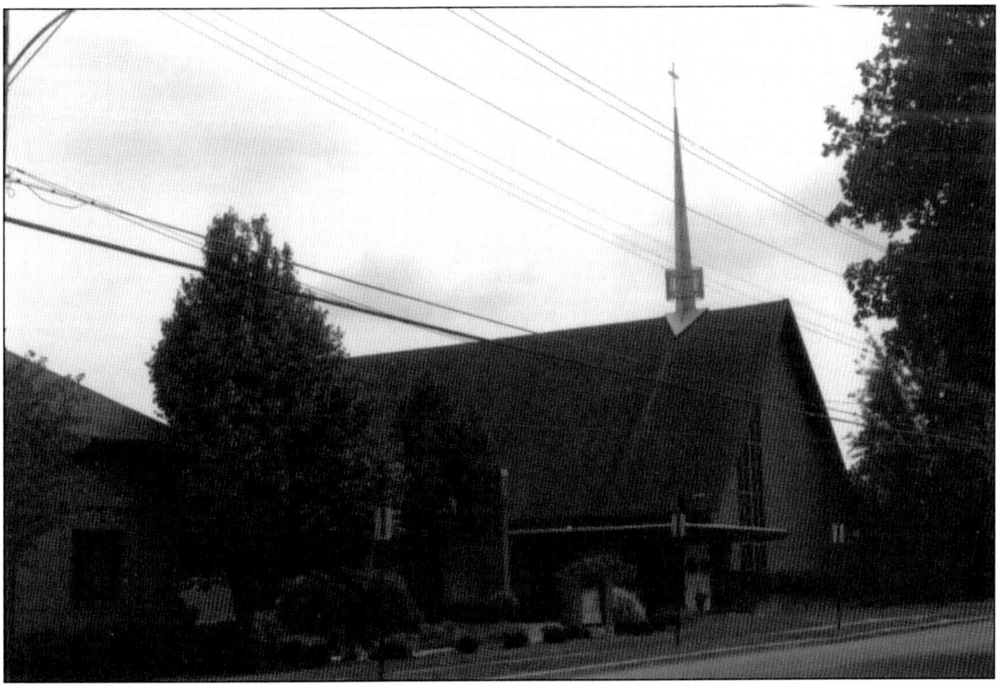
The Methodist church was rebuilt after the 1969 tornado. The old building was razed. (Courtesy of Larry and Marcia McCartt.)

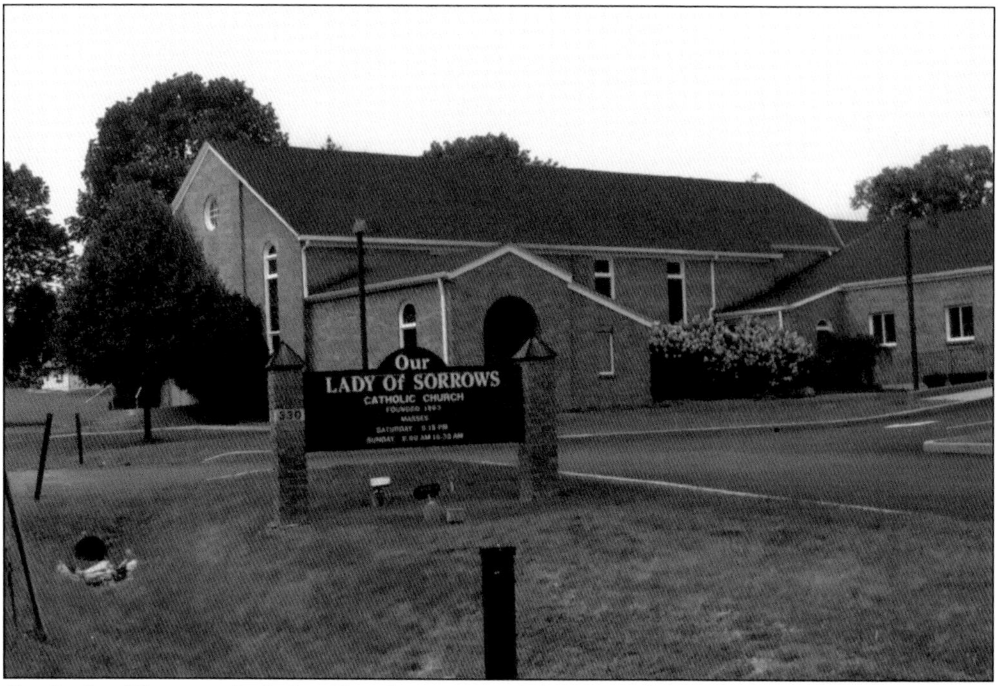

Our Lady of Sorrows Catholic Church was one of the original three congregations in Monroe. It was founded in 1883. (Courtesy of Larry and Marcia McCartt.)

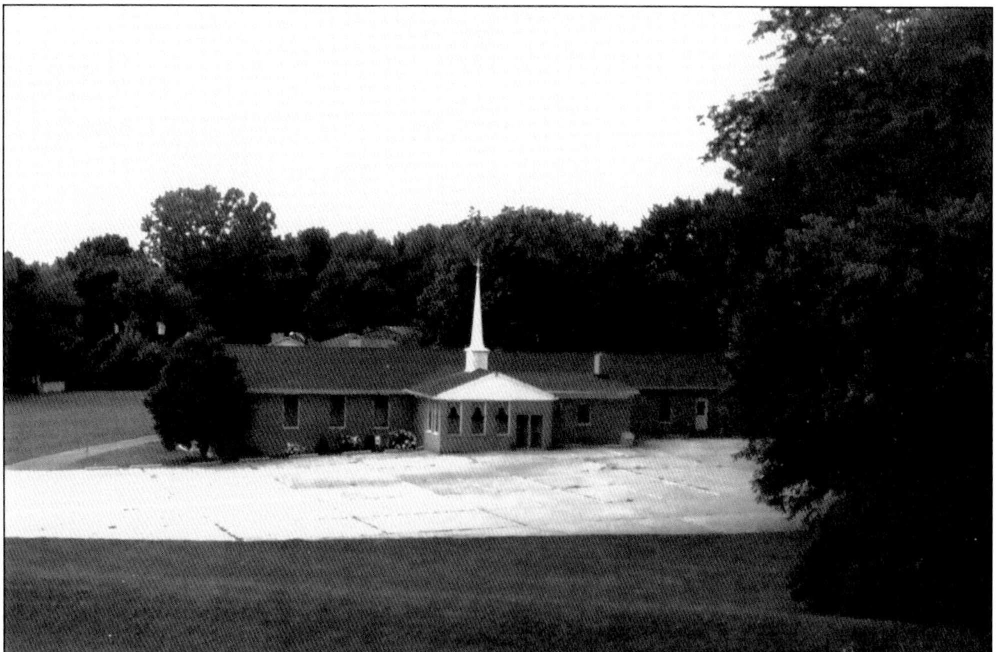

The First Baptist Church of Monroe began as a mission in 1958 at the home of Walter Carnes. A store by the old Sohio Station was rented and used for services until the land was purchased and the current building, located off Main Street, was completed in 1962. (Courtesy of Larry and Marcia McCartt.)

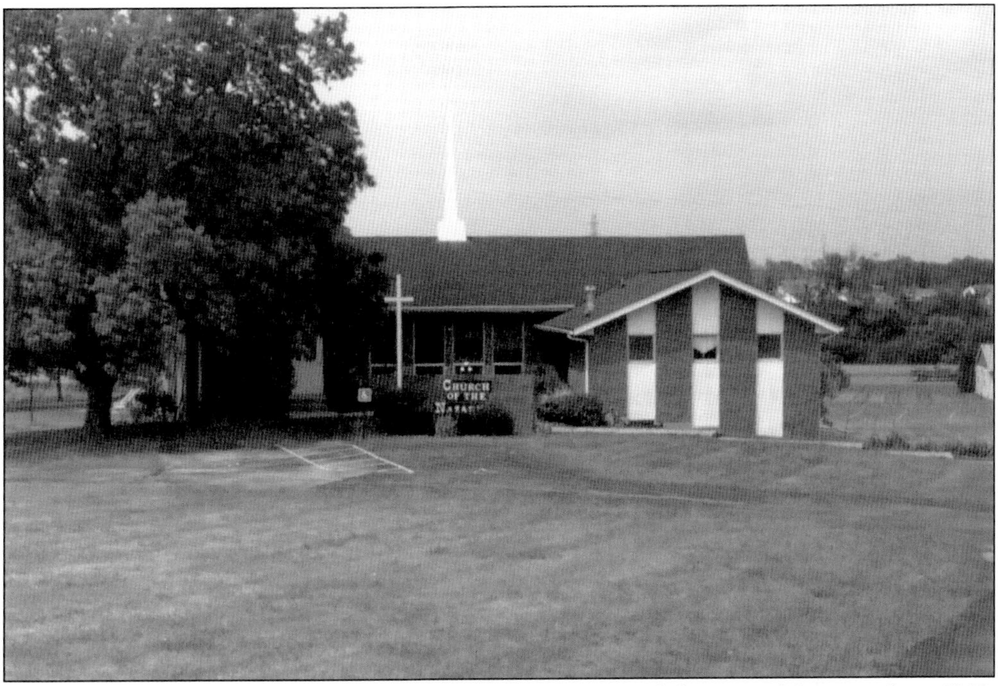

The Monroe Church of the Nazarene has its beginnings around the time of the tornado in 1969. The congregation met at a member's home on middle Sands Avenue until the current building and sanctuary was completed in 1970. (Courtesy of Larry and Marcia McCartt.)

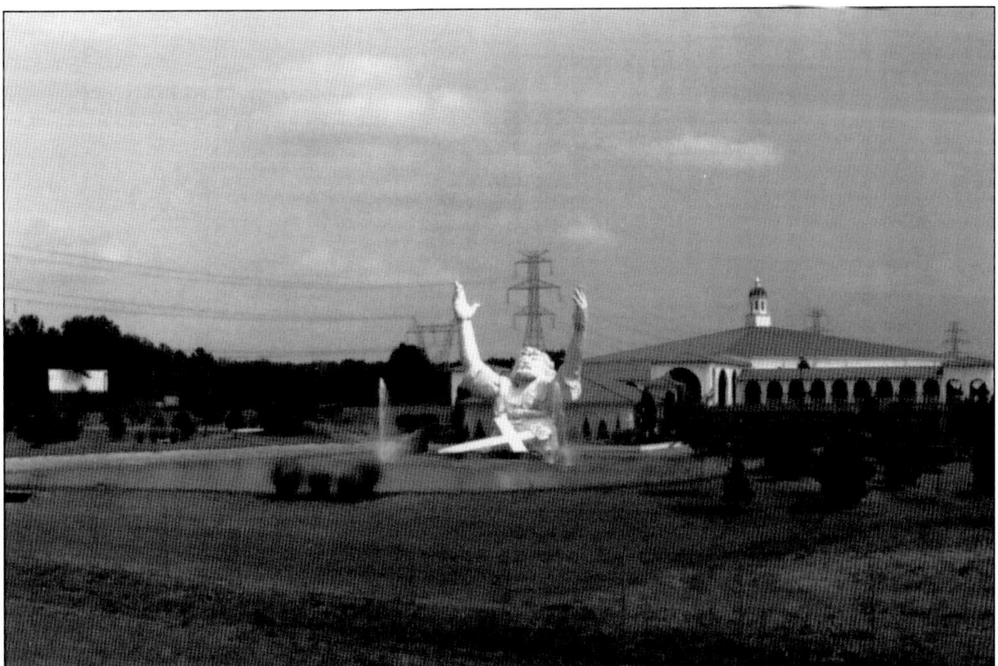

"Touchdown Jesus" at the Solid Rock Church on Union Road greets travelers on Interstate 75. (Courtesy of Larry and Marcia McCartt.)

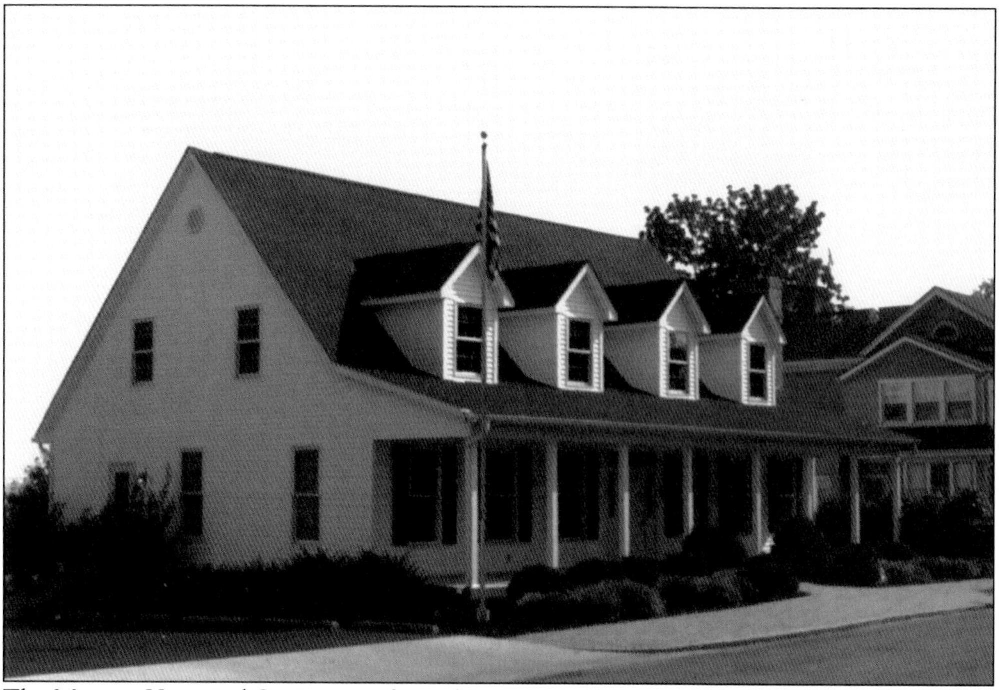

The Monroe Historical Society was formed in 1967 for the sesquicentennial celebration. The first officers were Mrs. G. W. McGohan, president; Paul Ramseyer, vice president; Mrs. Gordon Doty, recording secretary; Mrs. Mark A. Neu, corresponding secretary; Dale Forman, treasurer; Mrs. Kirtley W. Ervin, historian; Mrs. James L. Cast, curator; and Mrs. Charles F. Gorman, Dale Ridenour, Mrs. E. Eugene Switzer, and Dr. James M. Anderson, directors. (Courtesy of Larry and Marcia McCartt.)

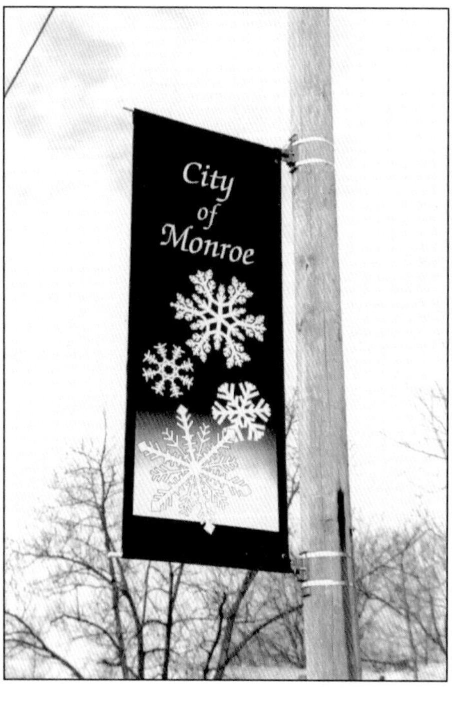

The City of Monroe changes its street banners seasonally. This one is displayed during the Christmas season. (Courtesy of Larry McCartt.)

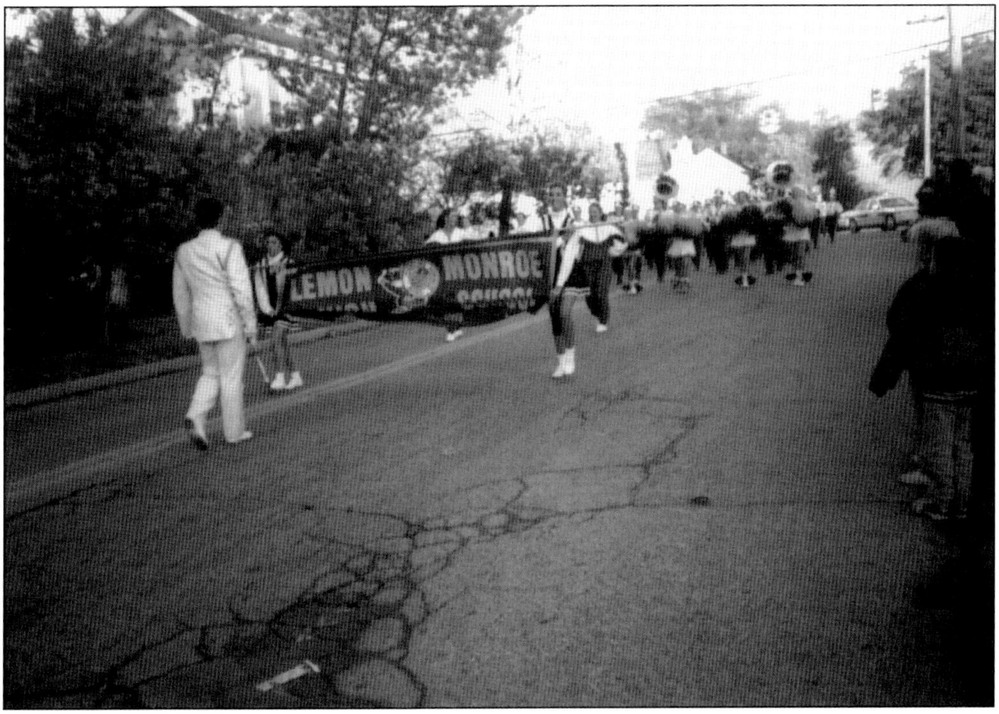

The Monroe cheerleaders are very energetic, hard-working young ladies and always appear in the parades. (Courtesy of Ed and Marge MacDonald.)

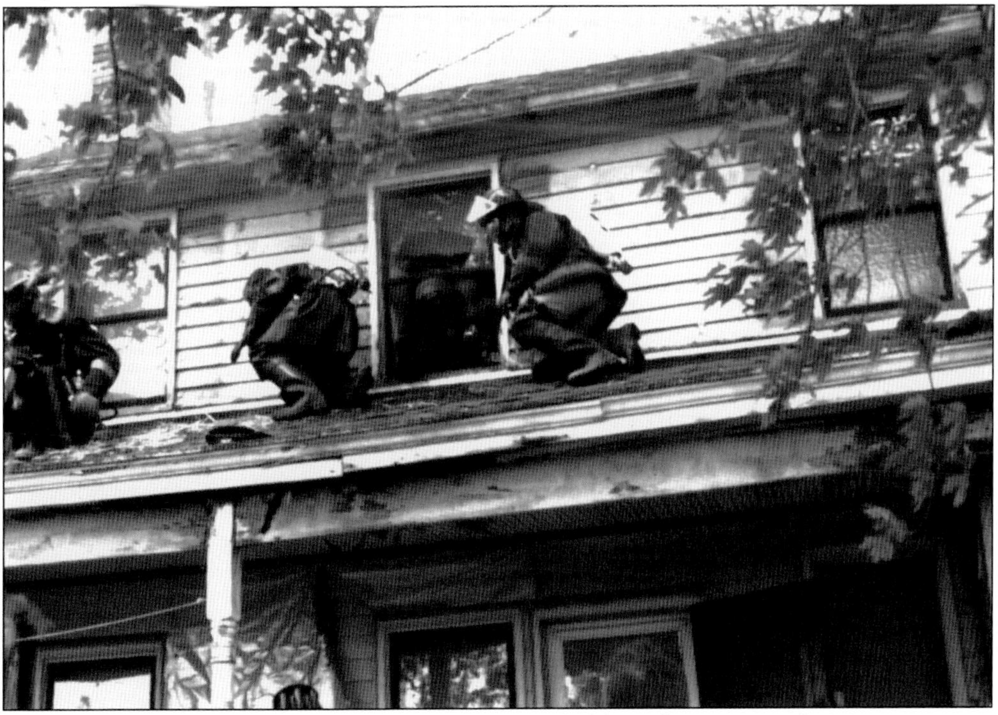
Monroe firefighters and police officers continue to work diligently to protect the Monroe citizens from danger. (Courtesy of the Monroe Fire Department.)

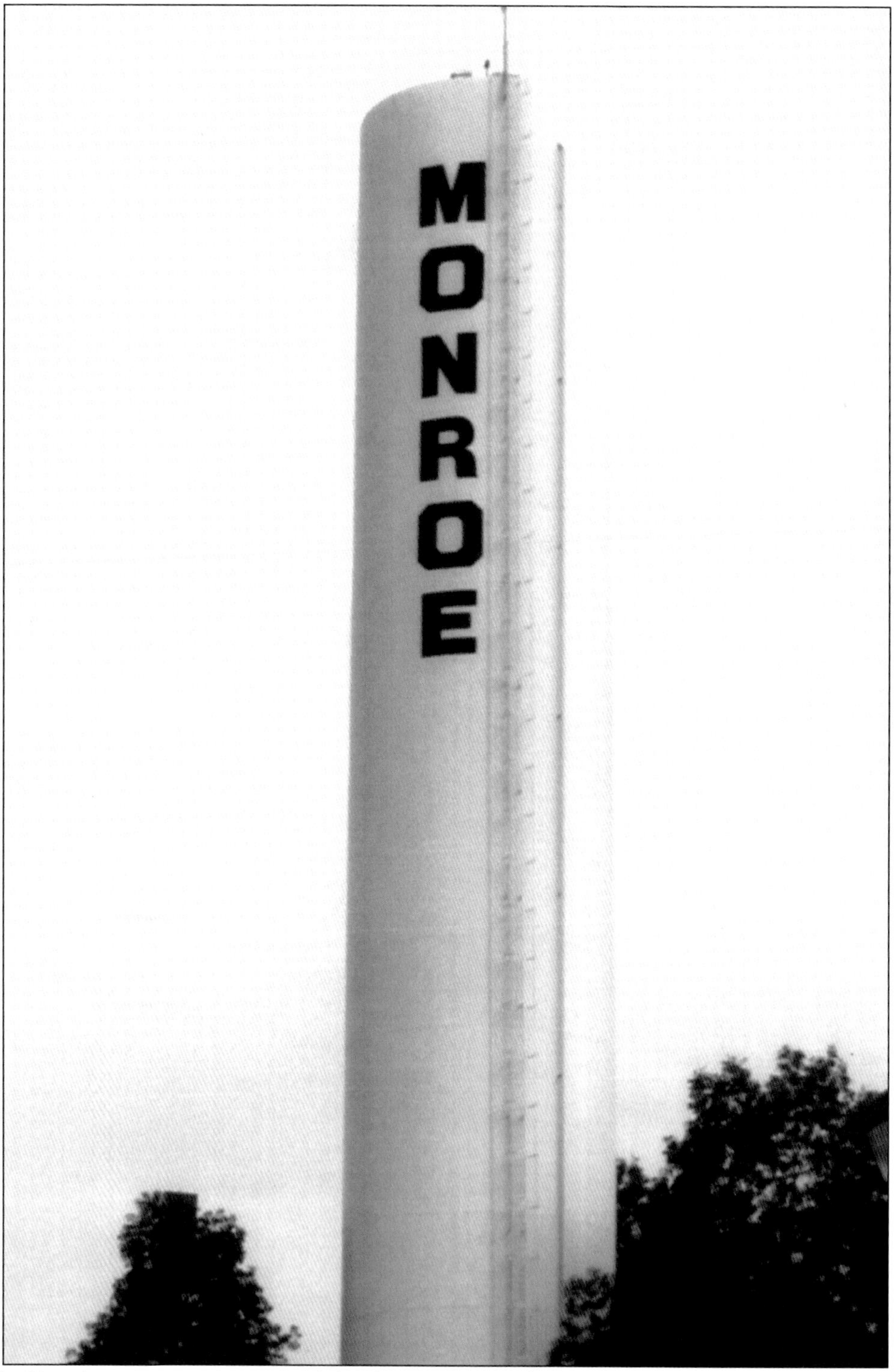

The East Avenue water tower stands by the Monroe Methodist Church, and for many years, the tower and church steeple were the first landmarks to greet travelers coming south on Cincinnati Dayton Road from Middletown. (Courtesy of the City of Monroe.)

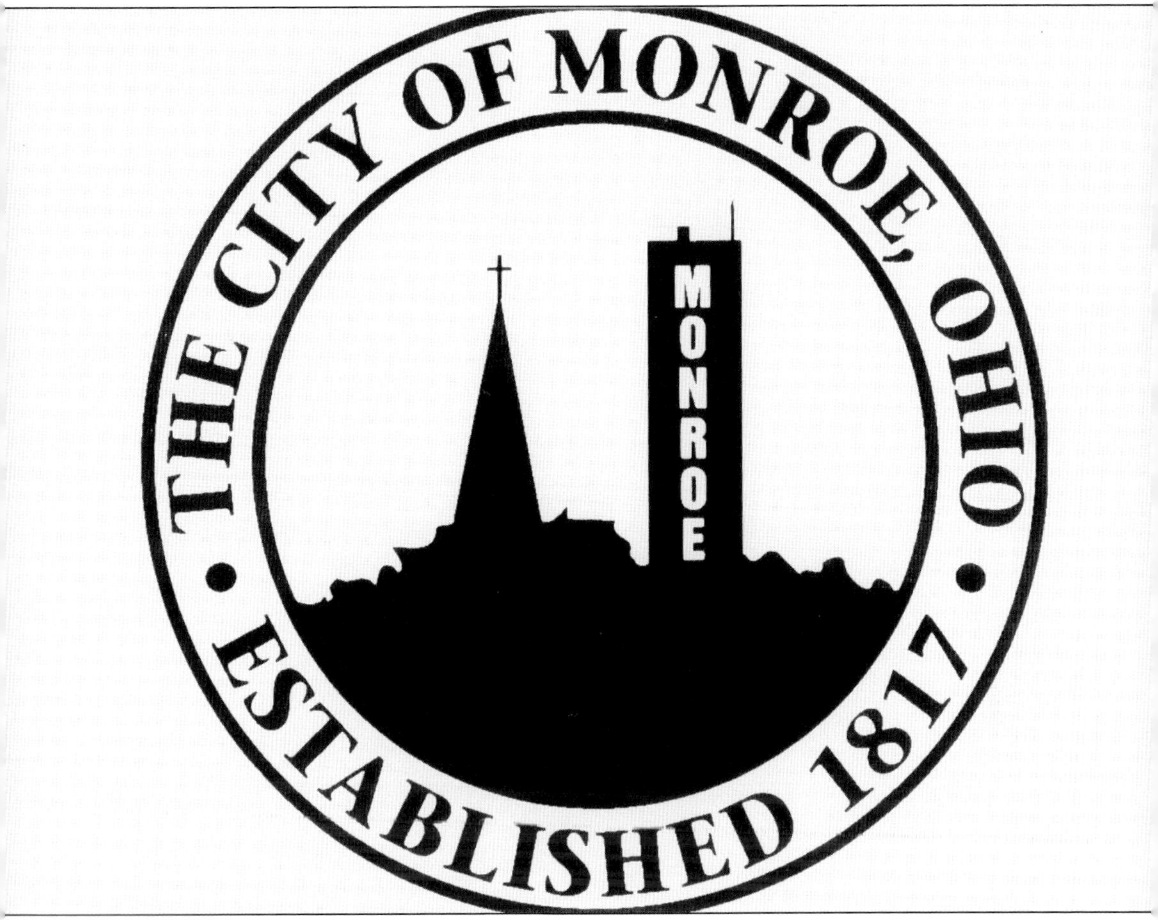

The Monroe city seal was designed by Larry McCartt in 1967 for the sesquicentennial celebration. The city officially adopted McCartt's design, the East Avenue water tower and the old steeple of the Monroe Methodist Church, for its city seal in February 2001. (Courtesy of the City of Monroe.)